Cooking
for the
Seasons

Photo Legend front cover:

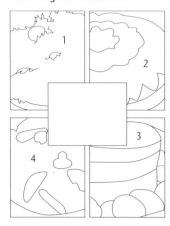

1. Garden Salad, page 20
2. Fresh Fruit Flan, page 86
3. Seasoned Sirloin, page 161
4. Roasted Vegetable Stew, page 109

Cooking for the Seasons
Copyright © Company's Coming Publishing Limited

Third Printing May 2002

Canadian Cataloguing in Publication Data

Paré, Jean
        Cooking for the seasons

(Special occasion series)
Includes indexes.
At head of title: Company's Coming.
ISBN 1-895455-91-X

        1. Cookery.   I. Title.   II. Series: Paré, Jean.   Special
occasion series.

TX714.P353 2002   641.5   C2001-903796-1

Published by
COMPANY'S COMING PUBLISHING LIMITED
2311 - 96 Street
Edmonton, Alberta, Canada T6N 1G3
Tel: 780.450.6223 Fax: 780.450.1857
www.companyscoming.com

Company's Coming is a registered trademark owned by
Company's Coming Publishing Limited

Printed in China

Pictured at left:

Center: Cream Of Asparagus Soup, page 22
Bottom: Meatless Taco Salad, page 20

Cooking for the Seasons was created thanks to the dedicated efforts of the people and organizations listed below.

COMPANY'S COMING PUBLISHING LIMITED

Author	Jean Paré
President	Grant Lovig
Vice President, Product Development	Kathy Knowles
Design Director	Jaclyn Draker
Publishing Coordinator	Shelly Willsey
Copy Editors	Debbie Dixon
	Karen Decoux

The Recipe Factory

Research & Development Manager	Nora Prokop
Editor	Laurel Hoffmann
Editorial Assistant	Rendi Dennis
Associate Editor	Sarah Campbell
Proofreaders	Audrey Dahl
	Audrey Whitson
Food Editor	Lynda Elsenheimer
Associate Food Editor	Suzanne Hartman
Researcher	Betty Chase
Test Kitchen Coordinator	Allison Dosman
Test Kitchen Staff	Jessica Pon
	Ellen Bunjevac
	Pat Yukes
	Janice Ciesielski
Photographer	Stephe Tate Photo
Assistant Photographer	John McDougall
Senior Food Stylist	Sherri Cunningham
Food Stylists	Leah Duperreault
	Debbie Duff
Prep Kitchen Staff	Audrey Smetaniuk
	Dana Royer
	Cathy Anderson
Prop Stylists	Paula Bertamini
	Snezana Ferenac
Nutrition Analyst	Margaret Ng, B.Sc., M.A., R.D.

Our special thanks to the following businesses for providing extensive props for photography.

Anchor Hocking Canada	Oaksmith Interiors
Bernardin Ltd.	Pfaltzgraff Canada
Browne & Co. Ltd.	Pier 1 Imports
Canhone Global	Pyrex Originials
Cherison Enterprises Inc.	The Bay
Dansk Gifts	The Paderno Factory Store
Linens 'N Things	Wal-Mart Canada Inc.
Michael's The Arts And Crafts Store	Winners Stores
Mikasa Home Store	

Digital Imagery on page 125 and on page 126 © copyright 2001 PhotoDisk, Inc.

Table of Contents

Foreword

Many of us have a favorite season, a point in time when everything is just the way we like it.

If someone asked me what my favorite time of year was, I would have to say that it's that one, indefinable moment when one season ends and a new one begins. For me, change is both a welcome and inspiring part of our four seasons, especially when it comes to cooking.

So, in creating this collection, we considered the availability of fresh vegetables and fruit, the many events and festivities that pop up throughout the year, and the different cooking trends that constantly shift in and out of style with each passing month.

Spring arrives—always—just in time. Despite a lingering chill in the air, we don sweaters and running shoes and head outdoors. Windows get washed, driveways are swept and lawns are raked as everyone says goodbye to the remains of winter. Although this is traditionally a rainy season, I always remember the Easter holidays as a sunny, warm event. Bring the festivities home with an Easter Brunch menu featured in our Spring section. Welcome this warm weather with some of the light, simple recipes we've put together for the spring season.

Summer is hot, and the pace changes. It's a time of year to keep things simple and cool, so many of us plan our meals around the barbecue. Appetites grow smaller and main course salads become popular alternatives to heavier meals. If you'd like a little adventure in outdoor cooking, then look through our selection of recipes created for the open campfire. Another summertime event is the family reunion, and I find that there's no greater challenge than creating a menu which doesn't include hot dogs and hamburgers. Take a moment to read our recipe ideas in the Summer section, and you may find just the right combination of dishes that you are looking for.

The draining heat seems to disappear overnight with the first chilly wind of fall. Appetites return and everyone's first instinct is to head indoors and eat. This is when I like to fill the house with scents of warm, fresh bread, simmering chowders and baked pies. Inside our Fall section are some recipes that might inspire you to turn the last vegetables and fruits of the season into sweet preserves and tangy pickles. Thanksgiving is one holiday event not to be missed. Keep the tradition alive with some of our classic and unique recipe selections.

When winter blows in, it truly gets cold. Skiers, skaters and children welcome the newly fallen snow, while the rest of us try not to think of bitter winds and frozen ears. Instead, we turn to whatever promises to bring us warmth and comfort. I pull out my cookbooks and start planning what to bake for the Christmas season. It's a time of year to take comfort in tempting casseroles, soul-warming hot drinks, and holiday treats. Enjoy this selection of winter recipes, along with some festive menu ideas for the season.

A wise person once said "a change is as good as a rest." The seasons as we experience them—Spring, Summer, Fall and Winter—feature dramatic, awe-inspiring changes.

That is what *Cooking for the Seasons* is all about—to reflect and celebrate the miraculous transformation that comes with each noble season.

Jean Paré

Each recipe has been analyzed using the most up-to-date version of the Canadian Nutrient File from Health Canada, which is based upon the United States Department of Agriculture (USDA) Nutrient Data Base.

Margaret Ng, B.Sc. (Hon), M.A.
Registered Dietitian

Spring

March	Shhhh—trees and plants are beginning to bud and grow and seeds are being ordered.
April	First sprigs of leafy herbs and hearty rhubarb are picked and seed germination begins underground.
May	Baby greens abound, sprouting seeds show their tips, some early vegetables are ready and breathtaking fruit blossoms have cameras snapping.

Just when you think Mother Nature has forgotten to turn her clock past winter, there's a change in the air and a warm breeze blows. Spring has arrived!

Everyone looks for the arrival of the "firsts"—the first bud on the trees, the first patch of green grass, the first song of the robin, and of course, the first delicate fruits and vegetables of the season. After a long winter of imported, canned and frozen foods, we are finally free to embrace a fresh, new and tender collection of produce.

The snow has yet to melt when chives bravely poke their heads up out of the ground, just in time to lend a savory flavor to salads. The leaves of the hardy mint plant bring a fresh, seasonal taste to salads, lamb and pork dishes. Baby greens are cut to make into delicate salads, while the rhubarb plant slowly blooms into long red stalks that will be used in delicious pies, cakes, muffins and other desserts.

March

In March, with each steady drip of melting snow off the roof, the winter gloom we have suffered through happily dissolves. Winter's grip is broken and the first rainfall of the year washes everything clean. In most parts of the country, tender perennials, planted nearest the house, will reach tentatively above the surface, searching for long lost heat and anxious for the longer hours of sunlight. Cooks everywhere also enjoy a rebirth in their cooking style—instead of stews, soups and casseroles, they now look forward to sampling lighter dishes featuring seasonal fruits and vegetables.

April

The month of April bears witness to a new season of planting. Depending on what area of the country you live in, peas, onions, carrots, beets and radishes can be planted. Some people plant lettuce in the fall and begin to see baby greens at this time of year. Cutting instead of pulling the greens will ensure regrowth. Plant a short row of radishes weekly for the next two months so that you'll have a continuous supply of this peppery red and white globe for salads or snacking.

Easter celebrations, whether in March or April, provide a welcome holiday respite and a chance to entertain. Families sit down to a traditional ham dinner or gather after church for a Sunday brunch. Regardless, spring colors abound at the table, especially with the pinks, greens, yellows and blues of Easter eggs.

For children, spring break heralds the true arrival of spring! Wearing only light jackets or T-shirts, their days are filled with playing outdoors. Skipping ropes appear on driveways, skateboards snake along sidewalks and bicycles become the welcomed mode of transportation once again.

May

April showers bring May flowers as the saying goes. In open fields, crocuses lift their purple heads upward, while in backyards, tulips, daffodils and fragrant lilac trees sprout with wild bursts of color. The heat of the month inspires a change in menu, away from the melded flavors of simmered stews, to lighter and fresher fare.

Mother's Day is the perfect time to have your mother, or any mother, over for a patio brunch. Cut vegetables and cheese for a quiche the day before, then pour into a pan with fork-beaten eggs that morning for an easy bake while you socialize over coffee, tea or juice. Complement the meal with a bowl of seasonal fruit.

Spring is the perfect time to get creative, so why not try your hand at cooking and garnishing with edible flowers? If you don't grow your own, you might find edible flowers in the produce section of grocery stores or at the farmers' market, but be sure to ask if they've been grown for eating. Float tea roses in fruit punch or hang a tuberous begonia flower on the rim of a tall glass of iced tea. Invite both a visual and taste surprise by mixing peppery nasturtiums with mild greens such as butter lettuce. Pansies have a delicate taste, a nice complement to the sharper flavors of certain greens like escarole or radicchio. Marigolds are edible, but only the pot and signet varieties taste good. You can use just the petals or the whole flower, depending on the size. Freeze violets and Johnny-jump-ups in ice cubes to decorate drinks. Lilacs add a hint of sweetness to salads and make a bright garnish on cakes and ice cream. Look to chive blossoms if you'd like both a mild onion flavor and a pretty purple display.

Victoria Day weekend is the seasonal benchmark for homeowners to tend gardens and rake yards. After a strenuous day of laying bedding plants, sweeping decks and washing windows, start up the barbecue for a quick and light meal. Enjoy the weather—sun or rain—because spring is here!

Mushroom Pastries

These are extra special. Good hot or cold.
An excellent appetizer that will disappear fast.

FILLING

Chopped fresh mushrooms	1 1/2 cups	375 mL
Medium onion, chopped	1	1
Cooking oil	1 1/2 tbsp.	25 mL
Light cream cheese, softened	8 oz.	250 g
Milk	1 tbsp.	15 mL
Dill weed	1 tsp.	5 mL
Green onions, finely chopped	2	2
Dried thyme	1/8 tsp.	0.5 mL
Tubes of refrigerator country-style biscuits (10 biscuits per tube)	2	2

Filling: Sauté mushrooms and onion in cooking oil in frying pan until onion is soft and liquid from mushrooms has evaporated. Remove to small bowl. Cool to room temperature.

Beat cream cheese, milk, dill weed, green onion and thyme in medium bowl until smooth. Stir in mushroom mixture. Makes 2 cups (500 mL) filling.

Separate biscuits. Split each biscuit in half. Flatten biscuit halves with rolling pin. Put about 2 tsp. (10 mL) filling on each. Fold over. Seal. Arrange in single layer on greased baking sheet. Bake in 400°F (205°C) oven for about 15 minutes until golden. Makes 40 appetizers.

1 appetizer: 65 Calories; 2.6 g Total Fat; 256 mg Sodium; 2 g Protein; 9 g Carbohydrate; trace Dietary Fiber

Pictured on page 11.

Rolled Asparagus

Golden toasted rounds of bread with
a spot of green through the middle.

White sandwich bread slices, crusts removed	10	10
Salad dressing (or mayonnaise)	1 tsp.	5 mL
Dijon (or grainy) mustard	1 tsp.	5 mL
Garlic herb spreadable cream cheese	1 tsp.	5 mL
Process cheese spread	1 tsp.	5 mL
Thousand Island salad dressing	1 tsp.	5 mL
Cooked fresh asparagus spears, trimmed to fit on bread	10	10
Grated Parmesan cheese	2 tbsp.	30 mL
Hard margarine (or butter), melted	1/4 cup	60 mL

Flatten each bread slice with rolling pin.

Spread 2 bread slices with 1/2 tsp. (2 mL) salad dressing each. Spread next 2 slices with 1/2 tsp. (2 mL) Dijon mustard each. Spread next 2 slices with 1/2 tsp. (2 mL) cream cheese each. Spread next 2 slices with 1/2 tsp. (2 mL) process cheese spread each. Spread remaining 2 slices with 1/2 tsp. (2 mL) Thousand Island salad dressing each.

Lay 1 asparagus spear on top of each bread slice. Roll up.

Spread Parmesan cheese evenly on large plate or waxed paper. Brush all sides of rolls with margarine. Roll in Parmesan cheese to coat completely. Cut each roll into 3 pieces. Arrange, seam side down, in single layer on greased baking sheet. Bake in 400°F (205°C) oven for 10 minutes until golden. Makes 30 appetizers.

1 appetizer: 40 Calories; 2.3 g Total Fat; 76 mg Sodium; 1 g Protein; 4 g Carbohydrate; trace Dietary Fiber

Pictured on page 11.

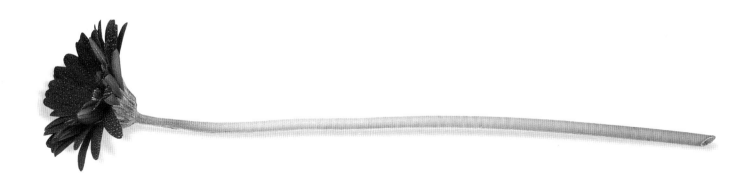

Top Left: Mushroom Pastries, page 10   Bottom: Beefy Phyllo Bites, below   Top Right: Rolled Asparagus, page 10

Beefy Phyllo Bites

Moist, flavorful filling in flaky pastry.

Lean ground beef	1 lb.	454 g
Finely chopped onion	1 1/2 cups	375 mL
Ketchup	1/2 cup	125 mL
Water	1/2 cup	125 mL
Garlic powder	1/2 tsp.	2 mL
Ground cinnamon	1/2 tsp.	2 mL
Ground nutmeg	1/4 tsp.	1 mL
Ground cloves	1/8 tsp.	0.5 mL
Salt	3/4 tsp.	4 mL
Pepper	1/2 tsp.	2 mL
Phyllo pastry sheets	6	6

Scramble-fry ground beef and onion in frying pan until beef is no longer pink and onion is soft and clear.

Add next 8 ingredients. Stir. Cover. Simmer for 5 minutes until thickened. Remove from heat. Cool.

Generously spray 3 phyllo sheets with cooking spray. Stack on top of one another. With long side of stack closest to you, evenly spread 1/2 of beef mixture on phyllo, leaving about 1 inch (2.5 cm) from edges on all 4 sides. Roll up, jelly roll-style, from long side. Repeat with remaining phyllo and filling. Carefully transfer rolls to greased baking sheet. Spray with cooking spray. Bake in 375°F (190°C) oven for about 20 minutes until golden. Let stand for 5 minutes. Cut into 1 inch (2.5 cm) slices. Makes about 30 appetizers.

1 appetizer: 52 Calories; 2.5 g Total Fat; 138 mg Sodium; 3 g Protein; 4 g Carbohydrate; trace Dietary Fiber

Pictured above.

Variation: For crispier pastry, freeze baked appetizers and reheat, partially thawed, on ungreased baking sheet in 350°F (175°C) oven for 15 minutes until heated through.

Avocado Dip

Smooth avocado flavor. So very easy and so very good. Surround with fresh veggies and an assortment of crackers and chips.

Bacon slices, diced	4	4
Light sour cream	1/3 cup	75 mL
Light mayonnaise	1/4 cup	60 mL
White vinegar	1 tbsp.	15 mL
Lime (or lemon) juice	1 tbsp.	15 mL
Dry mustard	1/8 tsp.	0.5 mL
Chopped onion	2 tbsp.	30 mL
Salt, just a pinch		
Cayenne pepper (optional)	1/4 tsp.	1 mL
Ripe avocado, peeled and cut up	1	1

Fry bacon in frying pan until crisp. Remove to paper towels to drain.

Put next 8 ingredients into blender. Add bacon. Process until smooth and bacon is very finely chopped.

With motor running, gradually add avocado, processing until smooth. Makes 1 1/3 cups (325 mL).

2 tbsp. (30 mL): 68 Calories; 6.2 g Total Fat; 79 mg Sodium; 1 g Protein; 3 g Carbohydrate; trace Dietary Fiber

Pictured on page 13.

Maple Lemon Fruit Dip

Serve this easy and quick dip with fruit or as a topping for ice cream. Excellent choice.

Golden corn syrup	1/2 cup	125 mL
Lemon juice	4 tsp.	20 mL
Maple flavoring	1 tsp.	5 mL
Frozen whipped topping, thawed	1 cup	250 mL

Combine corn syrup, lemon juice and maple flavoring in small bowl.

Fold in whipped topping. Makes 1 cup (250 mL).

2 tbsp. (30 mL): 90 Calories; 2.4 g Total Fat; 28 mg Sodium; trace Protein; 18 g Carbohydrate; trace Dietary Fiber

Pictured on page 13.

Asparagus Dip

Celebrate spring with fresh asparagus in this dip that has just a hint of heat. Serve with crackers and vegetables.

Fresh asparagus, trimmed of tough ends, cut up	3/4 lb.	340 g
Water		
Salad dressing (or mayonnaise)	1/4 cup	60 mL
Sour cream	1/2 cup	125 mL
Chopped fresh dill (or 1/4 tsp., 1 mL, dill weed)	1 tsp.	5 mL
Hot pepper sauce	1 tsp.	5 mL
Onion salt	1/4 tsp.	1 mL
Salt	1/8 tsp.	0.5 mL
Lime juice	1/2 tsp.	2 mL

Cook asparagus in water in large saucepan until very tender. Drain.

Put remaining 7 ingredients into blender. Add asparagus. Process until smooth. Makes 2 cups (500 mL).

2 tbsp. (30 mL): 35 Calories; 2.9 g Total Fat; 53 mg Sodium; 1 g Protein; 2 g Carbohydrate; trace Dietary Fiber

Pictured on page 13.

Tip *To have the most tender asparagus possible, trim the tough ends immediately prior to cooking, rather than when purchased. If not trimmed, the tough ends will stay hard and fibrous when cooked.*

Top: Asparagus Dip, above
Center: Avocado Dip, this page
Bottom: Maple Lemon Fruit Dip, this page

Rhubarb Loaf

Moist loaf with a sugar crust on top.

Hard margarine (or butter), softened	1/2 cup	125 mL
Brown sugar, packed	1 1/4 cups	300 mL
Large egg	1	1
Sour milk (see Note)	1 cup	250 mL
Vanilla	1 tsp.	5 mL
Chopped walnuts (optional)	1/2 cup	125 mL
Finely chopped fresh (or frozen, partially thawed) rhubarb	1 1/2 cups	375 mL
All-purpose flour	2 1/2 cups	625 mL
Baking soda	1 tsp.	5 mL
Salt	1 tsp.	5 mL
TOPPING		
Granulated sugar	1/3 cup	75 mL
Hard margarine (or butter), softened	1 tbsp.	15 mL

Cream margarine and brown sugar together in large bowl. Beat in egg. Add sour milk, vanilla and walnuts. Mix.

Add rhubarb. Stir.

Combine flour, baking soda and salt in medium bowl. Add to rhubarb mixture. Stir until just moistened. Turn into greased 9 x 5 x 3 inch (22 x 12.5 x 7.5 cm) loaf pan.

Topping: Mix granulated sugar and margarine well in small bowl. Sprinkle over batter. Bake in 350°F (175°C) oven for about 1 hour until wooden pick inserted in center comes out clean. Let stand in pan for 15 minutes. Turn out onto wire rack to cool. Cuts into 18 slices.

1 slice: 209 Calories; 6.6 g Total Fat; 291 mg Sodium; 3 g Protein; 35 g Carbohydrate; 1 g Dietary Fiber

Pictured on page 15.

Note: To make sour milk, add milk to 1 tbsp. (15 mL) white vinegar or lemon juice in 1 cup (250 mL) liquid measure. Stir.

Babka

Rich and wonderful. Perfectly browned and crisped crust on this fluffy light yellow bread. Flecks of color throughout.

Warm water	1/2 cup	125 mL
Granulated sugar	1 tsp.	5 mL
Active dry yeast (or 1/4 oz., 8 g, envelope)	2 1/2 tsp.	12 mL
Egg yolks (large)	6	6
Granulated sugar	1/3 cup	75 mL
Hard margarine (or butter), melted	6 tbsp.	100 mL
Grated lemon peel	4 tsp.	20 mL
Warm milk	1 cup	250 mL
Vanilla	1/2 tsp.	2 mL
Almond flavoring	1 tsp.	5 mL
All-purpose flour, approximately	5 1/4 cups	1.3 L
Golden raisins	1 cup	250 mL
Hard margarine (or butter), melted	1 tsp.	5 mL

Stir water and first amount of sugar in small bowl until sugar is dissolved. Sprinkle yeast over top. Let stand for 10 minutes. Stir to dissolve yeast.

Beat egg yolks in large bowl. Add second amount of sugar, margarine and lemon peel. Beat well. Add milk, vanilla and almond flavoring. Add yeast mixture. Mix.

Gradually work in flour and raisins until dough pulls away from sides of bowl. Turn out onto lightly floured surface. Knead for 6 to 8 minutes until smooth and elastic. Place dough in greased bowl, turning once to grease top. Cover with tea towel. Let stand in oven with light on and door closed for about 1 1/2 hours until doubled in bulk. Punch dough down. Divide into 2 equal portions. Shape each portion into loaf. Place in 2 greased 9 x 5 x 3 inch (22 x 12.5 x 7.5 cm) loaf pans. Cover with tea towel. Let stand in oven with light on and door closed for about 1 hour until doubled in size. Bake in 375°F (190°C) oven for about 30 minutes until golden. Turn out onto wire racks to cool.

Brush warm tops with margarine. Makes 2 loaves, each cutting into 16 slices, for a total of 32 slices.

1 slice: 138 Calories; 3.6 g Total Fat; 33 mg Sodium; 3 g Protein; 23 g Carbohydrate; 1 g Dietary Fiber

Pictured on page 15.

Variation: Bake in 1 greased bundt or tube pan.

Hot Cross Buns

Very nice soft buns filled with cinnamon and raisins.

Warm water	1/2 cup	125 mL
Granulated sugar	1 tsp.	5 mL
Active dry yeast (or 1/4 oz., 8 g, envelope)	2 1/2 tsp.	12 mL
Hard margarine (or butter), melted	1/4 cup	60 mL
Granulated sugar	1/3 cup	75 mL
Large eggs	2	2
Warm milk	1 cup	250 mL
Ground cinnamon	3/4 tsp.	4 mL
Salt	3/4 tsp.	4 mL
All-purpose flour	2 cups	500 mL
Raisins (or currants)	1 cup	250 mL
All-purpose flour, approximately	2 1/2 cups	625 mL
Hard margarine (or butter), melted	2 tsp.	10 mL
GLAZE		
Icing (confectioner's) sugar, approximately	1/2 cup	125 mL
Milk, approximately	2 1/2 tsp.	12 mL
Vanilla	1/8 tsp.	0.5 mL

Stir water into first amount of sugar in small bowl until sugar is dissolved. Sprinkle yeast over top. Let stand for 10 minutes. Stir to dissolve yeast.

Beat first amount of margarine, second amount of sugar and eggs together in large bowl. Add milk, cinnamon and salt. Stir. Add yeast mixture. Mix.

Add first amount of flour. Beat on low until just moistened. Beat on high for 1 minute.

Stir in raisins and enough of second amount of flour until dough pulls away from sides of bowl. Turn out onto floured surface. Knead for 5 to 8 minutes until smooth and elastic. Place dough in greased bowl, turning once to grease top. Cover with tea towel. Let stand in oven with light on and door closed for about 1 hour until doubled in bulk. Punch dough down. Cut off egg-size pieces and shape into balls. Arrange in single layer, about 3/4 inch (2 cm) apart, in greased 9 x 13 inch (22 x 33 cm) pan. Cover with tea towel. Let stand in oven with light on and door closed for about 45 minutes until doubled in size. Cut a cross on top of each bun about 1/4 inch (6 mm) deep using scissors, sharp knife or razor blade. Bake in 375°F (190°C) oven for about 15 minutes until golden. Turn out onto wire racks to cool.

Brush warm tops with second amount of margarine. Cool.

Glaze: Combine icing sugar, milk and vanilla in small bowl, adding more icing sugar or milk until barely pourable consistency. Drizzle or pipe over slashes. Makes 24 buns.

1 bun: 165 Calories; 3.2 g Total Fat; 114 mg Sodium; 4 g Protein; 30 g Carbohydrate; 1 g Dietary Fiber

Pictured below.

FRUITED HOT CROSS BUNS: Add about 2/3 cup (150 mL) finely chopped mixed glazed fruit.

To Make Ahead: Freeze unglazed buns in freezer container. Thaw. Drizzle or pipe glaze over slashes.

Left: Babka, page 14   Center: Hot Cross Buns, above   Right: Rhubarb Loaf, page 14

Left: Pancakes, page 17   Top Center: Rhubarb Strawberry Sauce, below   Right: Oven French Toast, this page

Rhubarb Strawberry Sauce

*Turn Pancakes, page 17, into something special
with this thick red sauce. Try it over wedges of
angel food cake, too, for a quick dessert.*

Fresh (or frozen, partially thawed) rhubarb, cut into small pieces	2 cups	500 mL
Water	1/2 cup	125 mL
Granulated sugar	1/2 cup	125 mL
Sliced fresh strawberries, mashed	1 cup	250 mL

Cook rhubarb in water in medium saucepan until tender and mushy. Remove from heat.

Add sugar. Stir until sugar is dissolved. Add strawberries. Stir. Makes 2 cups (500 mL).

2 tbsp. (30 mL): 31 Calories; 0.1 g Total Fat; 1 mg Sodium; trace Protein; 8 g Carbohydrate; trace Dietary Fiber

Pictured above.

Oven French Toast

*The sprinkle of cinnamon turns this brunch dish into
something special. Serve with mixed berries and bacon.*

Large eggs	4	4
Milk	2/3 cup	150 mL
Granulated sugar	1 tbsp.	15 mL
Hard margarine (or butter), softened	2 tbsp.	30 mL
Day-old white Texas toast bread slices	8	8

Icing (confectioner's) sugar, sprinkle
Ground cinnamon, sprinkle

Lightly beat eggs in medium bowl. Add milk and sugar. Mix well.

Spread margarine in 10 x 15 inch (25 x 38 cm) jelly roll pan.

Dip bread slices into egg mixture. Arrange in single layer over margarine. Bake in 425°F (220°C) oven for about 20 minutes until golden.

Sprinkle with icing sugar and cinnamon. Makes 8 slices.

1 slice: 145 Calories; 6.5 g Total Fat; 211 mg Sodium; 6 g Protein; 15 g Carbohydrate; 1 g Dietary Fiber

Pictured above.

Pancakes

Serve hot with butter and maple syrup or
Rhubarb Strawberry Sauce, page 16.

All-purpose flour	1 1/2 cups	375 mL
Granulated sugar	1 tbsp.	15 mL
Baking soda	1/4 tsp.	1 mL
Salt	1/4 tsp.	1 mL
Large egg	1	1
Cooking oil	1 tbsp.	15 mL
Sour milk (see Note)	1 1/4 cups	300 mL
Milk, approximately	1/2 cup	125 mL
Icing (confectioner's) sugar, sprinkle		

Combine flour, sugar, baking soda and salt in medium bowl. Make a well in center.

Put egg, cooking oil and sour milk into well. Stir until just moistened. Add enough milk to reach desired consistency. Heat frying pan until fairly hot. A few drops of water sprinkled on frying pan will bounce all over. If drops just sit there and sizzle, pan isn't hot enough. Spray frying pan with cooking spray for first batch only. Drop generous tablespoonful batter, for each pancake, into frying pan. Cook until bubbly and edges appear dry. Turn over. Cook until browned.

Sprinkle with icing sugar. Makes about 14 pancakes.

1 pancake: 78 Calories; 1.7 g Total Fat; 81 mg Sodium; 3 g Protein; 13 g Carbohydrate; trace Dietary Fiber

Pictured on page 16.

BLUEBERRY PANCAKES: Add 1 cup (250 mL) fresh (or frozen, thawed) blueberries to batter. Stir.

FRUIT CRÊPES: Add 1/2 to 2/3 cup (125 to 150 mL) milk to make thin batter. Drop 1 tbsp. (15 mL) batter in 7 or 8 inch (18 or 20 cm) frying pan. Immediately swirl to coat bottom of pan. Cook for 1 minute until top appears dry. Remove from pan. Repeat with remaining batter. Fill each crêpe with sliced fresh fruit. Roll up. Top with whipped cream. Makes about 24 crepes.

Note: To make sour milk, add milk to 1 tbsp. (15 mL) white vinegar or lemon juice in 1 cup (250 mL) liquid measure. Stir.

Asparagus With Pasta

Nice color contrast between the
asparagus and pimiento. Mild flavor.

Penne pasta (about 5 cups, 1.25 L)	1 lb.	454 g
Boiling water	16 cups	4 L
Salt	1 tbsp.	15 mL
Fresh asparagus, trimmed of tough ends, cut up	1 lb.	454 g
Grated lemon peel	1 tbsp.	15 mL
Water		

SAUCE		
Cans of skim evaporated milk (13 1/2 oz., 385 mL, each)	2	2
All-purpose flour	3 tbsp.	50 mL
Finely grated Parmesan cheese	1/2 cup	125 mL
Jar of chopped pimiento, drained	2 oz.	57 mL
Salt	1/2 tsp.	2 mL
Pepper	1/4 tsp.	1 mL
Ground nutmeg, just a pinch		
Coarsely grated Parmesan cheese, for garnish		

Cook pasta in boiling water and salt in large uncovered pot or Dutch oven for 12 to 14 minutes until tender but firm. Drain. Return to pot.

Cook asparagus and lemon peel in water in medium saucepan until asparagus is tender. Drain. Add to pasta.

Sauce: Stir evaporated milk into flour in medium saucepan until smooth.

Add next 5 ingredients. Heat and stir until boiling and thickened. Pour over pasta and asparagus. Stir gently.

Sprinkle with Parmesan cheese. Makes 11 cups (2.75 L).

1 cup (250 mL): 253 Calories; 2.4 g Total Fat; 289 mg Sodium; 14 g Protein; 43 g Carbohydrate; 2 g Dietary Fiber

Pictured on page 19.

SALMON AND ASPARAGUS WITH PASTA: Add 2 cans (6 1/2 oz., 184 g, each) salmon, drained, skin and round bones removed.

Shrimp Quiche

Great cheesy flavor with delicate dill and shrimp flavors.
A guaranteed hit.

Frozen cooked shrimp, thawed and blotted dry	4 oz.	113 g
Unbaked 9 inch (22 cm) pie shell	1	1
Grated Swiss cheese	1 cup	250 mL
Green onions, thinly sliced	4	4
Large eggs	3	3
All-purpose flour	2 tbsp.	30 mL
Milk	1/2 cup	125 mL
Mayonnaise	1/2 cup	125 mL
Chopped pimiento	2 tbsp.	30 mL
Curry powder	1/2 tsp.	2 mL
Fresh dill, chopped (or 1/4 tsp., 1 mL, dill weed)	1 tsp.	5 mL
Salt	1/4 tsp.	1 mL

Reserve 3 shrimp for top. Scatter remaining shrimp over bottom of pie shell. Sprinkle cheese and green onion over shrimp. Set aside.

Beat eggs in medium bowl until frothy. Beat in flour, milk, mayonnaise, pimiento, curry powder, dill and salt. Pour over shrimp mixture. Arrange reserved shrimp on top. Bake on bottom rack in 350°F (175°C) oven for about 40 minutes until knife inserted in center comes out clean. Let stand for 10 minutes before cutting. Cuts into 6 wedges.

1 wedge: 400 Calories; 30.8 g Total Fat; 457 mg Sodium; 15 g Protein; 15 g Carbohydrate; trace Dietary Fiber

Pictured on page 19.

Spinach Quiche

A must for spinach lovers. The nutmeg
is a noticeable (and nice!) addition.

Bag of fresh spinach, stems removed	10 oz.	300 g
Water		
Grated Swiss cheese	1 cup	250 mL
Green onions, thinly sliced	3	3
Unbaked 9 inch (22 cm) pie shell	1	1
Large eggs	3	3
All-purpose flour	1 tbsp.	15 mL
Salt	1/2 tsp.	2 mL
Pepper	1/8 tsp.	0.5 mL
Ground nutmeg	1/4 tsp.	1 mL
Half-and-half cream	1/2 cup	125 mL
Milk	1 1/4 cups	300 mL

Cook spinach in water in large saucepan until wilted. Drain. Squeeze dry. Chop finely.

Scatter cheese and green onion over bottom of pie shell. Scatter spinach over top.

Beat eggs in medium bowl until frothy. Beat in flour, salt, pepper and nutmeg. Add cream and milk. Beat on low until blended. Pour over spinach mixture. Bake on bottom rack in 350°F (175°C) oven for about 70 minutes until knife inserted in center comes out clean. Let stand for 10 minutes before cutting. Cuts into 6 wedges.

1 wedge: 282 Calories; 17.6 g Total Fat; 489 mg Sodium; 13 g Protein; 18 g Carbohydrate; 1 g Dietary Fiber

Pictured on page 19.

Top: Spinach Quiche, above
Center: Shrimp Quiche, this page
Bottom Left: Asparagus With Pasta, page 17
Bottom Right: Toasty Asparagus, page 20

Toasty Asparagus

Tasty combination of flavors and pretty contrasts of color.

CREAM SAUCE

Hard margarine (or butter)	1 tbsp.	15 mL
All-purpose flour	1/4 cup	60 mL
Salt	1/2 tsp.	2 mL
Pepper	1/8 tsp.	0.5 mL
Milk	2 cups	500 mL
Fresh asparagus, trimmed of tough ends and cut in half crosswise	1 lb.	454 g
Water		
Hard-boiled eggs	2	2
White bread slices, toasted and cut in half diagonally	8	8

Cream Sauce: Melt margarine in medium saucepan. Stir in flour, salt and pepper until smooth. Gradually stir in milk. Heat and stir until boiling and thickened.

Cook asparagus in water in large saucepan until tender. Drain. Keep warm.

Cut eggs in half. Remove yolks. Grate egg yolks onto small plate. Finely chop egg whites. Add egg whites to sauce.

Lay 4 halves of toast on each of 4 large individual plates. Divide asparagus halves over toast. If asparagus spears are a lot longer than toast, it looks much nicer to cut them to fit. Lay short pieces over asparagus already on toast. Spoon sauce over top. Divide and sprinkle grated egg yolk over sauce. Serves 4.

1 serving: 310 Calories; 9.1 g Total Fat; 701 mg Sodium; 15 g Protein; 43 g Carbohydrate; 2 g Dietary Fiber

Pictured on page 19.

Garden Salad

This salad shouts "Spring!" with its fresh taste and pretty mix of colors.

Fresh mixed greens (such as lettuce, chard, spinach and arugula), lightly packed	4 cups	1 L
Radishes, thinly sliced	6	6
Green onions (or chives), sliced	3	3
Chopped fresh parsley (or 1 1/2 tsp., 7 mL, flakes)	2 tbsp.	30 mL

DRESSING

Light salad dressing (or mayonnaise)	3 tbsp.	50 mL
White vinegar	1 tsp.	5 mL
Granulated sugar	1 tsp.	5 mL
Milk	2 tbsp.	30 mL
Small sprig of dill, finely chopped	1	1

Combine first 4 ingredients in large bowl.

Dressing: Mix all 5 ingredients well in small bowl. Makes 1/4 cup (60 mL) dressing. Drizzle over salad before serving. Toss, if desired. Makes 7 cups (1.75 L). Serves 4 to 6.

1 serving: 51 Calories; 3.1 g Total Fat; 128 mg Sodium; 1 g Protein; 5 g Carbohydrate; 1 g Dietary Fiber

Pictured on front cover and on page 23.

Meatless Taco Salad

A very tasty salad. Be sure to combine with dressing just before serving to prevent a soggy salad.

Medium head of iceberg lettuce, cut or torn	1	1
Grated sharp Cheddar cheese	3/4 cup	175 mL
Green onions, chopped	4	4
Medium radishes, sliced paper thin	6	6
Large tomato, seeded and diced	1	1
Crushed tortilla chips	1 cup	250 mL

DRESSING

Light salad dressing (or mayonnaise)	1/4 cup	60 mL
Milk	2 tbsp.	30 mL
Granulated sugar	1/2 tsp.	2 mL
White vinegar	1/2 tsp.	2 mL

Combine first 6 ingredients in large bowl.

Dressing: Mix salad dressing, milk, sugar and vinegar in small bowl. Add to salad just before serving. Toss until well coated. Makes 12 cups (3 L). Serves 8 to 10.

1 serving: 121 Calories; 7.8 g Total Fat; 200 mg Sodium; 4 g Protein; 9 g Carbohydrate; trace Dietary Fiber

Variation: Serve salad in tortilla bowl. Serves 12.

Pictured on page 2/3 and on page 22/23.

Coastal Rim Salad, below

Coastal Rim Salad

What a great combination of flavors!

DRESSING

Granulated sugar	2 tbsp.	30 mL
White vinegar	1 tbsp.	15 mL
Salt	1 tsp.	5 mL
Pepper	1/4 tsp.	1 mL
Olive (or cooking) oil	1 tbsp.	15 mL
Bacon slices, cooked crisp and crumbled	4	4
Green onions, sliced	4	4
Small head of iceberg lettuce, cut or torn, lightly packed (about 4 cups, 1 L)	1	1
Chow mein noodles	1/2 cup	125 mL
Sliced almonds, toasted (see Tip, page 28)	2 tbsp.	30 mL

Dressing: Combine first 5 ingredients in bowl or jar with tight-fitting lid. Stir or shake well. Chill until ready to serve. Makes about 2 tbsp. (30 mL) dressing.

Combine bacon, green onion, lettuce, noodles and almonds in large bowl. Just before serving, stir or shake dressing. Drizzle over salad. Makes 6 cups (1.5 L). Serves 4 to 6.

1 serving: 152 Calories; 10.3 g Total Fat; 727 mg Sodium; 4 g Protein; 12 g Carbohydrate; 1 g Dietary Fiber

Pictured above.

Broccoli Cheese Soup

Cheese at the bottom makes an interesting variation. For visual appeal the cheese can be put on top.

Tiny shell pasta	1 cup	250 mL
Boiling water	8 cups	2 L
Salt	1 tsp.	5 mL
Chopped fresh broccoli	2 cups	500 mL
Water		
Finely chopped onion	1/2 cup	125 mL
Hard margarine (or butter)	1 tbsp.	15 mL
Water	1 cup	250 mL
Chicken bouillon powder	4 tsp.	20 mL
Water	2 1/2 cups	625 mL
Salt	1/4 tsp.	1 mL
Pepper	1/16 tsp.	0.5 mL
Mozzarella cheese slices, cut into 1 inch (2.5 cm) wide strips	4	4
Mozzarella cheese slices, cut into thin strips, for garnish	2	2
Broccoli florets, for garnish	4	4

Cook pasta in boiling water and first amount of salt in large uncovered saucepan for 7 to 9 minutes until tender but firm. Drain.

Cook broccoli in water in medium saucepan until tender. Drain.

Sauté onion in margarine in frying pan until soft.

Put third amount of water, bouillon powder, broccoli and onion mixture into blender. Process until smooth. Add to pasta.

Add fourth amount of water, salt and pepper. Cook, stirring occasionally, until heated through.

Divide first amount of cheese among 4 individual empty bowls. Add soup.

Garnish with second amount of cheese and broccoli. Makes about 5 1/2 cups (1.4 L). Serves 4.

1 serving: 226 Calories; 9.2 g Total Fat; 935 mg Sodium; 10 g Protein; 26 g Carbohydrate; 2 g Dietary Fiber

Pictured on page 23.

Cream Of Asparagus Soup

Thick, pale green soup. Very good.

Fresh asparagus, trimmed of tough ends	1 1/2 lbs.	680 g
Water		
Chopped onion	3/4 cup	175 mL
Cooking oil	1 tbsp.	15 mL
Chicken bouillon powder	2 tsp.	10 mL
All-purpose flour	2 tbsp.	30 mL
Salt	3/4 tsp.	4 mL
Pepper (white is best)	1/4 tsp.	1 mL
Milk	2 cups	500 mL
Ground nutmeg, sprinkle (optional)		

Cook asparagus in water in large saucepan until tender. Drain. Reserve 4 spears for garnish. Cut remaining spears into 2 inch (5 cm) pieces. Return to saucepan.

Sauté onion in cooking oil in small frying pan until soft. Add to asparagus.

Combine bouillon powder, flour, salt and pepper in medium bowl. Stir in milk until smooth. Gradually stir into asparagus mixture. Heat and stir until boiling and thickened. Cool slightly. Put into blender. Process, in batches, until smooth. Return to saucepan. Heat through.

Garnish individual servings with reserved asparagus spears. Sprinkle with nutmeg. Makes 4 cups (1 L).

1 cup (250 mL): 155 Calories; 5.5 g Total Fat; 839 mg Sodium; 9 g Protein; 20 g Carbohydrate; 3 g Dietary Fiber

Pictured on page 2/3 and on page 22/23.

Top Left: Cream Of Asparagus Soup, above
Top Right: Broccoli Cheese Soup, page 21
Bottom Left: Meatless Taco Salad, page 20
Bottom Right: Garden Salad, page 20

Easter Brunch

Church celebrations, Easter egg hunts and Sunday brunch all come together on this uplifting and festive day. Enjoy mixing tradition with a little bit of fun as you prepare to serve family and friends—let everyone take delight in this wonderful springtime event.

Stuffed Cherry Tomatoes
Grassy Green Punch

Spring Salad
Simple Fruit Salad

Easter Egg Nests
Kulich

Asparagus Quiche
Roast Bacon

3-D Easter Bunny Cake

Stuffed Cherry Tomatoes

A burst of flavorful freshness in these pretty little circles. Serve with Roast Bacon, page 29.

Finely diced cooked potato	1 cup	250 mL
Hard-boiled egg, finely diced	1	1
Green onion, finely chopped	1	1
Finely diced celery	2 tbsp.	30 mL
Salad dressing (or mayonnaise)	2 tbsp.	30 mL
White vinegar	1 tsp.	5 mL
Onion salt	1/8 tsp.	0.5 mL
Pepper	1/4 tsp.	1 mL
Dry mustard	1/8 tsp.	0.5 mL
Salt	1/4 tsp.	1 mL
Cherry tomatoes, halved	34	34
Fresh sprigs of parsley (or dill), for garnish		

Combine potato, egg, green onion and celery in medium bowl.

Mix next 6 ingredients in small bowl. Add to potato mixture. Stir.

Cut tops off tomatoes. Scoop out and discard pulp. Stuff each shell with about 1 1/2 tsp. (7 mL) potato mixture.

Garnish each with parsley sprig. Makes 34 appetizers.

1 appetizer: 10 Calories; 0.5 g Total Fat; 25 mg Sodium; trace Protein; 1 g Carbohydrate; trace Dietary Fiber

Pictured on page 26 and on page 27.

Grassy Green Punch

Good even before the grass is green! Can easily be halved for a smaller group.

Packages of unsweetened lemon lime powdered drink mix (1/4 oz., 6 g, each)	2	2
Granulated sugar	1 1/2 cups	375 mL
Pineapple juice	6 cups	1.5 L
Water	6 cups	1.5 L
Lemon lime soft drink	6 cups	1.5 L

Measure first 4 ingredients into punch bowl. Stir until sugar is dissolved. Chill until ready to serve.

Just before serving, add soft drink. Stir gently. Makes 18 cups (4.5 L).

1 cup (250 mL): 152 Calories; 0.1 g Total Fat; 11 mg Sodium; trace Protein; 39 g Carbohydrate; trace Dietary Fiber

Pictured on page 27.

Easter Egg Nests

Easter-colored eggs nestled in soft, sweet bread.
Best if eaten the same day.

TINTED EGGS (per color)		
Large (or medium) eggs	12	12
Boiling water	1/2 cup	125 mL
White vinegar	1 tsp.	5 mL
Food coloring (your choice)	1/4 tsp.	1 mL
Cooking oil	1 tsp.	5 mL
EGG NESTS		
All-purpose flour	1 1/2 cups	375 mL
Granulated sugar	2 tbsp.	30 mL
Instant yeast (or 1/4 oz., 8 g, envelope)	2 1/2 tsp.	12 mL
Salt	3/4 tsp.	4 mL
Milk	1 cup	250 mL
Hard margarine (or butter)	2 tbsp.	30 mL
Large eggs	2	2
All-purpose flour, approximately	2 cups	500 mL

Tinted Eggs: Let eggs stand at room temperature for 30 minutes to reduce cracking when dipped. Warm liquid measure using hot water. Discard water. Combine boiling water, vinegar and food coloring in liquid measure. Dip eggs, 1 at a time, in colored water until desired color. Remove. Allow eggs to dry.

Brush each egg with cooking oil.

Egg Nests: Measure first amount of flour, sugar, yeast and salt into large bowl.

Heat milk and margarine in small saucepan until drop on inner wrist feels quite warm. Gradually add to flour mixture, beating on low, until just moistened.

Add eggs. Beat on medium for 2 minutes.

Work in enough of second amount of flour until dough pulls away from sides of bowl. Turn out onto floured surface. Knead for 5 to 8 minutes, adding more flour if necessary, until smooth and elastic. Place dough in greased bowl, turning once to grease top. Cover with tea towel. Let stand in oven with light on and door closed for about 1 hour until doubled in bulk. Punch dough down. Divide dough into 12 equal portions. Shape into balls. Press balls flat in center to form a "nest" to hold egg. Arrange 2 inches (5 cm) apart on greased baking sheet. Cover with tea towel. Let stand in oven with light on and door closed for about 30 minutes until doubled in size. Push colored eggs into nests.

Bake in 375°F (190°C) oven for about 30 minutes, pushing eggs down into nests after 10 minutes, until bread is golden. Eggs will be hard-cooked. Turn out onto wire racks to cool. Makes 12 egg nests.

1 egg nest: 267 Calories; 8.8 g Total Fat; 256 mg Sodium; 12 g Protein; 34 g Carbohydrate; 1 g Dietary Fiber

Pictured on page 26 and on page 27.

EGG BRAID: Divide dough into 3 portions. Roll each portion into 20 inch (50 cm) rope. Pinch 3 ends together. Loosely braid on greased baking sheet. Form into circle. Nestle about 8 colored eggs into braid. Cover with tea towel. Let stand in oven with light on and door closed for about 45 minutes until doubled in size. Bake as above.

Photo Legend next page:

1. Grassy Green Punch, page 24
2. Easter Egg Nests, this page
3. Asparagus Quiche, page 30
4. Stuffed Cherry Tomatoes, page 24
5. Spring Salad, page 28
6. Roast Bacon, page 29
7. 3-D Easter Bunny Cake, page 30

Kulich

Firm, dark brown upper crust with
golden crisp, flaky sides baked in a coffee can.

Warm milk	1 1/4 cups	300 mL
Granulated sugar	1 tsp.	5 mL
Active dry yeast (or 1/4 oz., 8 g, envelope)	2 1/2 tsp.	12 mL
Large eggs, room temperature	2	2
Granulated sugar	1/4 cup	60 mL
Hard margarine (or butter), melted	1/4 cup	60 mL
Salt	1/2 tsp.	2 mL
Vanilla	1/2 tsp.	2 mL
Ground nutmeg	1/4 tsp.	1 mL
Ground cardamom	1/2 tsp.	2 mL
All-purpose flour	2 cups	500 mL
All-purpose flour, approximately	2 1/2 cups	625 mL
Chopped almonds	1/3 cup	75 mL
Golden raisins	1/3 cup	75 mL
Chopped mixed glazed fruit	1/3 cup	75 mL
GLAZE		
Icing (confectioner's) sugar, approximately	1 cup	250 mL
Milk, approximately	1 tbsp.	15 mL
Almond flavoring (or vanilla)	1/4 tsp.	1 mL

Combine warm milk and first amount of sugar in small bowl. Sprinkle yeast over top. Let stand for 10 minutes. Stir to dissolve yeast.

Beat next 7 ingredients together in large bowl. Add yeast mixture. Mix.

Add first amount of flour. Beat well.

Work in enough of second amount of flour until dough pulls away from sides of bowl. Turn out onto floured surface. Knead for 8 to 10 minutes until smooth and elastic. Place dough in greased bowl, turning once to grease top. Cover with tea towel. Let stand in oven with light on and door closed for about 1 hour until doubled in bulk. Punch dough down.

Gradually knead almonds, raisins and fruit into dough. Divide into 4 equal portions. Shape each portion into a ball. Put balls into 4 greased 10 1/2 oz. (300 g) coffee cans. Cover with tea towel. Let stand in oven with light on and door closed for about 1 hour until doubled in size. Bake in 375°F (190°C) oven for 25 to 30 minutes until wooden pick inserted in center of each comes out clean and loaves are hollow-sounding when tapped. Turn out onto wire racks to cool.

Glaze: Combine icing sugar, milk and almond flavoring in small bowl, adding more icing sugar or milk until barely pourable consistency. Drizzle over bread, allowing some to run down sides. Makes 4 loaves, each cutting into 8 slices, for a total of 32 slices.

1 slice: 135 Calories; 2.9 g Total Fat; 67 mg Sodium; 3 g Protein; 24 g Carbohydrate; 1 g Dietary Fiber

Pictured on page 29.

Spring Salad

A sweet and sour dressing made just for spinach.

DRESSING		
Apple cider vinegar	3 tbsp.	50 mL
Granulated sugar	1/4 cup	60 mL
Worcestershire sauce	1/4 tsp.	1 mL
Sesame seeds, toasted (see Tip, below)	1 1/2 tbsp.	25 mL
Poppy seeds	2 tsp.	10 mL
Onion powder	1/4 tsp.	1 mL
Bag of fresh spinach, stems removed and leaves cut or torn	10 oz.	300 g
Fresh medium strawberries, halved	2 cups	500 mL

Dressing: Put first 6 ingredients into blender. Process until smooth. Pour into small bowl.

Combine spinach and strawberries in large bowl. Add as much dressing as needed just before serving. Toss until well coated. Makes 9 cups (2.25 L). Serves 6 to 8.

1 serving: 84 Calories; 2.1 g Total Fat; 42 mg Sodium; 2 g Protein; 16 g Carbohydrate; 3 g Dietary Fiber

Pictured on page 26.

Tip *To toast almonds and sesame seeds, place in single layer in ungreased shallow pan. Bake in 350°F (175°C) oven for 5 to 10 minutes, stirring or shaking often, until desired doneness.*

Left: Simple Fruit Salad, below

Top Right: Kulich, page 28

Simple Fruit Salad

*Fresh and canned fruit combine to make this salad.
Serve on a bed of shredded lettuce.*

Can of fruit cocktail, drained and juice reserved	14 oz.	398 mL
Medium orange, peeled and cut bite size	1	1
Fresh small strawberries, halved	8	8
Plain yogurt	2 tbsp.	30 mL
Granulated sugar	1 1/2 tsp.	7 mL
Reserved fruit cocktail juice	1/3 cup	75 mL
Shredded butter lettuce leaves, lightly packed	3 cups	750 mL

Toss fruit cocktail, orange and strawberry halves together in medium bowl.

Combine yogurt, sugar and reserved fruit cocktail juice in small bowl.

Divide and arrange lettuce on 4 individual salad plates. Divide fruit over lettuce. Drizzle dressing over top. Serves 4.

1 serving: 98 Calories; 0.3 g Total Fat; 14 mg Sodium; 2 g Protein; 24 g Carbohydrate; 2 g Dietary Fiber

Pictured above.

Roast Bacon

*An ideal way to serve bacon for a brunch or lunch.
Wonderful with Stuffed Cherry Tomatoes, page 24.*

Canadian back bacon, unsliced	1 1/2 lbs.	680 g
Brown sugar, packed	1/4 cup	60 mL
Prepared mustard	2 tsp.	10 mL
Prepared orange (or pineapple) juice	1/2 cup	125 mL
Sherry (or alcohol-free sherry), optional	2 tbsp.	30 mL

Score fat side of bacon about 4 times using sharp knife. Place in small roasting pan.

Combine brown sugar and mustard in small cup. Spread over top of bacon.

Mix orange juice and sherry in separate small cup. Pour into roasting pan. Cover. Bake in 350°F (175°C) oven for about 1 1/2 hours, basting at halftime, until golden. Cuts into 12 to 14 slices.

1 slice: 93 Calories; 3 g Total Fat; 525 mg Sodium; 10 g Protein; 6 g Carbohydrate; trace Dietary Fiber

Pictured on page 26.

Asparagus Quiche

One of the best quiches you will try. Great for company but treat your family once in awhile too!

Fresh asparagus spears, trimmed of tough ends and halved	1 lb.	454 g
Water		
Salt	1/2 tsp.	2 mL
Bacon slices, diced	8	8
Grated Swiss cheese (or your favorite)	1 cup	250 mL
Unbaked 9 inch (22 cm) pie shell	1	1
Large eggs	4	4
Milk	3/4 cup	175 mL
Skim evaporated milk	3/4 cup	175 mL
Ground nutmeg	1/8 tsp.	0.5 mL
Salt	1/2 tsp.	2 mL
Pepper	1/8 tsp.	0.5 mL

Cook asparagus in water and first amount of salt in large saucepan until tender. Drain. Cool. Chop.

Fry bacon in frying pan until golden. Drain. Cool.

Scatter cheese over bottom of pie shell. Lay asparagus over cheese in spiral pattern. Scatter bacon over top.

Beat eggs in medium bowl until frothy. Add both milks, nutmeg, second amount of salt and pepper. Beat on low until well blended. Pour over asparagus mixture. Bake on bottom rack in 350°F (175°C) oven for about 70 minutes until knife inserted in center comes out clean. Let stand for 10 minutes before cutting. Cuts into 6 wedges.

1 wedge: 336 Calories; 20.2 g Total Fat; 617 mg Sodium; 18 g Protein; 20 g Carbohydrate; 1 g Dietary Fiber

Pictured on page 27.

How To

3-D Easter Bunny Cake

This year the kids will actually get to see the Easter Bunny!

CAKE

Yellow cake mix (2 layer size)	1	1
Instant vanilla pudding powder (4 serving size)	1	1
Large eggs	4	4
Cooking oil	1/2 cup	125 mL
Water	1 cup	250 mL

ICING

Icing (confectioner's) sugar, approximately	6 cups	1.5 L
Hard margarine (or butter), softened	3/4 cup	175 mL
Vanilla	1 tbsp.	15 mL
Milk (or water), approximately	6 tbsp.	100 mL
Flake coconut	1 cup	250 mL
Drops of red food coloring	2 - 3	2 - 3
Flake coconut	1/4 cup	60 mL
Jelly bean	1	1
Black licorice strings	3	3
Multi-colored licorice candies	2	2
Large marshmallow	1	1

Cake: Empty cake mix into large bowl. Add pudding powder, eggs, cooking oil and water. Beat on low until just moistened. Beat on medium for about 2 minutes until smooth. Divide between 2 greased 9 inch (22 cm) round pans. Bake in 350°F (175°C) oven for about 30 minutes until wooden pick inserted in center comes out clean. Let stand for 15 minutes. Turn out onto wire racks to cool.

Icing: Beat first 4 ingredients together in medium bowl, adding more icing sugar or milk until desired spreading consistency.

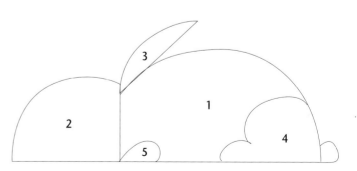

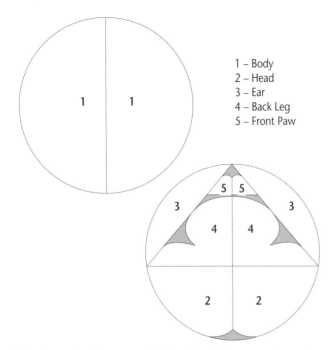

1 – Body
2 – Head
3 – Ear
4 – Back Leg
5 – Front Paw

Cut cakes as in diagrams. (**Note:** Shaded areas not used—so treat yourself as you assemble!)

For head and body, join 2 pieces for head and 2 pieces for body together, using icing. Set body, cut side down, on platter.

Place head in front of body, longer cut edge down. Ice both body and head with a thin layer of icing to seal in crumbs. Attach back legs, on either side of body, using icing. Thinly ice. Attach front paws, on either side of body, using icing. Thinly ice.

Thinly ice each ear. Attach curved side up in between head and body, using icing. Cover entire bunny with remaining icing in even layer.

Pat first amount of coconut, 2 to 3 tbsp. (30 to 50 mL) at a time, into icing.

Combine red food coloring with second amount of coconut in small plastic bowl with lid. Cover. Shake for about 2 minutes until coconut is colored. Pat onto ears.

Decorate using jelly bean, licorice strings and licorice candies. Use marshmallow for tail. Serves 12.

1 serving: 749 Calories; 33.4 g Total Fat; 581 mg Sodium; 3 g Protein; 113 g Carbohydrate; 1 g Dietary Fiber

Pictured on page 26 and above.

Top Left: Beef Oscar, below

Bottom Right: Round Steak Supreme, page 33

Beef Oscar

Decadent and rich with lots of sauce.

Fresh asparagus spears, trimmed of tough ends	16	16
Water		
Can of crabmeat, drained, cartilage removed	4 1/4 oz.	120 g
All-purpose flour	1/4 cup	60 mL
Salt	1/2 tsp.	2 mL
Pepper	1/8 tsp.	0.5 mL
Cooking oil	2 tsp.	10 mL
Hard margarine (or butter)	2 tsp.	10 mL
Beef tenderloin steaks (about 1 lb., 454 g)	4	4
JIFFY HOLLANDAISE		
Egg yolks (large)	3	3
Lemon juice	2 tbsp.	30 mL
Salt	1/4 tsp.	1 mL
Hot pepper sauce	1/16 tsp.	0.5 mL
Butter (not margarine)	3/4 cup	175 mL
Freshly ground pepper (optional)		
Chopped fresh parsley (optional)		

Cook asparagus in water in large saucepan until tender. Drain. Keep hot.

Heat crab in saucepan or in microwave. Keep hot.

Combine flour, salt and pepper in shallow bowl or on waxed paper.

Heat cooking oil and margarine in frying pan until hot. Press steaks with palm of hand to flatten. Press steaks in flour mixture to coat completely. Fry steaks on both sides in frying pan until browned. Cook until desired doneness. Transfer to 4 individual serving plates. Place 4 asparagus spears on each steak. Divide crab over asparagus. Keep warm.

Jiffy Hollandaise: Put egg yolks, lemon juice, salt and pepper sauce into blender. Process for 5 to 6 seconds until blended.

Heat butter in small saucepan until bubbling. With motor running, very slowly pour butter through hole in lid. Process until fluffy and thick. Spoon sauce over all.

Garnish with pepper and parsley. Serves 4.

1 serving: 651 Calories; 53.2 g Total Fat; 1000 mg Sodium; 34 g Protein; 10 g Carbohydrate; 1 g Dietary Fiber

Pictured above.

Veal Oscar: Omit beef. Use same amount of veal.

Round Steak Supreme

After browning, this economical cut of beef is cooked slowly to become tender and succulent.

Round steak, at least 1 inch (2.5 cm) thick	1 1/2 lbs.	680 g
Prepared mustard	2 tsp.	10 mL
All-purpose flour	3 tbsp.	50 mL
Salt	1 tsp.	5 mL
Pepper	1/4 tsp.	1 mL
Cooking oil	1 1/2 tbsp.	25 mL
Ketchup	1/4 cup	60 mL
Steak sauce	1 tsp.	5 mL
Chopped onion	1/2 cup	125 mL
Water	1 cup	250 mL

Score steak with knife on both sides. Brush with mustard.

Combine flour, salt and pepper in shallow dish or on waxed paper. Press steak into flour mixture to coat completely.

Brown both sides of steak in cooking oil in frying pan.

Combine ketchup, steak sauce, onion and water in small bowl. Add to steak. Cover. Cook on low for about 1 1/2 hours, adding more water if necessary, until very tender. To serve, cut into thin slices. Fan slices on serving platter. Spoon remaining sauce over slices. Serves 6.

1 serving: 253 Calories; 11.8 g Total Fat; 624 mg Sodium; 28 g Protein; 7 g Carbohydrate; 1 g Dietary Fiber

Pictured on page 32.

Two-Cupper Chicken Pie

You get a bit of everything with each bite. Use leftover chicken.

Cooked frozen peas	2 cups	500 mL
Cooked diced carrot (about 7 small)	2 cups	500 mL
Cooked diced potato (about 2 1/2 medium)	2 cups	500 mL
Cooked diced chicken	2 cups	500 mL
Salt, sprinkle		
Pepper, sprinkle		
Warmed chicken gravy	2 cups	500 mL

Two-Cupper Chicken Pie, below

TOPPING

All-purpose flour	1 1/2 cups	375 mL
Baking powder	1 tbsp.	15 mL
Salt	1/4 tsp.	1 mL
Water	1/2 cup	125 mL
Cooking oil	1 tbsp.	15 mL
Large egg	1	1
Water	1 tbsp.	15 mL

Layer peas, carrot, potato and chicken in ungreased 3 quart (3 L) casserole. Sprinkle with salt and pepper. Pour gravy evenly over top.

Topping: Combine flour, baking powder and salt in medium bowl. Make a well in center.

Pour water and cooking oil into well. Stir until soft ball forms. Turn out onto lightly floured surface. Knead 6 to 8 times. Roll or pat to size of casserole. Cut slits. Place over top.

Combine egg and water in small bowl. Brush over topping. Bake, uncovered, in 400°F (205°C) oven for 25 to 30 minutes until heated through and golden. Serves 6.

1 serving: 376 Calories; 7.3 g Total Fat; 808 mg Sodium; 23 g Protein; 54 g Carbohydrate; 6 g Dietary Fiber

Pictured above.

Mediterranean Chicken

A very tasty dish and so easy to prepare.
Spices are just right for all to enjoy.

Chicken parts, skin removed	3 lbs.	1.4 kg
Salt, sprinkle		
Pepper, sprinkle		
Chopped onion	1 1/2 cups	375 mL
Can of condensed cream of mushroom soup	10 oz.	284 mL
White vinegar	1 tbsp.	15 mL
Poultry seasoning	1/2 tsp.	2 mL
Dried whole oregano	1/2 tsp.	2 mL
Dried rosemary, crushed	1/2 tsp.	2 mL
Parsley flakes	1/2 tsp.	2 mL
Paprika	1/2 tsp.	2 mL

Arrange chicken in small roasting pan. Sprinkle with salt and pepper. Scatter onion over chicken.

Measure remaining 7 ingredients into medium bowl. Stir vigorously. Spoon over onion. Cover. Bake in 350°F (175°C) oven for 1 to 1 1/2 hours until chicken is tender. Serves 4.

1 serving: 299 Calories; 10.9 g Total Fat; 739 mg Sodium; 37 g Protein; 12 g Carbohydrate; 1 g Dietary Fiber

Pictured on page 34/35.

Left: Mediterranean Chicken, this page

Plum-Sauced Chicken

Delicate sweet flavor and tender moist chicken.

PLUM SAUCE		
Can of plums, drained and pitted	14 oz.	398 mL
Lemon juice	1 tbsp.	15 mL
Soy sauce	2 tsp.	10 mL
Granulated sugar	1 tsp.	5 mL
Chicken parts, skin removed	3 lbs.	1.4 kg

Plum Sauce: Put first 4 ingredients into blender. Process until smooth. Pour into small bowl. Makes 3/4 cup (175 mL) sauce.

Arrange chicken in single layer in ungreased 4 quart (4 L) casserole. Spoon sauce over chicken, being sure to get some on every piece. Cover. Bake in 350°F (175°C) oven for about 1 1/2 hours until chicken is very tender. Transfer sauce to frying pan. Bring sauce to a boil. Boil for about 10 minutes until reduced and thickened. Spoon over chicken. Serves 4.

1 serving: 244 Calories; 5 g Total Fat; 301 mg Sodium; 36 g Protein; 13 g Carbohydrate; 1 g Dietary Fiber

Pictured on page 35.

Top Center: Chicken Noodle With Ham, below

Right: Plum-Sauced Chicken, page 34

Chicken Noodle With Ham

*Great flavor combo. Satisfies a cream sauce craving
without adding the extra calories.*

Milk	3/4 cup	175 mL
All-purpose flour	3 tbsp.	50 mL
Chicken bouillon powder	1 1/2 tsp.	7 mL
Large eggs	2	2
Water	1 tbsp.	15 mL
Hard margarine (or butter)	1 tsp.	5 mL
Fettuccine	8 oz.	225 g
Boiling water	12 cups	3 L
Salt	2 tsp.	10 mL
Sliced fresh mushrooms	2 cups	500 mL
Hard margarine (or butter)	1 tbsp.	15 mL
Green onions, thinly sliced	6	6
Can of flaked chicken, drained and broken up	6 1/2 oz.	184 g
Can of ham flakes, drained and broken up	6 1/2 oz.	184 g
Grated Parmesan cheese, for garnish	2 tbsp.	30 mL
Dried whole oregano, for garnish	1/2 tsp.	2 mL

Stir milk into flour and bouillon powder in small saucepan until smooth. Heat and stir until boiling and thickened. It will be quite thick. Keep warm.

Beat eggs and water together in small bowl using fork. Melt first amount of margarine in frying pan. Add eggs. Cook on medium, without stirring, until set. Remove from pan. Roll up, jelly roll-style. Cut into thin strips.

Cook fettuccine in boiling water and salt in large uncovered pot or Dutch oven for 11 to 13 minutes until tender but firm. Drain. Return fettuccine to pot. Keep warm.

Sauté mushrooms in second amount of margarine in large pot or frying pan until liquid from mushrooms has evaporated. Add milk mixture and fettuccine. Stir. Heat through.

Add green onion, chicken and ham. Stir. Heat through. Turn into large bowl or platter. Top with egg strips.

Mix Parmesan cheese and oregano in small cup. Sprinkle over top. Makes 5 cups (1.25 L).

1 cup (250 mL): 369 Calories; 13.1 g Total Fat; 853 mg Sodium; 24 g Protein; 42 g Carbohydrate; 2 g Dietary Fiber

Pictured above.

Lamb Chops

Not your usual plain chops. The onion, tomato and sauce are good additions.

Shoulder lamb chops (see Note)	4	4
Hard margarine (butter browns too fast)	1 tbsp.	15 mL
Large onion rings	4	4
Slices of large tomato	4	4
Water	1 cup	250 mL
Garlic salt	1/4 tsp.	1 mL
Dried rosemary, crushed	1/8 tsp.	0.5 mL
Dill weed	1/8 tsp.	0.5 mL
Pepper	1/8 tsp.	0.5 mL
Salt, sprinkle		
Pepper, sprinkle		
Fresh dill sprigs (optional)		

Brown lamb chops on both sides in margarine in frying pan.

Place 1 onion ring on each chop. Top each with 1 tomato slice.

Combine next 5 ingredients in small cup. Pour over chops. Add enough additional water to reach halfway up chops. Bring to a boil. Reduce heat. Cover. Simmer for about 30 minutes until lamb is tender.

Sprinkle with salt and second amount of pepper. Garnish with dill sprigs. Serves 4.

1 serving: 383 Calories; 30.8 g Total Fat; 193 mg Sodium; 23 g Protein; 3 g Carbohydrate; 1 g Dietary Fiber

Pictured on page 37.

Note: Shoulder chops are larger than other lamb chops and are easily identified by the round bone in the center.

Lamb En Croûte

This attractive, golden, lightly glazed pastry is wonderful served with the tangy sauce. The dook-SEHL stuffing makes this an elegant, but simple, presentation.

Boneless lamb loin chops, trimmed of fat	4	4
Cooking oil	1 tbsp.	15 mL
DUXELLE		
Chopped fresh mushrooms	1 cup	250 mL
Finely chopped onion	1 tbsp.	15 mL
Cooking oil	1 tbsp.	15 mL
Green onions, chopped	2	2
Parsley flakes	1/2 tsp.	2 mL
White (or alcohol-free) wine	2 tbsp.	30 mL
Salt	1/2 tsp.	2 mL
Pepper	1/8 tsp.	0.5 mL
Box of frozen puff pastry (14 oz., 397 g), thawed	1/2	1/2
Large egg, fork-beaten	1	1
Milk	1 tbsp.	15 mL
SAUCE ROBERT		
Water	1 cup	250 mL
White vinegar	2 tbsp.	30 mL
Worcestershire sauce	1 tsp.	5 mL
Prepared mustard	1 tsp.	5 mL
Onion salt	1/4 tsp.	1 mL
Green onion, finely chopped	1	1
Parsley flakes	1/4 tsp.	1 mL

Brown lamb chops on both sides in cooking oil in frying pan. Reduce heat. Cook for 15 to 20 minutes, turning occasionally, until juices run clear. Remove lamb chops. Cool.

Duxelle: Sauté mushrooms and onion in cooking oil in same frying pan until onion is soft and liquid from mushrooms has evaporated.

Add green onion, parsley flakes, wine, salt and pepper. Stir. Bring to a boil. Reduce heat. Simmer, uncovered, until liquid is absorbed. Cool.

Divide pastry into 4 equal portions. Roll out each portion on lightly floured surface large enough to enclose chop. Spread 1/8 of Duxelle on each portion to size of chop. Set chops over Duxelle. Divide and cover each chop with remaining Duxelle. Dampen edges of pastry with water. Fold up pastry to make parcels. Gather and pinch pastry on top of chops. Arrange parcels in single layer on greased baking sheet.

Mix egg and milk in small cup. Brush liberally over parcels. Cut 3 or 4 slits in top of each to allow steam to escape. Bake on top rack of 425°F (220°C) oven for 15 to 20 minutes until pastry is golden.

Sauce Robert: Pour water into same frying pan. Stir to loosen any brown bits. Pour into small saucepan. Add remaining 6 ingredients. Bring to a boil. Makes generous 1 cup (250 mL) sauce. Serve with parcels. Serves 4.

1 serving: 540 Calories; 35.1 g Total Fat; 638 mg Sodium; 27 g Protein; 28 g Carbohydrate; trace Dietary Fiber

Pictured on page 37.

Top Right: Lamb En Croûte, this page
Center Left: Herbed Potatoes, page 38
Bottom: Lamb Chops, this page

Fish Anyway

When you have no luck on your fishing outing,
try this instead. If you were lucky, try this anyway.

Dry onion soup mix, stir before measuring	1 tbsp.	15 mL
Light sour cream	1/2 cup	125 mL
Fine dry bread crumbs	1/2 cup	125 mL
Grated Parmesan cheese	1 tbsp.	15 mL
Paprika	1/8 tsp.	0.5 mL
Fish fillets (4 oz., 113 g, each)	4	4
Hard margarine (or butter), melted	2 tbsp.	30 mL
Lemon peel twists (optional)		

Combine soup mix with sour cream in shallow bowl.

Mix bread crumbs, Parmesan cheese and paprika in separate shallow bowl or on waxed paper.

Dip fillets in sour cream mixture. Roll in crumb mixture to coat completely. Arrange in single layer in greased 9 x 13 inch (22 x 33 cm) dish.

Drizzle with margarine. Bake in 500°F (260°C) oven for 10 to 12 minutes until fish flakes easily when tested with fork.

Garnish with lemon peel. Serves 4.

1 serving: 254 Calories; 9.6 g Total Fat; 372 mg Sodium; 25 g Protein; 13 g Carbohydrate; 1 g Dietary Fiber

Pictured on page 39.

Veggie Pasta

Pleasing combination of shapes, textures, colors and flavors.

Rotini pasta	4 1/4 cups	1 L
Boiling water	12 cups	3 L
Salt	1 tbsp.	15 mL
Bacon slices, diced	5	5
Small fresh mushrooms, quartered	3 cups	750 mL
Fresh baby peas	1 cup	250 mL
Finely grated Parmesan cheese, sprinkle		

Cook pasta in boiling water and salt in large uncovered pot or Dutch oven for 10 to 12 minutes until tender but firm. Drain. Return to pot.

Fry bacon in frying pan until half cooked.

Add mushrooms and peas. Sauté until bacon is crispy and liquid from mushrooms has evaporated. Add to pasta. Stir.

Sprinkle with Parmesan cheese. Makes 9 cups (2.25 L). Serves 8.

1 serving: 219 Calories; 2.9 g Total Fat; 89 mg Sodium; 9 g Protein; 39 g Carbohydrate; 3 g Dietary Fiber

Pictured on page 39.

Herbed Potatoes

Tender golden-brown baby potatoes prepared in 10 minutes.

Baby potatoes	20	20
Cooking oil	2 tsp.	10 mL
Ground savory	1 tsp.	5 mL
Dried whole oregano	1 tsp.	5 mL
Parsley flakes	1 tsp.	5 mL
Seasoned salt	1/2 tsp.	2 mL

Rub potatoes with cooking oil until coated.

Combine remaining 4 ingredients in small resealable plastic bag. Add potatoes, in batches. Shake to coat. Arrange in single layer on ungreased baking sheet. Bake in 350°F (175°C) oven for about 45 minutes until tender. Serves 4.

1 serving: 134 Calories; 2.5 g Total Fat; 159 mg Sodium; 3 g Protein; 25 g Carbohydrate; 2 g Dietary Fiber

Pictured on page 37.

Variation: Omit savory, oregano, parsley flakes and seasoned salt. Sprinkle potatoes with 1/2 tsp. (2 mL) garlic and herb no-salt seasoning (such as Mrs. Dash).

Top Left: Veggie Pasta, page 38 — Bottom: Fish Anyway, page 38 — Top Right: Spinach Scallop, below

Spinach Scallop

Spinach done somewhat soufflé style.

Bag of fresh spinach, stems removed	10 oz.	300 g
Water		
Chopped onion	1/4 cup	60 mL
Hard margarine (or butter)	1 tbsp.	15 mL
Milk	3/4 cup	175 mL
All-purpose flour	2 tbsp.	30 mL
Egg yolks (large)	2	2
Ground nutmeg	1/16 tsp.	0.5 mL
Salt	1/2 tsp.	2 mL
Pepper	1/8 tsp.	0.5 mL
Egg whites (large), room temperature	2	2
TOPPING		
Hard margarine (or butter)	1 tbsp.	15 mL
Fine dry bread crumbs	1/4 cup	60 mL

Cook spinach in small amount of water in large saucepan until wilted and tender. Drain well. Cool. Finely chop. Transfer to medium bowl.

Sauté onion in margarine in frying pan until soft. Add to spinach.

Stir milk into flour in small bowl until smooth. Add egg yolks, nutmeg, salt and pepper. Stir. Stir into spinach mixture.

Beat egg whites in small bowl until stiff peaks form. Fold into spinach mixture. Turn into ungreased 1 quart (1 L) casserole.

Topping: Melt margarine in small saucepan. Stir in bread crumbs until well coated. Sprinkle over spinach mixture. Bake, uncovered, in 350°F (175°C) oven for about 25 minutes until set. Serves 4.

1 serving: 172 Calories; 9.5 g Total Fat; 539 mg Sodium; 8 g Protein; 14 g Carbohydrate; 2 g Dietary Fiber

Pictured above.

Berry Trifle

Mmm...Rich red raspberries, off-white cake, yellow custard and white whipped cream—incredible layered look!

CUSTARD

Milk	2 1/2 cups	625 mL
Vanilla pudding powder (not instant), 6 serving size	1	1
Salt	1/2 tsp.	2 mL
Milk	1/2 cup	125 mL

CAKE

All-purpose flour	1 1/2 cups	375 mL
Granulated sugar	3/4 cup	175 mL
Baking powder	1 1/2 tsp.	7 mL
Salt	1/2 tsp.	2 mL
Hard margarine (or butter), softened	1/2 cup	125 mL
Large egg	1	1
Vanilla	1 tsp.	5 mL
Milk	3/4 cup	175 mL
Sherry (or alcohol-free sherry or white grape juice)	1/2 cup	125 mL
Fresh raspberries (or sliced fresh strawberries)	3 cups	750 mL
Frozen whipped topping, thawed	2 cups	500 mL

Custard: Bring first amount of milk to a boil in medium saucepan.

Mix pudding powder, salt and second amount of milk in small bowl. Stir into boiling milk. Heat and stir until boiling and thickened. Cover with waxed paper directly on surface to prevent skin forming. Cool. Chill for 2 to 3 hours.

Cake: Beat first 8 ingredients together in large bowl until smooth. Turn into greased 9 x 9 inch (22 x 22 cm) pan. Bake in 350°F (175°C) oven for about 25 minutes until wooden pick inserted in center comes out clean. Cool. Cut into 3/4 inch (2 cm) cubes.

Put 1/2 of cake cubes into large trifle bowl. Drizzle 1/2 of sherry over top. Reserve a few raspberries for garnish. Scatter 1/2 of remaining raspberries over cake cubes. Spoon 1/2 of custard over raspberries. Repeat with remaining cake cubes, sherry, raspberries and custard. Spread whipped topping over custard. Arrange reserved raspberries over whipped topping. Chill. Serves 10 to 12.

1 serving: 404 Calories; 15.7 g Total Fat; 581 mg Sodium; 7 g Protein; 59 g Carbohydrate; 3 g Dietary Fiber

Pictured on page 41.

Rhubarb Cheese Dessert

Wonderful tart rhubarb flavor with creamy cream cheese and complementary graham crust. Dress up individual servings with mint leaves.

GRAHAM CRUST

Hard margarine (or butter)	1/3 cup	75 mL
Graham cracker crumbs	1 1/2 cups	375 mL
Icing (confectioner's) sugar	2 tbsp.	30 mL

FILLING

Granulated sugar	2/3 cup	150 mL
Chopped fresh rhubarb	3 cups	750 mL
Water	2 tbsp.	30 mL
Cornstarch	4 tsp.	20 mL
Light cream cheese, softened	12 oz.	375 g
Granulated sugar	1/2 cup	125 mL
Large eggs	2	2

Graham Crust: Melt margarine in medium saucepan. Add graham crumbs and icing sugar. Stir until well coated. Press into foiled-lined 9 x 9 inch (22 x 22 cm) pan.

Filling: Combine first amount of granulated sugar and rhubarb in small saucepan. Heat and stir until simmering. Simmer until rhubarb is soft.

Stir water into cornstarch in small cup until smooth. Stir into rhubarb mixture until simmering and thickened. Set saucepan in cold water, stirring to cool.

Beat cream cheese and second amount of granulated sugar together in medium bowl. Beat in eggs, 1 at a time. Spread smoothly over crust. Drop dabs of rhubarb mixture here and there onto cream cheese mixture. Swirl with knife to create marble effect. Bake in 350°F (175°C) oven for about 35 minutes until wooden pick inserted in center comes out clean. Cuts into 12 pieces.

1 piece: 272 Calories; 13.4 g Total Fat; 360 mg Sodium; 5 g Protein; 34 g Carbohydrate; trace Dietary Fiber

Pictured on page 41.

Top: Berry Trifle, this page
Center Left: Rhubarb Cobbler, page 42
Center Right: Rhubarb Cheese Dessert, above
Bottom: Strawberry Heaven, page 42

Rhubarb Cobbler

This is rhubarb at its best, especially if served with ice cream or cream.

Fresh rhubarb (or frozen, partially thawed), cut into 1/2 inch (12 mm) pieces	5 cups	1.25 L
Granulated sugar	1 cup	250 mL
TOPPING		
All-purpose flour	1 cup	250 mL
Baking powder	1 1/2 tsp.	7 mL
Granulated sugar	1/4 cup	60 mL
Salt	1/4 tsp.	1 mL
Hard margarine (or butter)	1/3 cup	75 mL
Quick-cooking rolled oats (not instant)	1/2 cup	125 mL
Milk	2/3 cup	150 mL
Granulated sugar, sprinkle (optional)		

Put rhubarb into ungreased 2 quart (2 L) casserole. Pour sugar over top. Stir until combined.

Topping: Combine flour, baking powder, first amount of sugar and salt in medium bowl. Cut in margarine until mixture is crumbly.

Add rolled oats. Stir. Add milk. Stir until just moistened. Drop dabs here and there onto rhubarb mixture.

Sprinkle with second amount of sugar. Bake, uncovered, in 375°F (190°C) oven for about 55 minutes until rhubarb is cooked and top is golden and crusty. Serve warm. Serves 6 to 8.

1 serving: 415 Calories; 12 g Total Fat; 336 mg Sodium; 6 g Protein; 73 g Carbohydrate; 2 g Dietary Fiber

Pictured on page 41.

Strawberry Heaven

A layered dessert with a bright red middle layer and strawberries in strawberry jelly. Excellent.

FIRST LAYER		
Hard margarine (or butter)	1/2 cup	125 mL
Graham cracker crumbs	2 cups	500 mL
Granulated sugar	1/4 cup	60 mL
SECOND LAYER		
Cream cheese, softened	8 oz.	250 g
Icing (confectioner's) sugar	1/3 cup	75 mL
Vanilla	1 tsp.	5 mL
THIRD LAYER		
Package of strawberry-flavored gelatin (jelly powder)	3 oz.	85 g
Boiling water	1 cup	250 mL
Package of frozen sliced strawberries in syrup, partially thawed	15 oz.	425 g
FOURTH LAYER		
Envelope of dessert topping (not prepared)	1	1
Milk	1/2 cup	125 mL
Vanilla	1/2 tsp.	2 mL

First Layer: Melt margarine in medium saucepan. Add graham crumbs and sugar. Stir until well coated. Reserve 1/4 cup (60 mL) graham crumb mixture. Pack remaining graham crumb mixture into ungreased 9 × 9 inch (22 × 22 cm) pan. Bake in 350°F (175°C) oven for 10 minutes. Cool.

Second Layer: Beat cream cheese, icing sugar and vanilla together in small bowl. Drop dabs here and there over first layer. Spread with back of wet spoon. Chill.

Third Layer: Combine gelatin and boiling water in medium bowl. Stir until gelatin is dissolved.

Add strawberries. Stir until berries are completely thawed and gelatin is syrupy. If necessary, chill for about 10 minutes until gelatin is syrupy. Pour over second layer. Chill until firm.

Fourth Layer: Beat dessert topping, milk and vanilla together in small bowl until stiff peaks form. Spread over third layer. Sprinkle reserved crumbs over top. Chill. Serves 9.

1 serving: 434 Calories; 24.5 g Total Fat; 366 mg Sodium; 5 g Protein; 51 g Carbohydrate; 1 g Dietary Fiber

Pictured on page 41.

Summer

Summer

June   Salad greens are abundant, vegetable stalks and vines stand tall and strong, berry picking begins and fruits replace blossoms; what we aren't growing, the farmers' markets will provide.

July   Salad greens continue to replenish, vegetables take shape, fruits start to fall into baskets and fresh herbs abound.

August   Above-ground vegetables and fruits are peaking and harvesting begins.

Summertime cooking is all about enjoying the weather outdoors as much as the food—and if the two can be combined, so much the better! What better time to enjoy potato, fruit, pasta or vegetable salads and cool drinks? It's the season to bring garden-fresh vegetables and fruits to your table, using fuss-free cooking methods that don't require your presence in a heated kitchen.

Sweet, aromatic tomatoes and crunchy carrots are what we crave as the summer offers up a garden's bounty, starting in June. The first harvests of the season are usually eaten raw, maybe with a dash of salt.

The next pickings are seasoned lightly with delicate herbs such as basil. Peas, shelled on the back porch, or wonderful baby potatoes go so well with fresh dill, which can overtake a garden.

If you don't have a growing space of your own, farmers' markets provide all the freshness you could wish for. Ask the vendors what will be available, and when, in your part of the country so you can plan ahead. Fresh, juicy cherries are a summer standard, eaten by the bowlful or made into mouthwatering pies.

June

June heralds the coming of what we truly call summer—the grass still has a touch of new lime green and the sun is busy climbing to its highest point in the sky. Biking to work and eating lunch outdoors becomes a routine treat for many people.

Now is the time to make sure the picnic basket is ready for those unexpectedly hot summer days. Whether you spread a blanket on the front lawn or bike to a nearby park, picnics can be as easy or elaborate as you want. Make a batch of sandwiches or wraps, an icy cold drink and a crisp salad. Pack it all in an insulated tote and you're off—for an afternoon tour of the countryside searching for antiques and flea market treasures, or a lazy day at the beach to read under an umbrella.

Bring a double recipe of a chilled dessert or fruit salad in a cooler to share with everyone at the family reunion by the lake. Unpack a chicken supper with a bottle of wine as the sun slowly sets, or meet a friend for a special outdoor breakfast before work one morning.

Choose paper plates and napkins along with plastic cups and cutlery for a casual, no-fuss get-together, or take cloth linens and fancier tableware to make the occasion more special. Wicker hampers will hold everything you need—use refreezable ice blocks and newspaper as insulation, but Styrofoam or insulated coolers work just as well. Resealable plastic bags with ice cubes or chilled drink cans or boxes will also help to keep everything cold.

Celebrate the beginning of summer holidays with a backyard party on the deck, patio or lawn. Decorate with ornamental lanterns or candles, and tempt guests with barbecued salmon or grilled sea bass. Make a special holiday by inviting cousins, aunts and uncles for a family reunion. Meet at a lake or campsite where everyone can set up a tent or camper. Dress up meal times with pretty plastic or cloth table linens that are easy to clean. Many of these summertime recipes can be doubled or tripled to feed a crowd.

July

July means summer vacation for most families, a perfect month to plan cottage or camping getaways, or to visit family and friends. As the mercury climbs above 85°F (30°C) outside, the kitchen stove is abandoned and the outdoor barbecue takes over as the preferred cooking method.

And what is summer without a camping trip? Just because you are roughing it doesn't mean your taste buds are left at home! Cook up the catch of the day or skewers of beef over an open fire. Heat up packets of rice, potatoes or vegetables that you've cooked at home. Food tastes so good in the great outdoors!

August

When July's sultry weather drifts lazily into August, gardeners and cooks watch with delight as the bounty of fruits and vegetables comes into its prime. As summer winds down and the first hint of cooler weather arrives, plan a backyard bash and prepare most of the food ahead of time so that you're able to enjoy the company of your guests.

Or how about a more elegant porch party? Remember to include freshly harvested fruits and vegetables, either on their own or as a colorful combination in salads, with rice or pasta. Round the meal off with a chilled soup and a refreshing dessert.

Either way, watch the sun set in a relaxed summer evening atmosphere as the countdown to fall begins.

Summer Food Safety

Foods such as meat and dairy products should not be left at room temperature for longer than one hour. Harmful bacteria, that cause food poisoning, grow between 40°F (4°C) and 140°F (60°C). Those foods require an internal temperature below or above these readings in order to kill or at least slow the growth of bacteria. This applies year round, not just in the summer. A heated car in the winter can promote growth just as easily as a hot kitchen in the summer. Shopping and storage must be done with care to prevent spoilage. Here are some suggestions:

* To prevent food from spoiling while sitting in a hot car, purchase produce at the farmers' market before heading to the grocery store.

* Chill or freeze perishable foods as soon as you get home.

* To keep eggs as fresh as possible and to keep them from absorbing flavor and odor from other foods, store them in their original carton. This way you will always have the best-before date handy.

* Eat or chill any food that contains raw egg immediately after preparation.

* Wash fruits and vegetables in soapy water to remove bacteria, rinse thoroughly before eating or using.

* Ground beef can spoil rapidly so be especially careful how long you take between putting it into your grocery cart and putting it into your refrigerator or freezer. Freeze ground beef immediately or chill and cook within two days of purchase.

* Serve plates of cold foods, such as deviled eggs, on a tray of ice cubes or crushed ice to keep them cold longer.

* Chill foods in smaller batches so that they will cool more quickly.

* When making a large quantity of potato salad, chill cooked and diced potato first before adding mayonnaise (which contains eggs). If adding hard-boiled eggs, make sure they have been well chilled after cooking and before adding to the salad.

Herbs

Fresh herbs, such as basil, chives (leaves and flowers), dill, mint, oregano, parsley, rosemary, sage, tarragon and thyme, can be found in many summer gardens or year round in pretty pots near bright kitchen windows. Use them in salads, soups and sauces and with meats and vegetables.

* Wash, air-dry and freeze fresh whole herb leaves in small resealable freezer bags or plastic wrap. They will turn dark and look limp when thawed but are delicious when added to recipes while cooking. They are about equal in taste to fresh herbs.

* Blanch fresh herbs to extend their freezer life. Tie ends of several sprigs of herbs together using string. Dip in boiling water for five seconds then in ice water for one minute. Dry gently by patting in tea towel or paper towel. Freeze in rigid airtight containers.

* Pick flowering herbs just after the flowers have opened. Wash, pat dry with paper towel and hang upside down in a dry, dark place for at least one week. Up to two weeks may be required, depending on size of sprigs. Herbs can also be arranged evenly on a rack to dry. Once herbs are dry, remove leaves and store in a tightly sealed container.

* Use 1/4 to 1/3 the amount of dried herbs as a substitute in a recipe that calls for fresh herbs.

Left: Crab Pizzas, below

Right: Curried Shrimp Tarts, below

Crab Pizzas

These attractive wedges are colorful, rich and creamy with a slight tang. Serve on a bed of lettuce.

Pizza Crust, page 52

Light cream cheese, softened	4 oz.	125 g
Fat-free sour cream	1/2 cup	125 mL
Cocktail sauce	1/3 cup	75 mL
Imitation crabmeat, broken into chunks (see Note)	8 oz.	225 g
Grated part-skim mozzarella cheese	3/4 cup	175 mL
Green onions, sliced	2	2

Divide pizza crust dough into 4 equal portions. Roll out and press each portion into 6 inch (15 cm) round, forming rim around edge. Place on greased baking sheet. Poke holes all over with fork. Bake in 425°F (220°C) oven for 5 minutes. Using paper towel to protect hands, press bumps down. Cool.

Mash or beat cream cheese and sour cream together. Spread over cooled crusts.

Carefully spread cocktail sauce over cream cheese mixture. Layer crab, cheese and green onion over top. Bake in 425°F (220°C) oven for 18 to 20 minutes until cheese is melted and crust is golden. Makes 4 pizzas, each cutting into 6 wedges, for a total of 24 wedges.

1 wedge: 74 Calories; 2.6 g Total Fat; 200 mg Sodium; 3 g Protein; 9 g Carbohydrate; trace Dietary Fiber

Pictured above.

Note: To use real crabmeat, omit imitation crabmeat. Substitute 2 cans (4 1/4 oz., 120 g, each) crabmeat with liquid.

Curried Shrimp Tarts

Be sure you have the rest of the meal ready when you serve these summer starters—they will disappear fast! Good hot or cold.

Hard margarine (or butter)	3 tbsp.	50 mL
All-purpose flour	3 tbsp.	50 mL
Milk	1 1/4 cups	300 mL
Anchovy paste	1 tsp.	5 mL
Curry powder	1 tsp.	5 mL
Salt	1/2 tsp.	2 mL
Pepper	1/8 tsp.	0.5 mL
Granulated sugar	1 tsp.	5 mL
Cooked small shrimp	1/2 lb.	225 g
Mini-tart shells, baked	34	34
Paprika, sprinkle		
Small fresh parsley sprigs, for garnish	34	34

Melt margarine in medium saucepan. Mix in flour until smooth. Gradually stir in milk until boiling and thickened.

Add next 5 ingredients. Stir. Cool.

Reserve 14 shrimp. Divide remaining shrimp among tart shells. Spoon sauce over shrimp.

Top each tart with 1 reserved shrimp, sprinkle of paprika and sprig of parsley. Chill for 1 to 2 hours until set. Makes 34 tarts.

1 appetizer tart: 59 Calories; 3.5 g Total Fat; 120 mg Sodium; 2 g Protein; 5 g Carbohydrate; trace Dietary Fiber

Pictured above.

Baked Bean Dip

Assemble this dip ahead and heat in the oven just before serving. A good hot dip. Serve with tortilla chips.

Can of condensed bean and bacon soup	10 oz.	284 mL
Light sour cream	3/4 cup	175 mL
Light salad dressing (or mayonnaise)	1/3 cup	75 mL
Minced onion flakes	4 tsp.	20 mL
Paprika	1/4 tsp.	1 mL
Hot pepper sauce	1/4 tsp.	1 mL
Worcestershire sauce	1 tsp.	5 mL
Grated light sharp Cheddar cheese	1 cup	250 mL
Grated light sharp Cheddar cheese	1/2 cup	125 mL

Combine first 8 ingredients in medium bowl. Turn into ungreased 9 inch (22 cm) pie plate or 1 quart (1 L) shallow casserole. Smooth top. Chill until ready to serve. Bake, uncovered, in 350°F (175°C) oven for about 20 minutes until bubbling around edges.

Sprinkle with second amount of cheese. Bake until cheese is melted. Makes 3 1/2 cups (875 mL).

2 tbsp. (30 mL): 39 Calories; 2.1 g Total Fat; 144 mg Sodium; 2 g Protein; 3 g Carbohydrate; trace Dietary Fiber

Pictured on page 49.

A Dipper's Dip

Intense yellow color with green flecks. Serve this tangy dip with assorted chips.

Light sour cream	1/2 cup	125 mL
Light mayonnaise	1/2 cup	125 mL
Prepared mustard	1/4 cup	60 mL
Prepared horseradish	2 tsp.	10 mL
Dill weed	2 tsp.	10 mL
Garlic powder	1/4 tsp.	1 mL

Combine all 6 ingredients in small bowl. Chill for 1 hour to blend flavors. Makes 1 1/2 cups (375 mL).

2 tbsp. (30 mL): 45 Calories; 4.1 g Total Fat; 140 mg Sodium; 1 g Protein; 2 g Carbohydrate; trace Dietary Fiber

Pictured on page 49.

Layered Dip

Makes a large quantity. Everyone will love this attractive dip.

Can of refried beans	14 oz.	398 mL
Envelope of taco seasoning mix	1 1/4 oz.	35 g
Can of diced green chilies, with liquid	4 oz.	113 mL
Ripe avocados, peeled, pitted and mashed	2	2
Lime juice	1 tbsp.	15 mL
Salsa	3 tbsp.	50 mL
Light sour cream	1/2 cup	125 mL
Light cream cheese, softened	4 oz.	125 g
Lime juice	1 tsp.	5 mL
Grated Dofino (or Havarti) cheese	1 cup	250 mL
Medium tomato, seeded and diced	1	1
Green onions, chopped	2	2

Combine beans, taco mix and chilies in medium bowl. Turn into ungreased 10 inch (25 cm) glass pie plate or 2 quart (2 L) shallow casserole. Smooth top.

Combine avocado, first amount of lime juice and salsa in small bowl. Spread over bean layer.

Beat sour cream, cream cheese and second amount of lime juice together in small bowl. Spread over avocado layer.

Sprinkle with Dofino cheese, tomato and green onion. Chill until ready to serve. Makes 7 1/2 cups (1.9 L).

2 tbsp. (30 mL): 32 Calories; 2.1 g Total Fat; 128 mg Sodium; 1 g Protein; 2 g Carbohydrate; 1 g Dietary Fiber

Pictured on page 49.

Top Left: Green Chili Dip, page 50
Top Right: Baked Bean Dip, this page
Center Left: Layered Dip, above
Center Right: Bean Salsa, page 50
Bottom: A Dipper's Dip, this page

Green Chili Dip

Not only an excellent dip but also great as a spread for bagels. Serve with chips, crackers or raw vegetables.

Can of diced green chilies, with liquid	4 oz.	113 mL
Light cream cheese, softened	8 oz.	250 g
Light sour cream	1 cup	250 mL
Lemon juice	1 tsp.	5 mL
Minced onion flakes	1 tbsp.	15 mL
Dry mustard	1/4 tsp.	1 mL
Salt	1/2 tsp.	2 mL

Beat all 7 ingredients together in medium bowl. Cover. Chill overnight. Makes 2 1/2 cups (625 mL).

2 tbsp. (30 mL): 39 Calories; 3.2 g Total Fat; 182 mg Sodium; 2 g Protein; 1 g Carbohydrate; trace Dietary Fiber

Pictured on page 49.

Bean Salsa

A mild-tasting salsa with a crunch and sweetness from kernel corn. Will keep in the refrigerator for up to one week in a sealed container. Serve with tortilla chips.

Can of stewed tomatoes, coarsely chopped, with juice	14 oz.	398 mL
Frozen kernel corn, thawed (or 12 oz., 341 mL, can, drained)	1 1/2 cups	375 mL
Can of black beans, drained and rinsed	19 oz.	540 mL
Chopped chives	1 tbsp.	15 mL
Chopped fresh parsley (or 3/4 tsp., 4 mL, flakes)	1 tbsp.	15 mL
Chili powder	3/4 tsp.	4 mL
Salt	1/2 tsp.	2 mL

Combine all 7 ingredients in medium bowl. Cover. Chill. Makes 4 1/2 cups (1.1 L).

2 tbsp. (30 mL): 19 Calories; 0.1 g Total Fat; 78 mg Sodium; 1 g Protein; 4 g Carbohydrate; 1 g Dietary Fiber

Pictured on page 49.

Patio Punch

For a pretty garnish, thinly slice several oranges. Cut slices into quarters. Spear orange piece and maraschino cherry with wooden pick. Repeat with remaining orange pieces and maraschino cherries. Serve in bowl for guests to garnish their drink.

Can of frozen concentrated lemonade (12 1/2 oz., 355 mL, size), thawed	1/2	1/2
Can of frozen concentrated orange juice, thawed	12 1/2 oz.	355 mL
Grenadine syrup	1/4 cup	60 mL
Water	2 cups	500 mL
Lemon lime soft drink	4 cups	1 L
Club soda	4 cups	1 L

Combine first 4 ingredients in pitcher. Cover. Chill.

Just before serving, pour concentrate mixture into punch bowl. Add lemon lime soft drink and club soda. Stir gently. Makes 12 1/2 cups (3.1 L).

1 cup (250 mL): 141 Calories; 0.1 g Total Fat; 33 mg Sodium; 1 g Protein; 36 g Carbohydrate; trace Dietary Fiber

Pictured on page 51.

Family Peach Chi Chi

A milder variation of a popular drink. A small section of fresh pineapple makes the perfect garnish.

Unsweetened pineapple juice	1/3 cup	75 mL
Coconut cream	3 tbsp.	50 mL
Ripe fresh peach half, peeled (or canned peach half), cut up	1	1
Ginger ale	1/2 cup	125 mL

Put all 4 ingredients into blender. Process for 30 seconds. Makes 1 1/3 cups (325 mL). Serves 1.

1 serving: 262 Calories; 16 g Total Fat; 14 mg Sodium; 2 g Protein; 31 g Carbohydrate; 2 g Dietary Fiber

Pictured on page 51.

ADULT PEACH CHI CHI: Add 1/4 cup (60 mL) vodka. Serves 2.

Left: Patio Punch, page 50   Top Center: Apricot Slush, this page   Bottom Center: Family Peach Chi Chi, page 50   Right: Fruit Cocktail Punch, this page

Fruit Cocktail Punch

This deep yellow punch is just a bit tart.

Prepared orange juice	2 cups	500 mL
Unsweetened pineapple juice	2 cups	500 mL
Unsweetened grapefruit juice	2 cups	500 mL
Apricot nectar	3 cups	750 mL
Lemon lime soft drink	2 cups	500 mL
Can of fruit cocktail, with juice	14 oz.	398 mL

Combine first 5 ingredients in pitcher. Chill.

Spoon fruit cocktail into ice cube tray. Divide juice evenly over top. Freeze for at least 3 hours. Just before serving, pour juice mixture into punch bowl. Add fruit cubes. Makes 12 cups (3 L).

1 cup (250 mL): 131 Calories; 0.2 g Total Fat; 9 mg Sodium; 1 g Protein; 33 g Carbohydrate; 1 g Dietary Fiber

Pictured above.

Apricot Slush

A large drink that is very satisfying. For an attractive garnish, cut a fresh lime into wedges. Cut wedges in half.

Apricot nectar	1/2 cup	125 mL
Lime juice	3 tbsp.	50 mL
Granulated sugar	3 tbsp.	50 mL
Ice cubes	10	10

Put all 4 ingredients into blender. Process until frozen slush consistency. Makes 1 3/4 cups (425 mL). Serves 1.

1 serving: 234 Calories; 0.2 g Total Fat; 5 mg Sodium; 1 g Protein; 61 g Carbohydrate; 1 g Dietary Fiber

Pictured above.

Family Reunion

When the gathering of the clan seems to grow larger each year, preparing to host a family reunion can become a daunting task. Take advantage of the variety in this menu idea, filled with recipes that have been specially selected to please everyone young and old.

Bacon And Scallop Pizzas
Curry Cheese Spread
Green Chili Appetizer

Rhubarb Punch
Pink Melonade

Beet Salad Mold
Black Bean And Corn Salad
Creamy Cucumbers
Macaroni Salad
Pineapple Bean Salad
Potato Caesar Salad

Square Biscuits

Crisp Parmesan Drumsticks
Picnic Beans
Sweet And Sour Meatballs
Wieners And Pasta Bake

Cool Melon Dessert Slice
Feed-A-Crowd Rhubarb Trifle

Watermelon Vase

Bacon And Scallop Pizzas

These pizzas are served as cold appetizers.

PIZZA CRUST

All-purpose flour, approximately	2 cups	500 mL
Instant yeast	1 1/4 tsp.	6 mL
Salt	1/4 tsp.	1 mL
Ground rosemary	1/4 tsp.	1 mL
Warm water	2/3 cup	150 mL
Cooking oil	2 tbsp.	30 mL

TOPPING

Bacon slices, diced	10	10
Large scallops, chopped	1/2 lb.	225 g
Boiling water, to cover		
Light salad dressing (or mayonnaise)	1/3 cup	75 mL
Sweet pickle relish	2 tsp.	10 mL
Lemon juice	1 tsp.	5 mL
Chopped fresh parsley (or 3/4 tsp., 4 mL, flakes)	1 tbsp.	15 mL
Grated part-skim mozzarella cheese	3/4 cup	175 mL
Ground rosemary, sprinkle		

Pizza Crust: Put flour, yeast, salt and rosemary into food processor. With motor running, add warm water and cooking oil through feed chute. Process for 50 to 60 seconds until dough forms ball. If very sticky, add 1/2 tsp. (2 mL) flour at a time until easy to handle. (No need to let dough rise, but you can if you want.) Divide dough into 4 equal portions. Roll out and press each portion into 6 inch (15 cm) round, forming rim around edge. Place on greased baking sheet. Poke holes all over with fork. Bake in 425°F (220°C) oven for 5 minutes. Using paper towel to protect hands, press bumps down. Bake for 7 minutes until cooked through. Cool.

Topping: Fry bacon in frying pan until crisp. Drain. Blot dry with paper towels.

Cook scallops in boiling water for 2 to 3 minutes until opaque. Do not overcook.

Mix salad dressing, relish and lemon juice together in small bowl. Spread over cooled crusts. Layer scallops and bacon over top.

Sprinkle with parsley, cheese and rosemary. Chill until ready to serve. Makes 4 pizzas, each cutting into 6 wedges, for a total of 24 wedges.

1 wedge: 95 Calories; 4.1 g Total Fat; 130 mg Sodium; 5 g Protein; 10 g Carbohydrate; trace Dietary Fiber

Pictured on page 53.

Left: Green Chili Appetizer, below
Top Right: Curry Cheese Spread, this page
Bottom Right: Bacon And Scallop Pizzas, page 52

Green Chili Appetizer

An attractive appetizer that will disappear fast.

CRUST

Hard margarine (or butter)	1/4 cup	60 mL
Soda cracker crumbs	1 cup	250 mL
Grated Parmesan cheese	2 tbsp.	30 mL

FILLING

Grated Monterey Jack cheese	1 cup	250 mL
Grated medium Cheddar cheese	1/2 cup	125 mL
Can of diced green chilies, with liquid	4 oz.	113 mL
Large eggs	4	4
Milk	1/2 cup	125 mL
Salt	1/2 tsp.	2 mL
Seasoned salt	1/2 tsp.	2 mL
Grated medium Cheddar cheese	1/2 cup	125 mL

Crust: Melt margarine in medium saucepan. Stir in cracker crumbs and Parmesan cheese. Press into ungreased 8 x 8 inch (20 x 20 cm) pan. Bake, uncovered, in 350°F (175°C) oven for 10 minutes. Cool slightly.

Filling: Scatter Monterey Jack cheese over crust. Scatter first amount of Cheddar cheese over top. Evenly spoon green chilies over Cheddar cheese.

Beat eggs in medium bowl. Beat in milk, salt and seasoned salt. Pour over chilies.

Sprinkle with second amount of Cheddar cheese. Bake, uncovered, in 350°F (175°C) oven for about 45 minutes until lightly browned and set. Cool completely before cutting. Cuts into 36 appetizers.

1 appetizer: 57 Calories; 4.4 g Total Fat; 171 mg Sodium; 3 g Protein; 2 g Carbohydrate; trace Dietary Fiber

Pictured on this page.

Curry Cheese Spread

Rich and creamy with a background of curry.
Serve with crackers, toast triangles or veggies.

Light cream cheese, softened	8 oz.	250 g
Mango chutney	1/3 cup	75 mL
Lemon juice	1 tsp.	5 mL
Curry powder	1/2 tsp.	2 mL
Chopped pimiento	2 tbsp.	30 mL
Finely chopped pecans (or walnuts), optional	1/4 cup	60 mL

Beat first 5 ingredients together in medium bowl. Turn into shallow bowl.

Sprinkle with pecans. Chill. Makes 1 1/2 cups (375 mL).

1 tbsp. (15 mL): 27 Calories; 2 g Total Fat; 70 mg Sodium; 1 g Protein; 2 g Carbohydrate; trace Dietary Fiber

Pictured on this page.

Variation: Try this spread on celery for a real flavor treat.

Photo Legend next page:

1. Pineapple Bean Salad, page 58
2. Rhubarb Punch, page 56
3. Watermelon Vase, page 64
4. Macaroni Salad, page 60
5. Crisp Parmesan Drumsticks, page 61
6. Black Bean And Corn Salad, page 57
7. Beet Salad Mold, page 57
8. Square Biscuits, page 56

Rhubarb Punch

Purple, pretty, flavorful and from your garden.

Finely chopped fresh (or frozen, thawed) rhubarb	2 lbs.	900 g
Water	4 cups	1 L
Granulated sugar	2/3 cup	150 mL
Prepared orange juice	1 cup	250 mL
Pineapple juice	1 cup	250 mL
Can of frozen concentrated lemonade	12 1/2 oz.	355 mL
Salt, just a pinch		
Club soda	3 cups	750 mL
Ginger ale	8 cups	2 L

Cook rhubarb in water in covered large pot or Dutch oven until rhubarb falls apart. Place rhubarb in colander over large bowl. Allow 30 minutes to drain. Discard rhubarb. Cool. Juice can be frozen at this point to be used later.

Add next 5 ingredients. Stir until sugar is dissolved. Pour into container. Chill.

Just before serving, pour rhubarb mixture into punch bowl. Add club soda and ginger ale. Stir gently. Makes 19 cups (4.75 L).

1 cup (250 mL): 130 Calories; 0.2 g Total Fat; 19 mg Sodium; 1 g Protein; 33 g Carbohydrate; trace Dietary Fiber

Pictured on page 54/55.

Pink Melonade

Uses up a lot of the watermelon taken out of the Watermelon Vase, page 64. Pretty color and very refreshing.

Watermelon chunks, seeds removed	8 cups	2 L
Can of frozen concentrated raspberry (or pink) lemonade, thawed	12 1/2 oz.	355 mL
Raspberry vodka (or raspberry ginger ale or soda water), optional	1 1/2 cups	375 mL

Put watermelon chunks into food processor. Process, in 2 batches, until juice consistency. Strain juice into medium bowl. Discard pulp.

Combine watermelon juice, lemonade and vodka in large pitcher. Makes 7 3/4 cups (1.9 L).

1 cup (250 mL): 154 Calories; 0.9 g Total Fat; 6 mg Sodium; 1 g Protein; 38 g Carbohydrate; 1 g Dietary Fiber

Pictured on page 65.

Square Biscuits

Make the smaller size as a go-with for salads. Use these to make Chicken Sandwiches, page 66, extra good. Can also be used as a base for different toppings.

All-purpose flour	3 cups	750 mL
Baking powder	1 1/2 tbsp.	25 mL
Salt	1 1/2 tsp.	7 mL
Cooking oil	1/2 cup	125 mL
Milk	1 cup	250 mL

Combine flour, baking powder and salt in large bowl.

Add cooking oil and milk. Stir until soft dough forms. Turn out onto lightly floured surface. Knead gently 6 times. Pat into 1/2 inch (12 mm) thick 8 x 12 inch (20 x 30 cm) rectangle. Cut into six 4 x 4 inch (10 x 10 cm) squares or sixteen 2 x 2 inch (5 x 5 cm) squares. Arrange 1 inch (2.5 cm) apart on ungreased baking sheet. Bake, uncovered, in 450°F (230°C) oven for 10 to 12 minutes until risen and golden. Makes 6 large biscuits or 16 small biscuits.

1 large biscuit: 430 Calories; 20.3 g Total Fat; 894 mg Sodium; 8 g Protein; 53 g Carbohydrate; 2 g Dietary Fiber

1 small biscuit: 161 Calories; 7.6 g Total Fat; 335 mg Sodium; 3 g Protein; 20 g Carbohydrate; 1 g Dietary Fiber

Pictured on page 54 and on page 67.

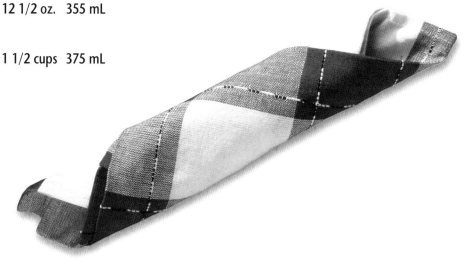

Black Bean And Corn Salad

Serve with salsa for an added touch.
Good chilled or at room temperature.

Long grain white rice	1 cup	250 mL
Water	2 cups	500 mL
Salt	1/2 tsp.	2 mL
Kernel corn, fresh (or frozen, thawed)	1 1/2 cups	375 mL
Can of black beans, drained and rinsed	19 oz.	540 mL
Jar of pimiento, drained and chopped	2 oz.	57 mL
Medium green pepper, coarsely chopped	1/2	1/2
DRESSING		
Water	1/2 cup	125 mL
Cornstarch	1 tbsp.	15 mL
White vinegar	3 tbsp.	50 mL
Granulated sugar	3 tbsp.	50 mL
Dry mustard	1/8 tsp.	0.5 mL
Worcestershire sauce	1/2 tsp.	2 mL
Onion salt	1/2 tsp.	2 mL
Salt	1/2 tsp.	2 mL
Pepper	1/8 tsp.	0.5 mL

Combine rice in water and salt in medium saucepan. Bring to a boil. Reduce heat. Cover. Simmer for about 20 minutes until tender and water is absorbed.

Combine corn, beans, pimiento and green pepper in large bowl. Add rice. Stir. Makes 7 cups (1.75 L).

Dressing: Stir water into cornstarch in small saucepan until smooth. Heat and stir until boiling and thickened.

Add remaining 7 ingredients. Stir until sugar is dissolved. Remove from heat. Makes about 3/4 cup (175 mL) dressing. Add to bean mixture. Stir until well coated. Chill. Serves 8.

1 serving: 190 Calories; 0.7 g Total Fat; 160 mg Sodium; 6 g Protein; 41 g Carbohydrate; 3 g Dietary Fiber

Pictured on page 54/55.

Beet Salad Mold

A molded salad is a must for a big "spread."
Tastes as good as it looks.

Can of crushed pineapple, drained, juice reserved	19 oz.	540 mL
Can of sliced beets, drained, julienned and juice reserved	14 oz.	398 mL
White vinegar	1/4 cup	60 mL
Water	1/4 cup	60 mL
Lemon juice	3 tbsp.	50 mL
Granulated sugar	2 tbsp.	30 mL
Packages of raspberry-flavored gelatin (jelly powder), 3 oz. (85 g), each	2	2
Chopped walnuts (or pecans)	1/2 cup	125 mL
TOPPING		
Salad dressing (or mayonnaise)	1/4 cup	60 mL
Frozen whipped topping, thawed	1/4 cup	60 mL

Combine reserved pineapple juice and beet juice in medium saucepan.

Add next 5 ingredients. Heat and stir until sugar and gelatin are dissolved. Chill, stirring and scraping down sides occasionally, until syrupy.

Add walnuts, pineapple and beets. Stir gently. Turn into lightly greased 6 cup (1.5 L) ring mold. Chill for several hours until firm.

Topping: Loosen salad in mold. Invert onto dampened serving plate. Dampness makes it easier to center mold on plate. Fold salad dressing into whipped topping in small bowl. Spoon into middle of salad. Serves 10 to 12.

1 serving: 200 Calories; 7.4 g Total Fat; 192 mg Sodium; 4 g Protein; 32 g Carbohydrate; 1 g Dietary Fiber

Pictured on page 54/55.

Tip
To keep food chilled for picnics, wait until just before leaving home to pack the cooler. Pack perishable foods in an insulated cooler with plenty of ice to surround them. Containers of frozen juice help keep foods cold as well.

Pineapple Bean Salad

Pretty! Sweet and tart with plenty of color.

Fresh whole green beans (6 oz., 170 g)	1 1/2 cups	375 mL
Fresh yellow wax beans (6 oz., 170 g)	1 1/2 cups	375 mL
Water		
Can of red kidney beans, drained and rinsed	14 oz.	398 mL
Can of pineapple tidbits, drained, juice reserved	14 oz.	398 mL
Thinly sliced celery	1 cup	250 mL
Chopped red (or yellow) pepper	1 cup	250 mL
DRESSING		
Reserved pineapple juice	2/3 cup	150 mL
Cornstarch	1 tbsp.	15 mL
White vinegar	1/4 cup	60 mL
Dry mustard	1 tsp.	5 mL
Granulated sugar	2 tbsp.	30 mL
Dill weed	1/2 tsp.	2 mL
Seasoned salt	1/2 tsp.	2 mL

Cook both beans in water in medium saucepan until tender-crisp. Drain. Cool.

Combine next 4 ingredients in medium bowl. Add bean mixture. Stir. Cover. Chill.

Dressing: Stir reserved pineapple juice into cornstarch in medium saucepan until smooth. Add remaining 5 ingredients. Heat and stir until boiling and thickened. Pour into small container. Cover. Chill. Just before serving, pour dressing over bean mixture. Gently stir until well coated. Makes 6 cups (1.5 L).

1/2 cup (125 mL): 74 Calories; 0.3 g Total Fat; 105 mg Sodium; 3 g Protein; 17 g Carbohydrate; 3 g Dietary Fiber

Pictured on page 54.

Potato Caesar Salad

Combine the best of two popular salads.

CROUTONS		
Hard margarine (or butter)	2 tbsp.	30 mL
Garlic powder	1/8 tsp.	0.5 mL
Bread cubes	2 cups	500 mL
DRESSING		
Cooking oil	1/4 cup	60 mL
Lemon juice	2 tbsp.	30 mL
Red wine vinegar	2 tbsp.	30 mL
Sliced green onion	1/4 cup	60 mL
Large egg	1	1
Worcestershire sauce	1 tsp.	5 mL
Garlic powder (or 1 clove, minced)	1/4 tsp.	1 mL
Salt	1 tsp.	5 mL
Pepper	1/4 tsp.	1 mL
Cubed cold cooked potato	4 cups	1 L
Medium head of Romaine lettuce, cut or torn	1	1
Grated Parmesan cheese	1/2 cup	125 mL

Croutons: Heat margarine and garlic powder in large frying pan. Add bread cubes. Stir-fry until browned and dried. Cool.

Dressing: Combine first 9 ingredients in small bowl. Makes 3/4 cup (175 mL) dressing.

Toss potato in large bowl with 1/3 of dressing until well coated.

Add lettuce, Parmesan cheese and croutons. Toss lightly. Add remaining dressing. Toss until well coated. Serve immediately. Serves 8.

1 serving: 237 Calories; 13.3 g Total Fat; 527 mg Sodium; 7 g Protein; 24 g Carbohydrate; 2 g Dietary Fiber

Pictured on page 59.

Top Left: Picnic Beans, page 61
Top Right: Potato Caesar Salad, above
Center Left: Wieners And Pasta Bake, page 61
Center Right: Sweet And Sour Meatballs, page 60
Bottom: Creamy Cucumbers, page 60

Macaroni Salad

Make this when you want to serve a large crowd.

Macaroni (or other pasta), 1 lb. (454 g)	4 cups	1 L
Boiling water	16 cups	4 L
Cooking oil (optional)	1 tbsp.	15 mL
Salt	1 tbsp.	15 mL
Diced red onion	1 cup	250 mL
Hard-boiled eggs, chopped	4	4
Cooked peas	1 1/4 cups	300 mL
Medium tomatoes, seeded and diced	2	2
DRESSING		
Salad dressing (or mayonnaise)	1 cup	250 mL
White vinegar	1 tbsp.	15 mL
Granulated sugar	1 tsp.	5 mL
Milk	1/4 cup	60 mL
Salt	1 tsp.	5 mL
Pepper	1/4 tsp.	1 mL

Cook macaroni in boiling water, cooking oil and salt in large uncovered pot or Dutch oven for 5 to 7 minutes until tender but firm. Drain. Rinse with cold water. Drain well.

Combine onion, egg, peas and tomato in large bowl. Add macaroni. Stir. Chill thoroughly.

Dressing: Mix all 6 ingredients in small bowl. Makes 1 1/3 cups (325 mL) dressing. Add to macaroni mixture. Toss until well coated. Cover. Chill. Makes 18 cups (4.5 L).

1/2 cup (125 mL): 98 Calories; 4.2 g Total Fat; 119 mg Sodium; 3 g Protein; 12 g Carbohydrate; 1 g Dietary Fiber

Pictured on page 55.

Creamy Cucumbers

Crunchy texture, creamy color, green flecks and fresh dill flavor.

Medium English cucumbers, with peel	2	2
Light sour cream	2/3 cup	150 mL
White vinegar	1 tbsp.	15 mL
Chopped chives	2 tbsp.	30 mL
Chopped fresh dill (or 1 1/2 tsp., 7 mL, dill weed)	2 tbsp.	30 mL
Salt	1/2 tsp.	2 mL
Pepper	1/16 tsp.	0.5 mL
Granulated sugar	2 tsp.	10 mL

Draw tines of fork down sides of cucumber. Thinly slice into medium bowl.

Combine remaining 7 ingredients in small bowl. Add to cucumber. Toss until well coated. Makes 5 cups (1.25 L).

1/2 cup (125 mL): 27 Calories; 1.2 g Total Fat; 127 mg Sodium; 1 g Protein; 4 g Carbohydrate; 1 g Dietary Fiber

Pictured on page 59.

Sweet And Sour Meatballs

Cooked in a barbecue-style sauce for a different variation.

Large egg, fork-beaten	1	1
Milk	1/4 cup	60 mL
Fine dry bread crumbs	1/2 cup	125 mL
Grated onion	1 tbsp.	15 mL
Salt	1/2 tsp.	2 mL
Pepper	1/4 tsp.	1 mL
Lean ground beef	1 lb.	454 g
Pineapple juice	2 cups	500 mL
All-purpose flour	3 tbsp.	50 mL
Barbecue sauce	1/2 cup	125 mL

Combine first 6 ingredients in large bowl. Stir.

Add ground beef. Mix. Shape into 1 inch (2.5 cm) balls. Arrange in single layer on baking sheet. Brown quickly under broiler. Transfer to ungreased 1 1/2 quart (1.5 L) casserole.

Stir pineapple juice into flour in small saucepan until smooth. Heat and stir until boiling and thickened. Remove from heat.

Add barbecue sauce. Stir. Pour over meatballs. Cover. Bake in 350°F (175°C) oven for about 1 hour until bubbling and meatballs are no longer pink inside. Serves 6.

1 serving: 299 Calories; 13.4 g Total Fat; 526 mg Sodium; 18 g Protein; 26 g Carbohydrate; 2 g Dietary Fiber

Pictured on page 59.

Crisp Parmesan Drumsticks

A crisp bread and cheese coating makes these delicious.

COATING

Fine dry bread crumbs	2/3 cup	150 mL
Grated Parmesan cheese	1/3 cup	75 mL
Parsley flakes	1/2 tsp.	2 mL
Poultry seasoning	1/4 tsp.	1 mL
Onion powder	1/8 tsp.	0.5 mL
Celery salt	1/8 tsp.	0.5 mL
Paprika	1/8 tsp.	0.5 mL
Salt	1/8 tsp.	0.5 mL
Pepper, just a pinch		
Chicken drumsticks, skin removed	20	20
Hard margarine (or butter), melted	1/3 cup	75 mL

Coating: Combine first 9 ingredients in shallow dish or on waxed paper.

Blot drumsticks dry with paper towel. Brush each with margarine. Roll in crumb mixture to coat completely. Arrange in single layer on large greased baking sheet with sides. Do not have drumsticks touching each other. Bake in 350°F (175°C) oven for about 50 minutes until golden and no longer pink inside. Makes 20 drumsticks.

1 drumstick: 135 Calories; 7.5 g Total Fat; 126 mg Sodium; 13 g Protein; 3 g Carbohydrate; trace Dietary Fiber

Pictured on page 55.

Picnic Beans

You'll definitely want a second helping of these beans.

Cans of baked beans in tomato sauce (14 oz., 398 mL, each)	3	3
Chili sauce	3/4 cup	175 mL
Chili powder	1/2 tsp.	2 mL
Brown sugar, packed	2 tbsp.	30 mL
Fancy (mild) molasses	2 tbsp.	30 mL
Minced onion flakes	2 tbsp.	30 mL
Liquid smoke	1/4 tsp.	1 mL
Steak sauce	1 1/2 tsp.	7 mL

Combine all 8 ingredients in ungreased 3 quart (3 L) casserole. Bake, uncovered, in 350°F (175°C) oven for about 1 3/4 hours, stirring once, until bubbling and showing signs of drying and browning around edges. Makes 5 cups (1.25 L).

1/2 cup (125 mL): 167 Calories; 0.7 g Total Fat; 814 mg Sodium; 7 g Protein; 38 g Carbohydrate; 11 g Dietary Fiber

Pictured on page 59.

Wieners And Pasta Bake

Little, medium and big kids like this yummy casserole.

Medium shell pasta	8 oz.	225 g
Boiling water	10 cups	2.5 L
Cooking oil (optional)	1 tbsp.	15 mL
Salt	2 tsp.	10 mL
Wieners (about 12), cut into 6 pieces each	1 lb.	454 g
Envelope of dry onion soup mix	1 1/4 oz.	38 g
Can of condensed tomato soup	10 oz.	284 mL
Worcestershire sauce	1 tsp.	5 mL
Water	1/4 cup	60 mL
Can of diced tomatoes, with juice	14 oz.	398 mL

TOPPING

Hard margarine (or butter)	2 tbsp.	30 mL
Fine dry bread crumbs	1/2 cup	125 mL

Cook pasta in boiling water, cooking oil and salt in large uncovered pot or Dutch oven for about 10 minutes until tender but firm. Drain. Transfer to ungreased 3 quart (3 L) casserole.

Add wieners to pasta. Stir.

Combine next 5 ingredients in medium bowl. Stir vigorously until well mixed. Pour over pasta and wieners. Stir gently.

Topping: Melt margarine in small saucepan. Add bread crumbs. Stir until well mixed. Sprinkle over pasta mixture. Bake, uncovered, in 350°F (175°C) oven for about 45 minutes until hot. Makes 9 cups (2.25 L).

1 cup (250 mL): 335 Calories; 15.9 g Total Fat; 1284 mg Sodium; 12 g Protein; 36 g Carbohydrate; 2 g Dietary Fiber

Pictured on page 59.

Variation: For a spicier version, use spicy onion soup or spicy tomato soup.

Feed-A-Crowd Rhubarb Trifle

A sharp tartness mellowed by a not-too-sweet custard makes this a popular dessert for a lot of people on a warm summer day. Keep chilled until ready to serve.

Diced fresh rhubarb (or rhubarb and fresh strawberries, mixed)	10 cups	2.5 L
Granulated sugar	2 1/2 cups	625 mL
Envelope of unflavored gelatin	1/4 oz.	7 g
Cold water	1/4 cup	60 mL
Vanilla custard powder	1/4 cup	60 mL
Granulated sugar	3 tbsp.	50 mL
Milk	3 cups	750 mL
Liquid whip topping (such as Nutriwhip)	2 cups	500 mL
White cake cubes (2 layer cake mix)	14 cups	3.5 L
Sliced fresh strawberries	1 cup	250 mL
Sliced fresh strawberries, for garnish	1/2 cup	125 mL
Chopped walnuts, for garnish	2 tbsp.	30 mL

Left: Feed-A-Crowd Rhubarb Trifle, this page

Put rhubarb into large saucepan. Evenly sprinkle with first amount of sugar. Do not stir. Cover. Let stand for 8 to 12 hours to release juices. Stir. Heat and stir on high until boiling. Reduce heat to low. Simmer for 8 to 10 minutes, stirring once or twice, until rhubarb is soft but still holds its shape. Remove from heat.

Sprinkle gelatin over cold water in small bowl. Let stand for 1 minute. Stir into rhubarb mixture until dissolved. Chill for about 2 hours, stirring several times, until syrupy. Makes about 6 cups (1.5 L).

Combine custard powder and second amount of sugar in medium saucepan. Gradually stir in milk until smooth. Heat and stir on medium until mixture comes to a rolling boil. Remove from heat. Cover with waxed paper directly on surface to prevent skin from forming. Cool to room temperature.

Beat liquid whip topping in large bowl until stiff peaks form.

Put 1/3 of cake cubes into large trifle bowl or 20 cup (5 L) deep glass bowl. Pour about 1/3 of rhubarb mixture over cake cubes. Scatter 1/3 cup (75 mL) strawberries over rhubarb mixture. Spoon 1/3 of custard over strawberries. Spread with 1/3 of whipped topping. Make another single layer of cake cubes, rhubarb mixture, strawberries and custard. Spread with 1/2 of remaining whipped topping. Repeat with remaining cake cubes, rhubarb mixture, 1/3 cup (75 mL) strawberries and remaining custard. Spread remaining whipped topping over all.

Arrange second amount of strawberries and walnuts over whipped topping. Serves about 30.

1 serving: 210 Calories; 6.6 g Total Fat; 81 mg Sodium; 3 g Protein; 36 g Carbohydrate; trace Dietary Fiber

Pictured above.

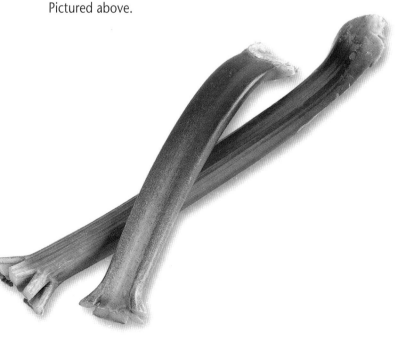

Right: Cool Melon Dessert Slice, this page

Cool Melon Dessert Slice

Truly melon and so, so cool! This can sit out at room temperature for about 4 hours with no visible effects, making it perfect for a buffet table.

Poppy seeds	3 tbsp.	50 mL
Water	1/2 cup	125 mL
White (or lemon) angel food cake mix	1	1
Icing (confectioner's) sugar	1/2 cup	125 mL
FILLING		
Envelope of unflavored gelatin	1/4 oz.	7 g
Cold water	1/4 cup	60 mL
Boiling water	1 cup	250 mL
Package of lemon-flavored gelatin (jelly powder)	3 oz.	85 g
Diced cantaloupe	1 cup	250 mL
Diced honeydew melon	1 cup	250 mL
Frozen whipped topping, thawed	2 cups	500 mL
Icing (confectioner's) sugar	1/4 cup	60 mL
Fresh mint sprigs, for garnish		

Bring poppy seeds and water to a boil in small saucepan. Boil for 5 minutes. Drain into small sieve. Rinse under cold water. Drain well.

Line 11 x 17 inch (28 x 43 cm) baking pan with waxed paper that has been cut to fit. Prepare cake mix according to package instructions. Add poppy seeds. Stir. Pour batter into pan. Smooth top. Bake on center rack in 400°F (205°C) oven for about 10 minutes until golden.

Immediately turn cake out onto large tea towel that has been covered with sifted icing sugar. Remove waxed paper. Roll up cake, jelly roll-style, with tea towel, from long side. Set aside to cool.

Filling: Sprinkle unflavored gelatin over cold water in medium bowl. Let stand for 1 minute.

Add boiling water and lemon-flavored gelatin. Stir until dissolved. Chill for about 1 hour, stirring and scraping down sides several times, until syrupy.

Fold cantaloupe, melon and whipped topping into gelatin. Makes 4 1/2 cups (1.1 L) filling. Unroll cake. Spread filling on cake almost to edges. Gently roll up, jelly roll-style, without tea towel. Cover in plastic wrap. Chill for at least 1 1/2 hours until firm.

To serve, sift icing sugar over top and garnish with mint. Cuts into 16 slices.

1 slice: 189 Calories; 3.4 g Total Fat; 209 mg Sodium; 4 g Protein; 37 g Carbohydrate; trace Dietary Fiber

Pictured above.

How To

Watermelon Vase

Take a little extra time to find just the right shape of watermelon and not only will you be able to make Pink Melonade, page 56, but also this beautiful picnic table centerpiece.

Materials: Oblong, evenly-shaped watermelon; large cutting board; large sharp knife; scoop or large spoon; large bowl; small plate; ruler; felt marker; small jar lid; paring knife; raffia or ribbon.

Slice watermelon horizontally about 1/3 from 1 end. Cut very thin slice from opposite end to allow vase to sit flat.

Scoop out flesh from larger section, leaving about 1 inch (2.5 cm) on sides and about 3 inches (7.5 cm) at bottom. Scoop out flesh from smaller section. Reserve flesh for Pink Melonade, page 56. Discard smaller shell.

To make scalloped edge, place larger section upright on small plate (to protect table surface). Using ruler and felt marker, measure and mark line all around about 2 inches (5 cm) down from cut edge and equal distance from table surface. Measure and mark diameter of jar lid. Holding lid flat against outside of shell, match marks on lid to line on shell. Trace arc of upper half of lid. Repeat evenly around shell. Carve out upper arcs using paring knife.

Push stems of cut flowers into watermelon base. Add water. Tie raffia or ribbon to hide marker line.

Pictured on page 55 and above.

Kneadless White Bread

Resist the urge to knead this bread—the texture will be soft and light.

Granulated sugar	3 tbsp.	50 mL
Warm water	1 1/4 cups	300 mL
Active dry yeast (or 1/4 oz., 8 g, envelope)	2 1/2 tsp.	12 mL
Hard margarine (or butter), softened	2 tbsp.	30 mL
Large egg	1	1
Salt	3/4 tsp.	4 mL
All-purpose flour	2 cups	500 mL
All-purpose flour, approximately	2 cups	500 mL
Hard margarine (or butter), softened	1 tsp.	5 mL

Stir sugar into warm water in large bowl. Sprinkle yeast over top. Let stand for 10 minutes. Stir to dissolve yeast.

Add first amount of margarine, egg, salt and first amount of flour. Beat on low until just moistened. Beat on high for 2 minutes.

Work in enough of second amount of flour until dough pulls away from sides of bowl. Do not knead. Place dough in greased bowl, turning once to grease top. Cover with tea towel. Let stand in oven with light on and door closed for about 1 hour until doubled in bulk. Punch dough down. Shape into loaf. Place in greased 9 × 5 × 3 inch (22 × 12.5 × 7.5 cm) loaf pan. Cover with tea towel. Let stand in oven with light on and door closed for about 30 minutes until doubled in size. Bake, uncovered, in 350°F (175°C) oven for about 35 minutes until golden. Turn out onto wire rack to cool.

Brush warm top with second amount of margarine. Cuts into 16 slices.

1 slice: 150 Calories; 2.4 g Total Fat; 136 mg Sodium; 4 g Protein; 28 g Carbohydrate; 1 g Dietary Fiber

Pictured on this page.

Tip *To avoid heating up the house on a warm summer day, make ahead as many meals as possible. Use a rainy day to make several meals ahead of time. Then on a day when it is just too hot to cook, simply reheat a premade meal in the microwave.*

Top Left: Pink Melonade, page 56
Top Right: Kneadless White Bread, this page
Bottom: Picnic Drumsticks, below

Picnic Drumsticks

You may need to increase this recipe, depending on the size of your picnic. Good cold as well as hot.

COATING		
All-purpose flour	1/2 cup	125 mL
Seasoned salt	2 tsp.	10 mL
Pepper	1/4 tsp.	1 mL
Onion powder	1/4 tsp.	1 mL
Paprika	2 tsp.	10 mL
Chicken drumsticks, skin removed	12	12
Italian dressing	1/4 cup	60 mL

Coating: Combine first 5 ingredients in shallow bowl or on waxed paper.

Blot drumsticks dry with paper towels. Brush each with Italian dressing. Roll in flour mixture to coat completely. Arrange in single layer on large greased foil-lined baking sheet. Do not have drumsticks touching each other. Bake in 350°F (175°C) oven for about 50 minutes until golden and no longer pink. Makes 12 drumsticks.

1 drumstick: 138 Calories; 7.3 g Total Fat; 280 mg Sodium; 13 g Protein; 5 g Carbohydrate; trace Dietary Fiber

Pictured above.

Rolled Beef Sandwiches

Have your beef and salad all rolled into a bun. Garnish with cucumber slices and orange pepper strips for added color.

Large thin deli (or cooked) roast beef slices (see Note)	6	6
Light salad dressing (or mayonnaise)	1/3 cup	75 mL
Prepared horseradish	1 tsp.	5 mL
Prepared mustard	2 tsp.	10 mL
Ketchup	1 tbsp.	15 mL
Grated carrot	1/2 cup	125 mL
Shredded cabbage	1 cup	250 mL
Hot dog buns, split and toasted (buttered, optional)	6	6

Lay beef slices flat on working surface.

Combine next 4 ingredients in small bowl. Spread 1 tbsp. (15 mL) dressing mixture on each beef slice.

Sprinkle with carrot and cabbage. Roll up, jelly roll-style.

Spread 2 tsp. (10 mL) remaining dressing mixture on each bun. Place 1 beef roll on bottom half of each bun. Replace tops. Makes 6 sandwiches.

1 sandwich: 271 Calories; 8.9 g Total Fat; 446 mg Sodium; 20 g Protein; 26 g Carbohydrate; 1 g Dietary Fiber

Pictured on page 67.

Note: If large beef slices aren't available, smaller ones can be used. Remember to overlap them so they will roll easily.

Chicken Sandwiches

Tender chicken with a tangy but sweet dressing. Serve with carrot and celery sticks.

Light salad dressing (or mayonnaise)	1/3 cup	75 mL
Sweet pickle relish	1 tsp.	5 mL
White vinegar	1 tsp.	5 mL
Parsley flakes	1 tsp.	5 mL
Curry powder	1/8 tsp.	0.5 mL
Sliced almonds, toasted (see Tip, page 28) and coarsely chopped	2 tbsp.	30 mL
Chopped cooked chicken, cooled	1 cup	250 mL
Square Biscuits (large), page 56, split horizontally (or bread slices), buttered (optional)	6	6
Shredded lettuce	1 cup	250 mL

Combine first 6 ingredients in small bowl.

Add chicken. Stir. Add more salad dressing if too dry.

Spread 1/6 of chicken mixture on bottom half of each biscuit. Divide lettuce over chicken mixture. Cover with top half of each biscuit. Makes 6 sandwiches.

1 sandwich: 521 Calories; 25.5 g Total Fat; 1008 mg Sodium; 16 g Protein; 56 g Carbohydrate; 2 g Dietary Fiber

Pictured on page 67.

Brunch Dish

Hash browns make the crust with an egg and cheese topping. An excellent brunch dish.

Bacon slices, diced	6	6
Chopped onion	1/4 cup	60 mL
Chopped green pepper	1/4 cup	60 mL
Frozen hash brown potatoes, thawed	2 cups	500 mL
Large eggs	4	4
Water (or milk)	1/4 cup	60 mL
Salt	1/2 tsp.	2 mL
Pepper	1/8 tsp.	0.5 mL
Grated medium Cheddar cheese	1/2 cup	125 mL
Grated part-skim mozzarella cheese	1/2 cup	125 mL

Sauté bacon, onion and green pepper in large non-stick frying pan until bacon is golden. Remove with slotted spoon to paper towel to drain. Drain fat from frying pan, reserving 1 tbsp. (15 mL) in pan.

Pack hash browns into frying pan in even layer. Cook, uncovered, on medium-low, without stirring, until crispy on bottom.

Beat eggs, water, salt and pepper together in small bowl. Add bacon mixture. Stir. Pour over hash browns.

Sprinkle with both cheeses. Cover. Cook for about 5 minutes, without stirring, until eggs are set. Cuts into 4 wedges.

1 wedge: 326 Calories; 17.8 g Total Fat; 701 mg Sodium; 19 g Protein; 23 g Carbohydrate; 2 g Dietary Fiber

Pictured on page 67.

Top Right: Brunch Dish, above
Center: Rolled Beef Sandwiches, this page
Bottom: Chicken Sandwiches, this page, in Square Biscuits, page 56

Summer Fruit Salad, below

Summer Fruit Salad

*Fruit can easily be changed, added to
or taken away from this pretty salad.*

Honeydew melon balls	1 cup	250 mL
Whole fresh raspberries	1 cup	250 mL
Fresh peach slices	1/2 cup	125 mL
Fresh blueberries	1 cup	250 mL
Fresh strawberries, halved	1/2 cup	125 mL
Bananas, sliced using crinkle cutter	2	2
Creamed cottage cheese	3 cups	750 mL
Bread slices, toasted and halved diagonally (buttered, optional)	6	6

FRUIT TOPPING

Frozen whipped topping, thawed	1 cup	250 mL
Light salad dressing (or mayonnaise)	4 tsp.	20 mL

Combine first 6 ingredients in large bowl. Toss gently.

Arrange 1/2 cup (125 mL) cottage cheese in center of 6 individual salad plates. Divide fruit among plates halfway around cottage cheese. Set toast on side of fruit.

Fruit Topping: Fold whipped topping and salad dressing together in small bowl. Divide and spoon over fruit. Serves 6.

1 serving: 314 Calories; 10.6 g Total Fat; 619 mg Sodium; 17 g Protein; 39 g Carbohydrate; 3 g Dietary Fiber

Pictured above.

Summer Jellied Salad

Red and green layers—Christmas in July! This is extraordinary.

Boiling water	1 1/2 cups	375 mL
Package of strawberry-flavored (or other red) gelatin (jelly powder)	3 oz.	85 g
Can of crushed pineapple, drained	8 oz.	225 mL
Boiling water	1 1/2 cups	375 mL
Package of lime-flavored gelatin (jelly powder)	3 oz.	85 g
Light cream cheese, softened and cubed	4 oz.	125 g
Frozen whipped topping, thawed (or whipped cream)	1 cup	250 mL

Stir first amount of boiling water into strawberry-flavored gelatin in medium bowl until gelatin is dissolved. Add pineapple. Stir. Chill, stirring and scraping down sides occasionally, until syrupy. Turn into lightly greased 6 cup (1.5 L) mold or deep bowl. Chill for about 10 minutes until slightly tacky on surface and almost firm.

Stir second amount of boiling water into lime-flavored gelatin in medium saucepan until gelatin is dissolved. Add cream cheese. Heat and stir until cream cheese is melted and mixture is blended. Chill until thick and syrupy.

Fold whipped topping into cream cheese mixture. Carefully pour over first layer. Chill for several hours until firm. Loosen salad in mold. Invert onto dampened serving plate. Dampness makes it easier to center mold on plate. Serves 4 to 6.

1 serving: 314 Calories; 11.1 g Total Fat; 331 mg Sodium; 7 g Protein; 49 g Carbohydrate; 1 g Dietary Fiber

Pictured on page 69.

Left: Cheesy Pea Salad, below

Right: Summer Jellied Salad, page 68

Cheesy Pea Salad

*A variety of ingredients makes this
a tasty and attractive choice.*

Cooked peas	2 cups	500 mL
Diced light sharp Cheddar cheese	1/2 cup	125 mL
Thinly sliced celery	1 cup	250 mL
Sweet pickle relish	1/3 cup	75 mL
Hard-boiled eggs, chopped	3	3
Salt, sprinkle		
Pepper, sprinkle		
DRESSING		
Light salad dressing (or mayonnaise)	1/4 cup	60 mL
Milk	1 1/2 tbsp.	25 mL
Granulated sugar	1/4 tsp.	1 mL

Combine first 7 ingredients in medium bowl.

Dressing: Mix salad dressing, milk and sugar in small bowl. Add to pea mixture. Toss until well coated. Makes 4 cups (1 L).

1/2 cup (125 mL): 121 Calories; 4.8 g Total Fat; 240 mg Sodium; 7 g Protein; 13 g Carbohydrate; 3 g Dietary Fiber

Pictured above.

Potato Vegetable Salad

*Not your typical potato salad look—shiny and colorful.
Also very good.*

Cooked baby red potatoes, halved (measure after cutting)	4 cups	1 L
Sliced cooked carrot	1 cup	250 mL
Cooked peas	1 cup	250 mL
Finely chopped celery	1 cup	250 mL
Sweet pickle relish	1/4 cup	60 mL
DRESSING		
Golden Italian dressing	1/2 cup	125 mL
Salad dressing (or mayonnaise)	1/4 cup	60 mL
Salt	1/4 tsp.	1 mL
Pepper	1/4 tsp.	1 mL

Combine first 5 ingredients in large bowl.

Dressing: Mix all 4 ingredients in small bowl. Add to salad. Toss until well coated. Cover. Chill. Makes 7 cups (1.75 L).

1 cup (250 mL): 329 Calories; 16.9 g Total Fat; 535 mg Sodium; 5 g Protein; 42 g Carbohydrate; 5 g Dietary Fiber

Pictured on page 71.

Summer Spinach Salad

Fresh spinach and fruit just seem to go together. The pumpkin and flax seeds are optional but give an appealing crunch.

MINT VINAIGRETTE

Olive (or cooking) oil	1/4 cup	60 mL
Apple cider vinegar	3 tbsp.	50 mL
Liquid honey	1 tbsp.	15 mL
Chopped fresh mint leaves (or 3/4 tsp., 4 mL, dried)	1 tbsp.	15 mL
Salt, just a pinch		
Freshly ground pepper, sprinkle		
Torn fresh spinach, lightly packed	6 cups	1.5 L
Paper-thin sliced red onion	3/4 cup	175 mL
Sliced fresh strawberries	1 cup	250 mL
Shelled pumpkin seeds (optional)	3 tbsp.	50 mL
Flax seeds (optional)	2 tsp.	10 mL

Mint Vinaigrette: Combine first 6 ingredients in small bowl or jar with tight-fitting lid. Cover or seal. Stir or shake vigorously. Let stand for 30 minutes to blend flavors. Makes 1/2 cup (125 mL).

Combine remaining 5 ingredients in large bowl. Shake vinaigrette. Drizzle over salad. Toss if desired. Serve immediately. Serves 4.

1 serving: 190 Calories; 14.9 g Total Fat; 72 mg Sodium; 3 g Protein; 14 g Carbohydrate; 4 g Dietary Fiber

Pictured on page 71.

Strawberry Soup

There is a fresh strawberry taste to this chilled soup.

Granulated sugar	3/4 cup	175 mL
Water	1 1/2 cups	375 mL
Fresh strawberries, halved (about 1 1/2 lbs., 680 g)	4 cups	1 L
Grated lemon peel	1 1/2 tsp.	7 mL
Grated orange peel	2 tsp.	10 mL
Sherry (or alcohol-free sherry or fresh orange juice)	1/4 cup	60 mL
Whipping cream (optional)	4 tsp.	20 mL

Combine sugar and water in small saucepan. Bring to a boil on medium, stirring occasionally. Reduce heat to medium-low. Simmer for 10 minutes. Cool.

Combine next 4 ingredients in large bowl. Add sugar mixture. Stir. Process, in 2 batches, in blender until smooth. Strain juice into large bowl. Discard seeds. Pour into container. Chill.

Garnish individual servings with swirls of whipping cream. Serve chilled. Makes 3 1/2 cups (875 mL). Serves 4.

1 serving: 212 Calories; 0.6 g Total Fat; 3 mg Sodium; 1 g Protein; 51 g Carbohydrate; 4 g Dietary Fiber

Pictured on page 71.

Cabbage Salad

Bright colors, mild taste.

Shredded green cabbage, packed	2 cups	500 mL
Shredded red cabbage, packed	2 cups	500 mL
DRESSING		
Sour cream	1/2 cup	125 mL
Mayonnaise	1/2 cup	125 mL
Lemon juice	1 tbsp.	15 mL
Salt	1/2 tsp.	2 mL
Onion powder	1/4 tsp.	1 mL

Combine green and red cabbage in large bowl.

Dressing: Mix all 5 ingredients in small bowl. Add to cabbage. Toss until well coated. Serves 8.

1 serving: 140 Calories; 13.9 g Total Fat; 236 mg Sodium; 1 g Protein; 3 g Carbohydrate; 1 g Dietary Fiber

Pictured on page 71.

Top Left: Strawberry Soup, above
Center Left: Potato Vegetable Salad, page 69
Center Right: Summer Spinach Salad, this page
Bottom Right: Cabbage Salad, above

Taco Burgers, below

Taco Burgers

Great taco flavor. Offer a choice of condiments such as salsa, tomato slices and hot pickled peppers.

Can of tomato sauce	7 1/2 oz.	213 mL
Envelope of taco seasoning mix	1 1/4 oz.	35 g
Finely chopped onion (optional)	1/4 cup	60 mL
Soda cracker crumbs	1 cup	250 mL
Lean ground beef	1 1/2 lbs.	680 g
Hamburger buns, split (toasted and buttered, optional)	8	8
Grated medium Cheddar cheese	1/2 cup	125 mL

Combine first 4 ingredients in large bowl.

Add ground beef. Mix well. Shape into 8 patties. Barbecue, pan-fry or broil for 4 to 5 minutes per side until patties are no longer pink in center.

Place 1 patty on bottom half of each bun.

Sprinkle each with 1 tbsp. (15 mL) cheese. Replace top half of each bun. Makes 8 burgers.

1 burger: 348 Calories; 13.5 g Total Fat; 1130 mg Sodium; 22 g Protein; 34 g Carbohydrate; 1 g Dietary Fiber

Pictured above.

Bean Dog Joes

Fabulous flavor to this dark rusty colored topping. Serve with baby carrots instead of the usual potato chips.

Can of baked beans in tomato sauce	14 oz.	398 mL
Can of condensed tomato soup	10 oz.	284 mL
Hickory smoked barbecue sauce	1/4 cup	60 mL
Brown sugar, packed	1/2 cup	125 mL
Prepared mustard	1 tsp.	5 mL
Onion powder	1/2 tsp.	2 mL
Wieners (about 12), cut into 1/4 inch (6 mm) coins	1 lb.	454 g
Hot dog buns (or French rolls), split (buttered, optional)	6	6

Combine first 6 ingredients in medium saucepan. Heat, stirring often, until simmering. Simmer, stirring often, for 2 minutes.

Add wieners. Stir. Simmer for about 4 minutes until wieners are very hot. Makes 5 1/4 cups (1.3 L) topping.

Arrange 2 bun halves, cut sides up, on each plate. Divide topping over all halves. Serves 6.

1 serving: 526 Calories; 21.3 g Total Fat; 1739 mg Sodium; 17 g Protein; 68 g Carbohydrate; 7 g Dietary Fiber

Pictured on page 73.

Bottom Left: Popeye Burgers, below

Top Right: Bean Dog Joes, page 72

Popeye Burgers

*Add condiments such as spinach leaves, carrot strips,
yellow pepper rings and tomato slices. Potato chips
on the side complete this burger.*

Bulgur	1/3 cup	75 mL
Milk	1/3 cup	75 mL
Small onion, chopped	1	1
Garlic clove, peeled and quartered (or 1/4 tsp., 1 mL, powder), optional	1	1
Medium green pepper, chopped	1	1
Large egg	1	1
Dried whole oregano	1 tsp.	5 mL
Ground nutmeg	1/8 tsp.	0.5 mL
Salt	1 tsp.	5 mL
Pepper	1/8 tsp.	0.5 mL
Box of frozen chopped spinach, thawed and squeezed dry	10 oz.	300 g
Whole wheat cracker crumbs	1 cup	250 mL
Lean ground beef	3/4 lb.	340 g
Lean ground chicken	3/4 lb.	340 g
Hamburger buns, split (toasted and buttered, optional)	10	10

Put first 10 ingredients into blender. Process until almost smooth. Pour into large bowl.

Add spinach and cracker crumbs. Stir.

Add ground beef and ground chicken. Mix well. Divide and shape into 10 patties. Barbecue, pan-fry or broil for 9 minutes per side until no pink remains in center.

Place 1 patty on bottom half of each bun. Replace top half of each bun. Makes 10 burgers.

1 burger: 325 Calories; 12.2 g Total Fat; 606 mg Sodium; 19 g Protein; 35 g Carbohydrate; 2 g Dietary Fiber

Pictured above.

Tip *To keep food chilled when packing the picnic cooler, put the heavier items in the bottom of the cooler and pack the immediately necessary items on top so you don't have to keep the lid open longer than necessary.*

Smothered Halibut

The taste isn't smothered—that's for sure. Top notch!

Halibut fillets (about 1 1/4 lbs., 560 g)	4	4
Large onion, thinly sliced and separated into rings	1	1
Hard margarine (not butter)	1 1/2 tsp.	7 mL
Medium carrot, grated	1	1
Medium parsnip, grated	1	1
Hard margarine (not butter)	1 1/2 tsp.	7 mL
Small zucchini, with peel, cut into thin strips	1	1
Medium-small tomatoes, quartered, seeded and diced	2	2
Dried sweet basil	3/4 tsp.	4 mL
Salt	1/2 tsp.	2 mL
Pepper	1/4 tsp.	1 mL
Grated Parmesan cheese	2 tbsp.	30 mL

Arrange fillets in single layer in greased 8 × 8 inch (20 × 20 cm) dish.

Sauté onion in first amount of margarine in frying pan until soft. Spoon over fillets.

Add carrot, parsnip and second amount of margarine to frying pan. Sauté for 2 minutes until tender. Spoon and spread over onion.

Add zucchini to frying pan. Sauté for 2 minutes until soft. Spoon and spread over vegetable mixture.

Place tomato in medium bowl. Sprinkle with basil, salt and pepper. Toss until well coated. Spoon over zucchini.

Sprinkle with cheese. Cover. Bake in 450°F (230°C) oven for 30 to 35 minutes until fillets flake easily when tested with fork. Serves 4.

1 serving: 252 Calories; 7.5 g Total Fat; 482 mg Sodium; 32 g Protein; 13 g Carbohydrate; 3 g Dietary Fiber

Pictured on page 75.

Salmon On Cedar

Wonderful light smoky salmon taste with a yummy lemon and nut topping.

Cedar plank (see Note)	1	1
Mayonnaise (not salad dressing)	3 tbsp.	50 mL
Finely chopped fresh parsley (or 1 1/2 tsp., 7 mL, flakes)	2 tbsp.	30 mL
Minced garlic (optional)	1/2 tsp.	2 mL
Lemon juice	2 tsp.	10 mL
Grated lemon peel	1/2 tsp.	2 mL
Salmon fillets, with skin	1 1/2 lbs.	680 g
Pine nuts, finely chopped	1 tbsp.	15 mL

Soak cedar plank in water for at least 8 hours or overnight, turning several times to soak both sides or weighting down with heavy object to keep submerged.

Combine first 5 ingredients in small bowl.

Spread mayonnaise mixture evenly on skinless side of fillets. Sprinkle with pine nuts. Remove cedar plank from water. Place on preheated grill, rough side down. Reduce heat to low. (Or use indirect cooking method. See Tip, below.) Close lid for 1 to 2 minutes until plank is heated through and looks dry in places. Lay salmon, skin side down, on cedar plank. Close lid. Cook for 10 to 12 minutes for 3/4 inch (2 cm) fillets until fillets flake easily when tested with fork in thickest part. Cooking time will vary with thickness of fillets. Serves 6.

1 serving: 269 Calories; 18.8 g Total Fat; 104 mg Sodium; 23 g Protein; 1 g Carbohydrate; trace Dietary Fiber

Pictured on page 75.

Note: Purchase either a cedar plank designed specifically for cooking food or an untreated cedar plank at least 1/2 inch (12 mm) thick.

Tip To cook salmon using indirect cooking method, turn off one burner on your grill once it has been preheated and leave one burner on medium. Place cedar plank on grill over unlit side.

Top: Salmon On Cedar, above
Center: Smothered Halibut, this page
Bottom: Smoky Fish, page 76

Grilled Sea Bass

Dressed up with a sauce, this can be cooked on the barbecue or in the oven. Baby red potatoes and steamed pea pods complete this meal.

MUSTARD SAUCE

Fat-free salad dressing (or mayonnaise)	3 tbsp.	50 mL
Dijon mustard	1 1/2 tbsp.	25 mL
Chopped fresh parsley (or 3/4 tsp., 4 mL, flakes)	1 tbsp.	15 mL
Chopped fresh chives (or 3/4 tsp., 4 mL, dried)	1 tbsp.	15 mL
Lemon juice	1 tbsp.	15 mL
Salt	1/2 tsp.	2 mL
Cayenne pepper	1/8 tsp.	0.5 mL
Sea bass steaks (about 1 lb., 454 g) 2		2

Mustard Sauce: Mix first 7 ingredients together in small bowl until smooth.

Using double thickness of foil, make "pan" for fish. Spray with cooking spray. Poke several holes through foil to allow liquid to drip through. Place fish on foil. Spread sauce over top. Carefully place foil on grill. Close lid. Cook over medium-high (375°F, 190°C) for 8 to 10 minutes until fish flakes easily when tested with fork in thickest part. Serves 4.

1 serving: 131 Calories; 3 g Total Fat; 582 mg Sodium; 21 g Protein; 3 g Carbohydrate; trace Dietary Fiber

Pictured on page 77.

Smoky Fish

A mixture of grilled red peppers and red onion chunks complete this dish. The liquid smoke adds a lot of flavor.

SMOKY BARBECUE SAUCE

Ketchup	2 1/2 tbsp.	37 mL
White vinegar	1 1/2 tbsp.	25 mL
Granulated sugar	1 tbsp.	15 mL
Cooking oil	1 1/2 tsp.	7 mL
Worcestershire sauce	1/2 tsp.	2 mL
Liquid smoke	1-1 1/2 tsp.	5-7 mL
Onion powder	1/8 tsp.	0.5 mL
Garlic powder	1/8 tsp.	0.5 mL
Dry mustard	1/8 tsp.	0.5 mL
Salt	1/8 tsp.	0.5 mL
Red snapper fillets (or your choice), about 1 lb. (454 g)	4	4

Smoky Barbecue Sauce: Combine first 10 ingredients in small bowl. Makes about 1/3 cup (75 mL) sauce.

Brush fillets with sauce. Place fillets on greased grill. Cook, with lid open, for 3 minutes, basting occasionally with sauce. Turn fillets over. Cook for about 4 minutes until fillets flake easily when tested with fork. Serves 4.

1 serving: 143 Calories; 3.2 g Total Fat; 290 mg Sodium; 22 g Protein; 6 g Carbohydrate; trace Dietary Fiber

Pictured on page 75.

Variation: Arrange fillets in single layer on greased baking sheet. Bake in 400°F (205°C) oven for about 15 minutes until fillets flake easily when tested with fork.

Baked Trout

A subtle flavor change is in store when you use this topping on the catch-of-the-day. Serve with rice and grilled peppers.

Fresh lake (or rainbow) trout fillets or halves, with skin on	1 1/2 lbs.	680 g
Salt, sprinkle		
Pepper, sprinkle		
Sour cream	2 tbsp.	30 mL
Salad dressing (such as Miracle Whip)	1 1/2 tsp.	7 mL
Grated Parmesan cheese	1 tbsp.	15 mL
Soy sauce	1 tsp.	5 mL
Lemon juice	1/2 tsp.	2 mL
Paprika, sprinkle		
Chopped fresh dill (or chives), for garnish		

Arrange fillets in single layer, skin side down, on greased baking sheet. Sprinkle with salt and pepper.

Combine next 5 ingredients in small bowl. Spread thinly over fillets.

Sprinkle with paprika. Bake, uncovered, in 400°F (205°C) oven for 8 to 10 minutes until fillets flake easily when tested with fork.

Garnish with dill. Serves 6.

1 serving: 187 Calories; 9.1 g Total Fat; 146 mg Sodium; 24 g Protein; 1 g Carbohydrate; 0 g Dietary Fiber

Pictured on page 77.

Top Left: Baked Trout, page 76   Bottom: Grilled Sea Bass, page 76   Top Right: Sole Divan, below

Sole Divan

The broccoli is tender-crisp for a pleasing crunch.

Chopped onion	1/3 cup	75 mL
Chopped mushrooms	1 cup	250 mL
Hard margarine (or butter)	2 tsp.	10 mL
All-purpose flour	2 tbsp.	30 mL
Water	1/2 cup	125 mL
Skim evaporated milk	2/3 cup	150 mL
Sherry (or alcohol-free sherry) or white (or alcohol-free) wine	2 tbsp.	30 mL
Chicken (or seafood) bouillon powder	1 tsp.	5 mL
Fresh (or frozen, thawed and blotted dry) sole fillets	1 lb.	454 g
Lemon pepper, sprinkle		
Chopped fresh broccoli (or 15 oz., 500 g, bag of frozen broccoli, thawed and drained)	5 cups	1.25 L

Sauté onion and mushrooms in margarine in medium non-stick frying pan until onion is golden and liquid from mushrooms has evaporated.

Sprinkle with flour. Stir until well mixed.

Add water, evaporated milk, sherry and bouillon powder. Heat and stir on medium until boiling and thickened.

Sprinkle fillets with lemon pepper. Fold fillets in half crosswise. Arrange in single layer in ungreased 2 quart (2 L) shallow casserole.

Arrange broccoli around fillets. Dab sauce over broccoli and fillets. Cover with foil or lid. Bake in 400°F (205°C) oven for 30 to 35 minutes until fillets flake easily when tested with fork. Do not overcook. Serves 4.

1 serving: 221 Calories; 4 g Total Fat; 361 mg Sodium; 29 g Protein; 17 g Carbohydrate; 5 g Dietary Fiber

Pictured above.

Herbed Spaghetti Primavera

Use the season's best new vegetables. So colorful! So yummy!

Garlic cloves, minced (or 1/2 tsp., 2 mL, powder)	2	2
Fresh small mushrooms	1 cup	250 mL
Medium red pepper, slivered	1	1
Olive (or cooking) oil	1 tbsp.	15 mL
Green onions, sliced	3	3
Fresh peas	1 cup	250 mL
Finger-size zucchini pieces, cut into thirds diagonally	8	8
Finger-size carrot pieces, halved	8	8
Dry white (or alcohol-free) wine	1/3 cup	75 mL
Half-and-half cream	2/3 cup	150 mL
Coarsely shredded fresh spinach, packed	1 cup	250 mL
Diced fresh tomato	1 cup	250 mL
Chopped fresh sweet basil (or 3/4 tsp., 4 mL, dried)	1 tbsp.	15 mL
Chopped fresh oregano leaves (or 3/4 tsp., 4 mL, dried)	1 tbsp.	15 mL
Chopped fresh dill (or 3/4 tsp., 4 mL, dill weed)	1 tbsp.	15 mL
Chopped fresh parsley (or 3/4 tsp., 4 mL, flakes)	1 tbsp.	15 mL
Salt	1/2 tsp.	2 mL
Freshly ground pepper, sprinkle		
Freshly grated Romano cheese	1/3 cup	75 mL
Spaghetti	12 oz.	340 g
Boiling water	12 cups	3 L
Salt	1 tbsp.	15 mL
Freshly grated Romano cheese	2 tbsp.	30 mL

Sauté garlic, mushrooms and red pepper in olive oil in large frying pan for 1 minute.

Add green onion, peas, zucchini and carrot. Stir-fry for 2 to 3 minutes until vegetables are brightly colored.

Add wine. Simmer for 1 minute to avoid curdling. Add cream. Cover. Bring to a boil. Reduce heat. Simmer for 3 to 4 minutes until vegetables are tender-crisp.

Add next 8 ingredients. Toss. Cover. Bring to a boil. Reduce heat. Simmer for about 5 minutes until tomato is soft.

Stir in first amount of cheese.

Cook spaghetti in boiling water and salt in large uncovered pot or Dutch oven for 9 to 10 minutes until tender but firm. Drain. Turn into serving dish. Pour sauce over spaghetti. Toss gently.

Sprinkle with second amount of cheese. Serves 6.

1 serving: 367 Calories; 8.7 g Total Fat; 328 mg Sodium; 15 g Protein; 57 g Carbohydrate; 5 g Dietary Fiber

Pictured on this page.

Top Right: Summer Tomato And Cheese Topping, below
Bottom Left: Herbed Spaghetti Primavera, this page

Summer Tomato And Cheese Topping

Serve over hot pasta. Garnish with fresh Parmesan shavings and a sprig of fresh sweet basil.

Olive (or cooking) oil	1 tbsp.	15 mL
Garlic cloves, minced (or 1/2 tsp., 2 mL, powder)	2	2
Fresh sweet basil, shredded and packed (or 1 tbsp., 15 mL, dried)	1/4 cup	60 mL
Salt	1/2 tsp.	2 mL
Freshly ground pepper, sprinkle		
Seeded and diced ripe roma (plum) tomato	3 cups	750 mL
Diced roasted red pepper (optional)	2/3 cup	150 mL
Thinly sliced green onion	1/4 cup	60 mL
Non-fat creamed cottage cheese, slightly mashed with fork	1 cup	250 mL
Grated light Parmesan cheese	1 tbsp.	15 mL

Combine first 8 ingredients in medium bowl. Cover. Let stand at room temperature for at least 1 hour to blend flavors. Turn into medium saucepan. Heat through.

Add cottage cheese and Parmesan cheese. Stir. Makes 3 cups (750 mL).

3/4 cup (175 mL): 117 Calories; 4.1 g Total Fat; 489 mg Sodium; 13 g Protein; 8 g Carbohydrate; 2 g Dietary Fiber

Pictured above.

Chard Rolls

Freeze rolls individually in resealable freezer bags to use up the chard from your garden.

Large Swiss (or red) chard leaves	10	10
Boiling water	16 cups	4 L
Chopped onion	1 cup	250 mL
Diced fresh jalapeño pepper, ribs and seeds removed for less heat if desired (see Note)	1	1
Cooking oil	1 tbsp.	15 mL
Water	2 cups	500 mL
Diced sun-dried tomato	1/4 cup	60 mL
Vegetable (or chicken) bouillon powder	2 tbsp.	30 mL
Coarsely ground pepper	1/4 tsp.	1 mL
Brown medium (or long) grain rice	3/4 cup	175 mL
Water	2/3 cup	150 mL

Cut chard leaves in half lengthwise. Remove central ribs. Stack leaves. Gently push, all at once, into boiling water in large pot or Dutch oven. Boil for 10 seconds until soft. Drain. Cool. Restack leaves. Set aside.

Sauté onion and jalapeño pepper in cooking oil in medium saucepan until onion is soft.

Add second amount of water, sun-dried tomato, bouillon powder and pepper. Bring to a boil. Stir in rice. Reduce heat. Cover. Simmer on low for about 50 minutes until rice is tender and liquid is absorbed. Cool on counter until able to handle. Makes 2 cups (500 mL) filling. Place 1 1/2 tbsp. (25 mL) filling on each chard leaf. Roll each leaf, tucking in sides to enclose filling. Arrange rolls in single layer in greased 2 quart (2 L) shallow casserole.

Pour third amount of water over rolls. Cover. Bake in 375°F (190°C) oven for about 1 hour until chard is very tender and water is absorbed. Makes 20 rolls.

1 roll: 47 Calories; 1.1 g Total Fat; 262 mg Sodium; 1 g Protein; 8 g Carbohydrate; 1 g Dietary Fiber

Pictured on this page.

Note: Wear gloves when chopping jalapeño peppers and avoid touching your eyes.

Spiced Green Beans

Mmm...green beans from the garden are simply the best! Use your favorite mustard to give them a bit of pep.

Water	1/2 cup	125 mL
Salt	1/2 tsp.	2 mL
Fresh young whole green beans, trimmed (see Note)	1 lb.	454 g
Hard margarine (or butter)	1/4 cup	60 mL
Worcestershire sauce	1 tbsp.	15 mL
Grainy (or Dijon or prepared) mustard	1 tbsp.	15 mL
Garlic salt, sprinkle		

Combine water and salt in large saucepan. Bring to a boil. Add beans. Reduce heat to medium-low. Cover. Cook for 5 to 6 minutes until tender-crisp. Remove from heat. Do not drain.

Add margarine, Worcestershire sauce, mustard and garlic salt. Stir until well coated. Serve immediately. Serves 4.

1 serving: 150 Calories; 12.6 g Total Fat; 544 mg Sodium; 3 g Protein; 9 g Carbohydrate; 2 g Dietary Fiber

Pictured below.

Note: Or use 1 can (14 oz., 398 mL) whole green beans, drained, instead of fresh beans.

Left: Chard Rolls, this page   Right: Spiced Green Beans, above

Campfire Cooking

It's a true summer tradition to gather around the campfire for warmth, friendship and maybe a song or two. Why not use this time to try your hand at cooking over wood? These recipe selections are simple and fun, and everyone will savor the natural, smoky flavors that can only come from a wood fire.

Campfire Oatmeal Bread

Fajita Chicken-In-A-Packet

Pork Satay

Fire-Fried Rice

Campfire Oatmeal Bread

Good just as is, hot from the fire, but simply great served with butter and jam or peanut butter.

All-purpose flour	1 1/4 cups	300 mL
Quick-cooking rolled oats (not instant)	1/2 cup	125 mL
Skim milk powder	2 tbsp.	30 mL
Baking powder	1 tsp.	5 mL
Baking soda	1/2 tsp.	2 mL
Salt	1/2 tsp.	2 mL
Hard margarine (or butter), cold	1/4 cup	60 mL
Water, approximately	1/2 cup	125 mL

Combine first 6 ingredients in medium bowl.

Cut in margarine with pastry cutter until consistency of small peas. Place in resealable plastic bag.

Turn bag contents into medium bowl. Add water. Stir with fork until dough forms a ball. Do not add too much water or dough will be too soft. Knead 8 or 9 times. Divide into 8 portions. Form each portion into about 1/2 inch (12 mm) thick discs on 2-pronged roasting sticks or around sturdy twigs chosen for cooking over a fire. Hold about 12 inches (30 cm) above hot coals in fire pit for about 6 minutes, turning 2 or 3 times, until bread is very brown and dry looking. Serves 4.

1 serving: 324 Calories; 13.5 g Total Fat; 714 mg Sodium; 8 g Protein; 43 g Carbohydrate; 3 g Dietary Fiber

Pictured on page 82.

Variation: Divide dough into 2 portions. Form into 1/2 inch (12 mm) thick discs. Cook on heavy-duty foil placed on grate over hot coals. Turn once to brown both sides. Length of cooking time will be about 20 minutes but depends on heat from the coals and the position of the grate.

Fajita Chicken-In-A-Packet

Extra good, especially with cheese.

Italian dressing	1/4 cup	60 mL
Salsa	1/4 cup	60 mL
Lime juice	2 tsp.	10 mL
Finely grated lime peel (optional)	1/2 tsp.	2 mL
Ground cumin	1/4 tsp.	1 mL
Hot pepper sauce (optional)	1/4 tsp.	1 mL
Sliced fresh mushrooms	1 1/2 cups	375 mL
Large onion, cut lengthwise into wedges	1	1
Sliced red, green or yellow pepper	1 1/2 cups	375 mL
Boneless, skinless chicken breast halves (about 3), cut into strips	12 oz.	340 g
Whole wheat flour tortillas (10 inch, 25 cm, size)	4	4
TOPPINGS (optional)		
Shredded lettuce	1/2 cup	125 mL
Grated cheese	1/2 cup	125 mL
Chopped tomato	1/2 cup	125 mL
Sour cream	1/2 cup	125 mL

Combine first 6 ingredients in small bowl. Makes 2/3 cup (150 mL) sauce.

Lay out 2 lengths of heavy-duty or double layer of foil about 24 inches (60 cm) long each. Spoon 2 tbsp. (30 mL) salsa mixture in center of each. Divide and layer mushrooms, onion, red pepper and chicken strips on each. Divide remaining salsa mixture over each. Bring up 2 short sides of 1 length of foil to meet over chicken. Fold together downwards several times to seal very well. Fold sides in at an angle. Roll up from end to seal and create handles for turning with tongs. Repeat with remaining length of foil. Lay packets on top of grill over hot coals in fire pit or on rack in hot barbecue. Cook for about 30 minutes, turning carefully several times being careful not to puncture foil, until chicken is no longer pink and vegetables are tender.

Carefully open packets. Divide filling among tortillas.

Toppings: Top with choice of toppings. Roll, folding up bottom and sides of tortilla to contain filling. Makes 4 fajitas.

1 fajita: 404 Calories; 14.3 g Total Fat; 635 mg Sodium; 27 g Protein; 45 g Carbohydrate; 7 g Dietary Fiber

Pictured on page 82.

Pork Satay, below

Pork Satay

Having these frozen in the marinade makes them safer to take for camping or picnics.

Frozen concentrated orange juice	1/4 cup	60 mL
Low-sodium soy sauce	1 tbsp.	15 mL
Cooking oil	1 tbsp.	15 mL
Garlic cloves, minced (or 1/2 tsp., 2 mL, powder)	2	2
Finely grated gingerroot (or 1/2 tsp., 2 mL, ground ginger)	2 tsp.	10 mL
Hot pepper sauce	1/4 tsp.	1 mL
Pork loin, cut into 1 inch (2.5 cm) cubes	1 lb.	454 g

Combine first 6 ingredients in small bowl.

Place pork cubes in large resealable freezer bag. Pour marinade over top. Seal. Turn to coat. Freeze. Defrost. Remove pork cubes. Discard marinade. Push about 4 or 5 pork cubes onto each of 4 roasting sticks. Lay on top of grill over hot coals in fire pit. Cook for 10 minutes, turning several times, until no longer pink inside. Serves 4.

1 serving: 193 Calories; 7.8 g Total Fat; 186 mg Sodium; 25 g Protein; 4 g Carbohydrate; trace Dietary Fiber

Pictured above.

Left: Fire-Fried Rice, below   Bottom Left & Top Right: Campfire Oatmeal Bread, page 80   Right: Fajita Chicken-In-A-Packet, page 81

Fire-Fried Rice

Have several of these packets frozen for up to 2 months.
They'll always be available for those weekend camping trips.

Chopped onion	1 1/2 cups	375 mL
Chopped celery	1 1/2 cups	375 mL
Sliced fresh mushrooms	2 cups	500 mL
Diced red pepper	3/4 cup	175 mL
Cooking oil	2 tbsp.	30 mL
Soy sauce	2 tbsp.	30 mL
Salt	1/2 tsp.	2 mL
Pepper	1/4 tsp.	1 mL
Cold cooked long grain rice, broken up (about 1 1/2 cups, 375 mL, uncooked)	3 cups	750 mL

Sauté onion, celery, mushrooms and red pepper in cooking oil in large frying pan until onion is soft. Remove from heat. Turn into large bowl.

Add soy sauce, salt and pepper. Stir well. Let stand until cool.

Add rice to onion mixture. Use wet hands to break up any large chunks. Mix well. Makes about 6 1/2 cups (1.6 L). Divide into 2 resealable freezer bags. Freeze. Makes 2 packets containing 3 1/4 cups (800 mL) each. Defrost. Turn rice mixture into small greased foil container. Cover with foil. Lay container directly on top of grill over hot coals in fire pit or on rack in hot barbecue for 10 minutes. Remove foil. Stir gently. Cover. Heat for about 10 minutes until hot. Serves 4.

1 serving: 327 Calories; 7.8 g Total Fat; 866 mg Sodium; 7 g Protein; 57 g Carbohydrate; 3 g Dietary Fiber

Pictured above.

Fresh Cherry Dessert Sauce

This richly colored, richly flavored sauce is perfect for topping frozen yogurt, cheesecake, fresh fruit salad or even ice cream.

Sweet fresh cherries (such as Bing) (4 - 5 cups, 1 - 1.25 L)	1 1/2 lbs.	680 g
Granulated sugar	1 cup	250 mL
Water	1/3 cup	75 mL
Corn syrup	1/3 cup	75 mL
Almond-flavored liqueur (such as Amaretto) or water	2 tbsp.	30 mL
Cornstarch	1 tbsp.	15 mL
Lemon juice	2 tsp.	10 mL

Pit cherries. Discard pits. Coarsely chop. Put into large saucepan.

Sprinkle with sugar. Let stand for 2 hours, stirring once or twice.

Stir in water and corn syrup. Heat on medium-high for 15 minutes, stirring frequently, until simmering and richly colored.

Stir liqueur into cornstarch in small dish until smooth. Stir into cherry mixture until boiling and slightly thickened. Remove from heat.

Stir in lemon juice. Makes 3 cups (750 mL).

2 tbsp. (30 mL): 72 Calories; 0.3 g Total Fat; 6 mg Sodium; trace Protein; 17 g Carbohydrate; trace Dietary Fiber

Pictured on page 86.

Fresh Peach Tart

The fresh peach flavor permeates the custard and the flaky crust gives just a hint of cinnamon. If you don't have a pan with a removable bottom, a deep-dish pizza pan can be used.

All-purpose flour	3/4 cup	175 mL
Whole wheat flour	2/3 cup	150 mL
Brown sugar, packed	3 tbsp.	50 mL
Ground cinnamon	1/8 tsp.	0.5 mL
Hard margarine (or butter), cold	2/3 cup	150 mL
Large egg, fork-beaten	1	1
Cold water	1 1/2 tbsp.	25 mL
Minute tapioca	2 tsp.	10 mL
Fresh medium peaches (about 2 lbs., 900 g)	6	6
Boiling water		
Ice water		
Granulated sugar	1/2 cup	125 mL
All-purpose flour	2 tbsp.	30 mL
Large egg	1	1
Egg yolk (large)	1	1
Whipping cream	1 cup	250 mL
Vanilla	1/2 tsp.	2 mL
Sliced almonds, toasted (see Tip, page 28)	2 tbsp.	30 mL

Combine both flours, brown sugar and cinnamon in medium bowl. Cut in margarine until mixture is crumbly.

Combine first egg and cold water together in small dish. Slowly add to flour mixture while tossing and mixing with fork until flour is completely moistened. Add more cold water, 1 tsp. (5 mL) at a time, as needed to make pastry that is not too moist but will hold together. Shape into disc. Cover in plastic wrap. Chill for 15 minutes. Turn out onto lightly floured surface. Roll out into 12 1/2 inch (31.2 cm) circle. Fit into 11 inch (28 cm) tart tin with removable bottom. Trim excess dough or flute edge attractively.

Sprinkle tapioca over bottom of pastry. Set aside.

Drop peaches, 2 at a time, into large saucepan half filled with boiling water. Scald for 30 seconds, turning several times. Remove to an ice water bath with slotted spoon. Remove and discard skins. Cut in half. Discard pit. Cut into thin slices. Arrange close together in two layers in spiral pattern on pastry.

Combine granulated sugar and flour in medium bowl.

Combine second egg, egg yolk, whipping cream and vanilla in small bowl. Slowly stir into sugar mixture until smooth. Spoon over and in between peaches, filling almost to top edge of tart tin. Bake, uncovered, on bottom rack in 375°F (190°C) oven for about 55 minutes until set and knife comes out clean when inserted in center.

Sprinkle with almonds. Cool on wire rack for 15 minutes before cutting. Serve warm or cold. Cuts into 10 pieces.

1 piece: 389 Calories; 23.5 g Total Fat; 176 mg Sodium; 5 g Protein; 42 g Carbohydrate; 3 g Dietary Fiber

Pictured on page 86.

Golf Course Cake, below

Golf Course Cake

Something for the enthusiastic golfer in your house.

CAKE

All-purpose flour	2 1/4 cups	550 mL
Granulated sugar	1 2/3 cups	400 mL
Cocoa, sifted if lumpy	1/2 cup	125 mL
Baking powder	2 tsp.	10 mL
Baking soda	2 tsp.	10 mL
Salt	1 tsp.	5 mL
Hard margarine (or butter), softened	1/2 cup	125 mL
Large eggs	2	2
Vanilla	2 tsp.	10 mL
Milk	2 cups	500 mL

ICING

Icing (confectioner's) sugar	3 cups	750 mL
Hard margarine (or butter), softened	6 tbsp.	100 mL
Vanilla	1 tsp.	5 mL
Drops of green food coloring	3	3
Milk	2 tbsp.	30 mL

SAND TRAP

Brown sugar, packed	3 tbsp.	50 mL

WATER HAZARD

Long black licorice string	1	1
Drops of blue food coloring	4	4
Water	1/8 tsp.	0.5 mL
Medium coconut	2 tbsp.	30 mL

GRASS

Green food coloring	1/4 tsp.	1 mL
Water	1/2 tsp.	2 mL
Medium unsweetened coconut	1 1/2 cups	375 mL
Drops of green food coloring	4	4

Cake: Combine all 10 ingredients in large bowl. Beat on low until moistened. Beat on medium for about 2 minutes until smooth. Grease bottom of 3 1/2 x 1 3/4 x 1 1/2 inch (9 x 4.5 x 3.8 cm) foil pan. Spoon in 1/4 cup (60 mL) batter. Pour remaining batter into greased 9 x 13 inch (22 x 33 cm) pan. Bake in 350°F (175°C) oven for 30 to 40 minutes until wooden pick inserted in center comes out clean. (Cake in small foil pan will cook in about 15 minutes.) Let each cake stand in pan for about 20 minutes. Remove small cake to small plate. Remove large cake to wire rack. Cool both completely.

Icing: Beat all 5 ingredients together in medium bowl, adding more icing sugar or milk until desired spreading consistency. Use some icing to attach small cake in center at one end to make the tee. Ice top and sides of cake.

Sand Trap: Cut out shallow kidney-shaped hole about halfway between tee and first hole. Line with brown sugar. Lightly pack down.

Water Hazard: Make indent in cake and make outline using licorice string. Combine blue food coloring and water with coconut in small plastic bowl with lid. Cover. Shake for 2 minutes until coconut is colored. Pat into indent on cake.

Grass: Combine first amount of green food coloring and water with coconut in large plastic bowl with lid. Cover. Shake for about 2 minutes until coconut is colored. Reserve 1/3 cup (75 mL) green coconut. Pat remaining coconut over top and sides of cake, around sand trap and water hazard, leaving space around tee area and for "green" at opposite end. Add second amount of green food coloring to reserved green coconut. Cover. Shake for about 2 minutes until coconut is colored. Pat darker green coconut in tee area and on "green." To make flag, print number 1 on small paper triangle and glue to wooden pick. Make small hole in center of "green," about 1/2 inch (12 mm) deep. Insert flag. Cuts into 12 pieces.

1 piece: 594 Calories; 24.2 g Total Fat; 678 mg Sodium; 7 g Protein; 92 g Carbohydrate; 3 g Dietary Fiber

Pictured on this page.

Strawberry Parfait

A good easy, elegant looking dessert.

Can of crushed pineapple, well drained	14 oz.	398 mL
Granulated sugar	3 tbsp.	50 mL
Almond flavoring	1/4 tsp.	1 mL
Envelope of dessert topping (prepared)	1	1
Frozen sliced strawberries in syrup, thawed	15 oz.	425 g
Grenadine syrup (or 2 tbsp., 30 mL, granulated sugar)	2 tbsp.	30 mL
Maraschino cherries	6	6

Combine first 4 ingredients in medium bowl.

Combine strawberries with syrup and grenadine in separate medium bowl. Divide 1/3 of pineapple mixture among 6 parfait glasses. Divide 1/2 of strawberry mixture over top. Repeat layers with remaining pineapple mixture and strawberry mixture, ending with pineapple mixture.

Top each with cherry. Chill. Serves 6.

1 serving: 193 Calories; 3.7 g Total Fat; 30 mg Sodium; 2 g Protein; 42 g Carbohydrate; 2 g Dietary Fiber

Pictured on this page.

Strawberry Parfait, above

Top Left: Fresh Peach Tart, page 83   Top Right: Fresh Cherry Dessert Sauce, page 83   Bottom Right: Fresh Fruit Flan, below

Fresh Fruit Flan

Buttery sponge cake makes the perfect base to showcase summer fruits.

SPONGE CAKE

Egg whites (large), room temperature	3	3
Cream of tartar	1/4 tsp.	1 mL
Granulated sugar	1/3 cup	75 mL
Butter (not margarine), softened	1/2 cup	125 mL
Granulated sugar	1/2 cup	125 mL
Vanilla	1/2 tsp.	2 mL
Egg yolks (large)	3	3
All-purpose flour	3/4 cup	175 mL
Baking powder	1/4 tsp.	1 mL
Salt	1/4 tsp.	1 mL
Instant vanilla pudding powder (4 serving size)	1	1
Milk	1 1/3 cups	325 mL
Sliced and whole seasonal fresh fruit (such as peaches, raspberries, blueberries, strawberries, grapes and blackberries)	2 cups	500 mL
Red currant (or apple) jelly	3 tbsp.	50 mL

Sponge Cake: Beat egg whites and cream of tartar together in medium bowl (not plastic) until soft peaks form. Gradually beat in first amount of sugar until glossy and stiff. Set aside.

Beat butter, second amount of sugar and vanilla together in large bowl, using same beaters, until creamy and light. Add egg yolks. Beat well until thick and fluffy.

Combine flour, baking powder and salt in small bowl. Gradually add to butter mixture, beating well after each addition. Batter will be very stiff. Fold in egg white mixture, 1/3 at a time, until no streaks remain. Spoon and spread evenly into well greased or parchment paper-lined 10 or 11 inch (25 or 28 cm) flan or springform pan. Bake on bottom rack in 350°F (175°C) oven for about 20 minutes until wooden pick inserted in center comes out clean. Cool. Turn out onto serving plate.

Beat pudding powder and milk together in medium bowl for 2 minutes. Spread evenly over cake. Let stand for 5 minutes until set.

Arrange fruit in single layer over pudding.

Gently warm jelly over hot water or in microwave for about 30 seconds until smooth. Brush layer of jelly over all fruit to seal and prevent darkening. Chill for at least 1 hour until set. Serves 10 to 12.

1 serving: 297 Calories; 11.9 g Total Fat; 353 mg Sodium; 4 g Protein; 45 g Carbohydrate; 1 g Dietary Fiber

Pictured on front cover and above.

Fall

Fall

September	Root vegetables are ready and vine fruits are allowed to finish ripening.
October	The bounty is in and the ground is prepared for winter hibernation.
November	Frost patterns across the country will begin to dictate final production of the heartiest of vegetables and fruits.

Fall arrives and nature's growth comes to an end. But it's also a time for new beginnings: a new school year, the opening of the theater season, registration for hobby class or bridge club. As the days get shorter and people pick up the busy-ness of life, they look for quicker meals. Cooking styles adapt, from fresh salads and barbecues to one-dish meals and other simmering creations.

Winter squash, turnips, beets and potatoes lend themselves to soups, salads and side dishes flavored mildly with dill, sage and other herbs. Surplus ripe tomatoes are turned into canned or frozen sauces and salsas.

September

September days remain warm as the last of summer's bounty is finally harvested. Freshly made into pies, the welcoming sweet aromas of apples and peaches waft gently from the kitchen. As students return to school, bag lunches start appearing in the fridge each morning. Cold, crisp carrot sticks, sandwiches made from leftover ham or turkey, and an apple or orange can be put together quickly. For adults, a slice of quiche or container of soup can be heated in the microwave in the lunch room. Or leave some soup warming in the slow cooker for after-school hunger pangs.

Preserving brings back the taste of summer during the frigid depths of winter when store-bought tomatoes pale by comparison. Whether you choose to make a small batch of salsa to last only a few months or pails of pickles to last throughout the year, don't forget to think about making up pretty little sample jars of salsa, pickles and spiced fruit for family and friends as gifts. After all, Christmas season is just around the corner!

October

October's first real frost of the season, if it hasn't come already, brings an unconscious desire for heartier dinnertime meals. A cook's thoughts turn to stews served with a fresh loaf of warm bread. Harvested root vegetables simmer in a rich, meat-filled broth to provide comfort and warmth as the chill of fall nights settles in.

and their pumpkins over, and serve up apple cider punch and hot appetizers while everyone carves. Or gather friends to your home and take turns giving out treats at the door and enjoying the parade of costumes. Give the children an unexpected surprise by dressing up in costumes yourselves. Serve stew in small pumpkins and complement the meal with pumpkin pie.

November

November is a great time to plan casserole-type dinners. Inexpensive cuts of meat or seafood turn tender and savory when simmered in a concoction of herbs, spices, sauce and vegetables. Hearty casseroles can often also be made ahead and popped in the oven to heat while you sort mail or throw in a load of laundry. Many one-dish recipes are also great for entertaining. Enjoy the deep, rich melded flavors of fall!

Thanksgiving celebrations in mid-October usher in a new season of entertaining, bringing family and friends once again to the dinner table. Satisfy them with a classic turkey dinner, surrounded by a bounty of root vegetables that celebrate the best of the crop: potatoes, steaming carrots and sweet turnips. Just remember to tell everyone to leave room for pie!

When Halloween rolls around, don't forget to make a trip to a local pumpkin patch—even if it's the neighborhood grocery store. Everyone can pick out a big pumpkin to carve into a jack-o'-lantern. Turn the evening into a truly festive party—invite the neighbors

Chicken Crisps

Moist tender chicken coated with crispy crumbs and dipped in thick yellow sweet, sour and mustard-flavored sauce. Serve hot or cold.

All-purpose flour	1/4 cup	60 mL
Large egg	1	1
Water	2 tbsp.	30 mL
Fine dry bread crumbs	1 cup	250 mL
Salt	1 tsp.	5 mL
Paprika	2 tsp.	10 mL
Boneless, skinless chicken breast halves (about 4), cut into strips	1 lb.	454 g
Cooking oil, for deep-frying		

HONEY MUSTARD DIP

Water	1/2 cup	125 mL
Liquid honey	1/4 cup	60 mL
White vinegar	3 tbsp.	50 mL
Dijon mustard	2 tbsp.	30 mL
Garlic powder	1/8 tsp.	0.5 mL
Water	2 tbsp.	30 mL
Cornstarch	1 tbsp.	15 mL

Measure flour into small bowl.

Fork-beat egg and water together in separate small bowl.

Combine bread crumbs, salt and paprika in third small bowl. Dip chicken strips in flour, then in egg mixture, then in crumb mixture to coat completely.

Deep-fry, a few strips at a time, in hot (375°F, 190°C) cooking oil for about 1 minute until browned and no longer pink inside. Makes 35 chicken strips.

Honey Mustard Dip: Heat and stir first 5 ingredients together in small saucepan until boiling.

Stir second amount of water into cornstarch in small cup until smooth. Stir into mustard mixture until boiling and thickened. Makes 1 cup (250 mL) dip.

1 chicken strip with 1 1/2 tsp. (7 mL) dip: 65 Calories; 2.9 g Total Fat; 110 mg Sodium; 4 g Protein; 6 g Carbohydrate; trace Dietary Fiber

Pictured on page 91.

Curried Chicken Puffs

Fill a tray with these puffed shells packed with hot chicken for an elegant appetizer. Both shells and filling can be made ahead and assembled when needed.

Can of condensed cream of chicken soup	10 oz.	284 mL
Chopped cooked chicken	2 cups	500 mL
Curry powder	1 tbsp.	15 mL
Salt	1/4 tsp.	1 mL
Pepper	1/16 tsp.	0.5 mL
CREAM PUFFS		
Boiling water	1 cup	250 mL
Hard margarine (or butter)	1/2 cup	125 mL
Salt	1/4 tsp.	1 mL
All-purpose flour	1 cup	250 mL
Large eggs	4	4

Combine first 5 ingredients in large saucepan. Heat on medium-low until hot.

Cream Puffs: Combine boiling water, margarine and salt in medium saucepan. Stir until margarine is melted. Bring to a boil.

Add flour all at once. Stir vigorously until dough forms a ball and pulls away from sides of saucepan. Remove from heat.

Add eggs, 1 at a time, beating thoroughly after each addition. Drop, by 2 tsp. (10 mL) amounts, 3 inches (7.5 cm) apart onto greased baking sheet. Bake in 425°F (220°C) oven for 30 minutes until cream puffs look dry with no beads of moisture showing. Remove to wire rack to cool. Gently cut off top 1/3 of each cream puff. Fill each cream puff with 2 tsp. (10 mL) chicken mixture. Replace tops. Serve immediately. Makes 48 filled cream puffs.

1 filled cream puff: 49 Calories; 3 g Total Fat; 103 mg Sodium; 3 g Protein; 3 g Carbohydrate; trace Dietary Fiber

Pictured on page 91.

Top Center: Soy-Slim Shake, below   Top Right: Goblin's Glogg, this page   Bottom Right: Curried Chicken Puffs, page 90   Bottom Left: Chicken Crisps, page 90

Soy-Slim Shake

Pretty pink shake. Easy to add more berries.

Soy (or skim) milk	2 cups	500 mL
Liquid honey	1 tbsp.	15 mL
Sliced fresh (or frozen, thawed) strawberries	1 cup	250 mL
Medium banana, cut up	1	1
Crushed ice	1 cup	250 mL

Put all 5 ingredients into blender. Process until smooth. Makes 4 cups (1 L).

1 cup (250 mL): 98 Calories; 2.7 g Total Fat; 16 mg Sodium; 4 g Protein; 16 g Carbohydrate; 2 g Dietary Fiber

Pictured above.

Variation: Omit strawberries or banana. Use same amount of peaches, raspberries or melons.

Goblin's Glogg

Halloween orange. Mild flavor and smooth taste.

Can of frozen concentrated orange juice, thawed	12 1/2 oz.	355 mL
Lemon juice	1 cup	250 mL
Club soda	4 cups	1 L
Orange sherbet	8 cups	2 L
Maraschino cherries	1/3 cup	75 mL
Ginger ale	5 cups	1.25 L

Measure orange juice concentrate, lemon juice and club soda into large punch bowl. Add sherbet and cherries. Stir.

Add ginger ale. Stir gently. Makes about 16 cups (4 L).

1 cup (250 mL): 219 Calories; 2.1 g Total Fat; 67 mg Sodium; 2 g Protein; 51 g Carbohydrate; trace Dietary Fiber

Pictured above.

Zucchini Mini Loaves

Soft and moist loaves with a hint of cinnamon.
Great for gift giving.

Cooking oil	1 cup	250 mL
Granulated sugar	2 cups	500 mL
Large eggs	3	3
Grated zucchini, with peel	2 cups	500 mL
Vanilla	1 tsp.	5 mL
All-purpose flour	3 cups	750 mL
Baking soda	1 tsp.	5 mL
Baking powder	1/4 tsp.	1 mL
Ground cinnamon	1 tsp.	5 mL
Salt	1/2 tsp.	2 mL
Chopped walnuts (or pecans, dates or raisins)	1/2 cup	125 mL

Beat cooking oil and sugar together in large bowl. Beat in eggs, 1 at a time. Add zucchini and vanilla. Stir.

Add remaining 6 ingredients. Stir until just moistened. Pour 1 1/4 cups (300 mL) batter into each of 5 foiled-lined greased 5 3/4 x 3 1/4 x 2 inch (14 x 8 x 5 cm) mini-loaf pans. Bake in 350°F (175°C) oven for about 40 minutes until wooden pick inserted in center comes out clean. Makes 5 mini loaves.

1/2 mini loaf: 580 Calories; 28.7 g Total Fat; 27 mg Sodium; 9 g Protein; 75 g Carbohydrate; 2 g Dietary Fiber

Pictured on page 93.

Fruity Almond Ring

Absolutely delicious for very special occasions.
Lots of almond flavor complements the fruit filling.

Frozen white bread dough, thawed according to package directions	1 lb.	454 g
FILLING		
Almond paste	4 oz.	113 g
Light cream cheese, softened	1/4 cup	60 mL
Granulated sugar	2 tbsp.	30 mL
Mixed dried fruit (such as blueberries, cherries, apricots, apples), diced	1/2 cup	125 mL
Large egg, fork-beaten	1	1

Let bread dough stand in oven with light on and door closed for about 2 hours until doubled in size.

Filling: Crumble almond paste in small bowl. Add cream cheese. Mash. Add sugar and dried fruit. Stir. Set aside.

Punch dough down. Roll out into 10 x 15 inch (25 x 38 cm) rectangle. Spoon and spread filling evenly over dough almost to edges. Tightly roll up, jelly roll-style, from long side. Pinch seam together. Place roll, seam side down, on greased baking sheet. Curve around to form ring. Pinch ends together to seal. Using scissors, make 12 cuts from outside edge to within about 1 inch (2.5 cm) of center. Turn each cut wedge on its side, all in same direction, allowing them to overlap. Cover ring with tea towel. Let stand in oven with light on and door closed for 1 1/2 hours until doubled in size. Carefully brush egg over entire ring. Bake on center rack in 375°F (190°C) oven for about 25 minutes until golden. Remove to wire rack to cool. Cuts into 12 pieces.

1 piece: 182 Calories; 5.4 g Total Fat; 247 mg Sodium; 5 g Protein; 28 g Carbohydrate; 3 g Dietary Fiber

Pictured on page 93.

Top: Fruity Almond Ring, above
Center Left: Parmesan Herb Bread, page 94
Center Right: Jalapeño Biscuit Squares, page 94
Bottom: Zucchini Mini Loaves, this page

Parmesan Herb Bread

Prepare this early in the day or the day before.

Hard margarine (or butter), softened	1/2 cup	125 mL
Grated Parmesan cheese	1/4 cup	60 mL
Dried sweet basil	1/4 tsp.	1 mL
Dried whole oregano	1/4 tsp.	1 mL
Garlic powder	1/8 tsp.	0.5 mL
Dried thyme	1/8 tsp.	0.5 mL
French bread loaf	1	1

Cream first 6 ingredients together in small bowl.

Cut bread into 1 inch (2.5 cm) slices. Spread both sides of each slice with margarine mixture. Reshape into loaf on large piece of foil. Wrap tightly. Heat in 350°F (175°C) oven for 25 to 30 minutes until hot. Makes about 16 slices.

1 slice: 139 Calories; 7.4 g Total Fat; 275 mg Sodium; 3 g Protein; 15 g Carbohydrate; 1 g Dietary Fiber

Pictured on page 93.

Herbal Tomato Bread

Orange bread with flavorful herbs and tomato juice. Quick and tasty.

Finely chopped onion	1/2 cup	125 mL
Cooking oil	1 tsp.	5 mL
Granulated sugar	1 tsp.	5 mL
Warm water	1/4 cup	60 mL
Active dry yeast (or 1/4 oz., 8 g, envelope)	2 1/2 tsp.	12 mL
Warm tomato juice	1 1/4 cups	300 mL
Salt	1 tsp.	5 mL
Dried whole oregano	1 tsp.	5 mL
Dried sweet basil	1 tsp.	5 mL
Olive oil	1 tbsp.	15 mL
Granulated sugar	1 tbsp.	15 mL
Whole wheat flour	1 1/2 cups	375 mL
Cornmeal	1/4 cup	60 mL
All-purpose flour, approximately	2 cups	500 mL
Hard margarine (or butter), melted (optional)	1/2 tsp.	2 mL

Sauté onion in cooking oil in frying pan until clear. Do not brown. Cool. Scrape into large bowl.

Stir first amount of sugar into warm water in small bowl. Sprinkle with yeast. Let stand for 10 minutes. Stir. Add to onion.

Add next 6 ingredients. Mix.

Add whole wheat flour and cornmeal. Stir. Slowly work in enough all-purpose flour until dough pulls away from sides of bowl. Turn out onto lightly floured surface. Knead for 8 to 10 minutes, adding more flour if necessary to prevent dough from sticking, until smooth and elastic. Place dough in greased bowl, turning once to grease top. Cover with tea towel. Let stand in oven with light on and door closed for about 1 hour until doubled in bulk. Punch dough down. Shape into loaf. Place in greased 9 x 5 x 3 inch (22 x 12.5 x 7.5 cm) loaf pan. No second rising needed. Bake in 350°F (175°C) oven for 45 minutes until firm, golden and hollow-sounding when tapped.

Turn out onto wire rack. Brush warm top with margarine. Cuts into 16 slices.

1 slice: 130 Calories; 1.6 g Total Fat; 223 mg Sodium; 4 g Protein; 26 g Carbohydrate; 3 g Dietary Fiber

Pictured on page 95.

Jalapeño Biscuit Squares

Nice biscuit flavor with a hint of cheese and a nice bite from the jalapeño peppers. Use for Sausage On Biscuits, page 95.

All-purpose flour	2 cups	500 mL
Whole wheat flour	1 cup	250 mL
Baking powder	2 tbsp.	30 mL
Granulated sugar	1 tbsp.	15 mL
Salt	1 tsp.	5 mL
Cooking oil	1/2 cup	125 mL
Grated sharp Cheddar cheese	1 cup	250 mL
Large egg	1	1
Milk	3/4 cup	175 mL
Finely diced canned jalapeño peppers, blotted dry	3 tbsp.	50 mL

Combine first 5 ingredients in large bowl. Add cooking oil. Mix well with fork. Add cheese. Stir.

Beat egg and milk together in small bowl. Add jalapeño pepper. Stir. Pour over flour mixture. Stir with fork until flour is just moistened. Turn out onto lightly floured surface. Gently knead 5 times. Roll or pat out into 9 x 9 inch (22 x 22 cm) square. Cut into thirds. Cut again crosswise into thirds making nine 3 x 3 inch (7.5 x 7.5 cm) biscuits. Arrange 2 inches (5 cm) apart on greased baking sheet. Bake in 425°F (220°C) oven for about 15 minutes until golden. Makes 9 biscuits.

1 biscuit: 346 Calories; 18.5 g Total Fat; 646 mg Sodium; 10 g Protein; 36 g Carbohydrate; 3 g Dietary Fiber

Pictured on page 93.

Tuna And Apple Melt

Smothered in cheese and served open-faced,
these are sure to be a favorite Saturday lunch.

Can of flaked tuna, drained	6 oz.	170 g
Small cooking apple (such as McIntosh), with peel, diced (about 1 1/3 cups, 325 mL)	1	1
Lemon juice	2 tsp.	10 mL
Salad dressing (or mayonnaise)	3 tbsp.	50 mL
Liquid honey	2 tsp.	10 mL
Bread slices (or 2 bagels cut in half), toasted	4	4
Process cheese slices	4	4

Combine first 5 ingredients in medium bowl. Toss until well coated. Makes 2 cups (500 mL) tuna mixture.

Spoon about 1/2 cup (125 mL) tuna mixture over each toast slice. Top each with 1 cheese slice. Place on ungreased baking sheet. Broil until cheese is melted. Makes 4 melts.

1 melt: 318 Calories; 17.3 g Total Fat; 793 mg Sodium; 18 g Protein; 22 g Carbohydrate; 1 g Dietary Fiber

Pictured on this page.

Variation: Add 1 tbsp. (15 mL) finely chopped onion and 1 tbsp. (15 mL) finely chopped celery to tuna mixture. Stir.

Top Left: Sausage On Biscuits, this page
Top Right: Herbal Tomato Bread, page 94
Bottom: Tuna And Apple Melt, this page

Sausage On Biscuits

You may have sampled a similar dish
in the southern United States.

Sausage meat	3/4 lb.	340 g
Diced red pepper	1/2 cup	125 mL
Sliced green onion	1/4 cup	60 mL
All-purpose flour	3 tbsp.	50 mL
Paprika	1/4 tsp.	1 mL
Pepper	1/8 tsp.	0.5 mL
Milk	2 cups	500 mL
Jalapeño Biscuit Squares, page 94, warmed, split	6	6

Scramble-fry sausage meat, red pepper and green onion in frying pan until sausage is no longer pink. Drain.

Add flour, paprika and pepper to sausage mixture. Mix well. Stir in milk. Heat and stir until boiling and thickened. Makes 3 cups (750 mL) sausage mixture.

Spoon 1/2 cup (125 mL) sausage mixture onto 2 biscuit halves. Repeat with remaining sausage mixture and biscuits. Serves 6.

1 serving: 518 Calories; 30.1 g Total Fat; 925 mg Sodium; 17 g Protein; 46 g Carbohydrate; 3 g Dietary Fiber

Pictured above.

Tip *Just about any variety of apple can be termed a cooking apple but their flavor will vary. Some, such as Granny Smith, produce a more tart taste while McIntosh and Spartan, for example, have a nicer balance between tart and sweet.*

Crustless Broccoli Quiche, below

Crustless Broccoli Quiche

A smooth white filling that looks like ice cream.
Broccoli and tomato add color. So satisfying.

Box of frozen chopped broccoli	10 oz.	300 g
Water		
Medium tomatoes, sliced	2	2
Light cream cheese, softened	8 oz.	250 g
Large eggs	5	5
Skim evaporated milk	1/2 cup	125 mL
Chopped green onion	1/4 cup	60 mL
Parsley flakes	1 tsp.	5 mL
Garlic powder	1/4 tsp.	1 mL
Salt	1/4 tsp.	1 mL

Cook broccoli in water until tender-crisp. Drain. Cool slightly. Spread in greased 10 inch (25 cm) pie plate.

Arrange tomato over top.

Beat cream cheese and 1 egg together in medium bowl until smooth. Add remaining eggs, 1 at a time, beating after each addition. Add evaporated milk, green onion, parsley, garlic and salt. Stir. Pour over broccoli and tomato. Bake in 350°F (175°C) oven for about 45 minutes until knife inserted near center comes out clean. Let stand for 5 minutes before serving. Serves 6.

1 serving: 196 Calories; 12.6 g Total Fat; 484 mg Sodium; 13 g Protein; 9 g Carbohydrate; 2 g Dietary Fiber

Pictured above.

Cheesy Asparagus Chowder

A tasty pairing of cheese and asparagus.

Medium onion, chopped	1	1
Cooking oil	1 tbsp.	15 mL
Medium potatoes, diced	2	2
Medium carrot, thinly sliced (or diced)	1	1
Water	3 cups	750 mL
Worcestershire sauce	1 tsp.	5 mL
Chicken bouillon powder	1 tbsp.	15 mL
Salt	1 tsp.	5 mL
Pepper	1 tsp.	5 mL
Can of skim evaporated milk	13 1/2 oz.	385 mL
Grated sharp Cheddar cheese	1 1/2 cups	375 mL
Can of asparagus pieces, drained	12 oz.	341 mL
Instant potato flakes	1/2 cup	125 mL
Grated sharp Cheddar cheese, for garnish	6 tbsp.	100 mL

Sauté onion in cooking oil in large saucepan until soft.

Add next 7 ingredients. Bring to a boil, stirring often. Reduce heat. Cover. Simmer for 20 to 30 minutes until vegetables are tender.

Stir in evaporated milk. Add first amount of cheese. Heat and stir until melted.

Add asparagus and potato flakes. Heat and stir gently until heated through.

Garnish individual servings with 1 tbsp. (15 mL) second amount of cheese. Makes 7 1/2 cups (1.9 L).

1 cup (250 mL): 214 Calories; 10.4 g Total Fat; 966 mg Sodium; 13 g Protein; 18 g Carbohydrate; 2 g Dietary Fiber

Pictured on page 99.

Manhattan Clam Chowder

This tomato-based chowder is thick with vegetables and clams and has a very pleasant background of spices.

Bacon slices, diced	4	4
Medium onion, chopped	1	1
Diced green pepper	1/4 cup	60 mL
Diced celery	1/3 cup	75 mL
Water	3 cups	750 mL
Medium potatoes, diced	2	2
Can of diced tomatoes, with juice	14 oz.	398 mL
Salt	1 tsp.	5 mL
Pepper	1/4 tsp.	1 mL
Chicken bouillon powder	1 tbsp.	15 mL
Ground thyme	1/2 tsp.	2 mL
Bay leaf	1	1
Can of whole baby clams, with liquid	5 oz.	142 g
Instant potato flakes	1/2 cup	125 mL

Sauté bacon, onion, green pepper and celery in large pot or Dutch oven until onion is soft.

Add next 8 ingredients. Stir. Cover. Bring to a boil. Reduce heat. Simmer for 20 to 30 minutes until potato is tender. Remove and discard bay leaf.

Add clams with liquid and potato flakes. Heat and stir gently until heated through. Makes 8 cups (2 L).

1 cup (250 mL): 132 Calories; 5.8 g Total Fat; 764 mg Sodium; 8 g Protein; 13 g Carbohydrate; 1 g Dietary Fiber

Pictured on this page.

 Tip *To reduce the saltiness of a soup, drop in a peeled potato. The potato will absorb the excess salt.*

Manhattan Clam Chowder, this page

Borscht

Gorgeous clear wine color. Economical as well.

Grated beets (about 1 1/2 lbs., 680 g)	5 cups	1.25 L
Chopped onion	1 1/2 cups	375 mL
Hot water	10 cups	2.5 L
Vegetable bouillon powder	2 tbsp.	30 mL
Coarsely grated cabbage	2 cups	500 mL
Celery rib, diced	1	1
Medium carrot, grated	1	1
Medium potato, grated	1	1
Granulated sugar	1 tsp.	5 mL
Salt	1 tsp.	5 mL
Pepper	1/4 tsp.	1 mL
Bay leaf	1	1
Dill weed	1 1/2 tsp.	7 mL
Garlic powder	1/4 tsp.	1 mL
Apple cider vinegar	1/4 cup	60 mL
Sour cream, for garnish	3/4 cup	175 mL

Combine first 15 ingredients in large heavy pot or Dutch oven. Bring to a boil, stirring often. Reduce heat. Cover. Boil gently for about 1 hour, stirring occasionally, until slightly reduced. Remove and discard bay leaf.

Top individual servings with dollop of sour cream. Makes about 15 cups (3.74 L).

1 cup (250 mL): 42 Calories; 0.3 g Total Fat; 446 mg Sodium; 2 g Protein; 9 g Carbohydrate; 2 g Dietary Fiber

Pictured on page 99.

Minestrone

Serve as a meal with Parmesan Herb Bread, page 94.

Italian sausage (casing removed)	1/2 lb.	225 g
Garlic clove, minced (or 1/4 tsp., 1 mL, powder)	1	1
Chopped onion	1/2 cup	125 mL
Chopped celery	1/2 cup	125 mL
Condensed beef broth	4 cups	1 L
Can of diced tomatoes	28 oz.	796 mL
Chopped carrot	1/2 cup	125 mL
Can of white kidney beans, drained and rinsed	19 oz.	540 mL
Dried sweet basil	1 tsp.	5 mL
Ground oregano	1/2 tsp.	2 mL
Freshly ground pepper	1/8 tsp.	0.5 mL
Granulated sugar	1 tbsp.	15 mL
Tiny shell pasta	1/2 cup	125 mL
Finely grated Parmesan cheese (optional)	6 tbsp.	100 mL

Scramble-fry sausage, garlic, onion and celery in large pot or Dutch oven until sausage is no longer pink. Drain.

Add next 8 ingredients. Stir to combine. Bring to a boil. Reduce heat. Cover. Simmer for 15 minutes.

Add pasta. Stir. Cook, uncovered, for 20 minutes until pasta is tender but firm.

Sprinkle individual servings with about 2 tsp. (10 mL) Parmesan cheese. Makes about 10 cups (2.5 L).

1 cup (250 mL): 120 Calories; 3.6 g Total Fat; 960 mg Sodium; 8 g Protein; 15 g Carbohydrate; 1 g Dietary Fiber

Pictured on page 99.

Zucchini Cream Soup

Slightly sweet with a hint of onion.

Chopped onion	2 cups	500 mL
Hard margarine (or butter)	1 tbsp.	15 mL
Water	3 cups	750 mL
Grated zucchini, with peel	4 cups	1 L
Chicken bouillon powder	4 tsp.	20 mL
Ground nutmeg	1/8 tsp.	0.5 mL
Salt	1 tsp.	5 mL
Pepper	1/8 tsp.	0.5 mL
Worcestershire sauce (optional)	3/4 tsp.	4 mL
Skim evaporated milk	1/2 cup	125 mL

Grated zucchini, for garnish

Sauté onion in margarine in large saucepan until soft. Do not brown.

Add next 7 ingredients. Stir. Bring to a boil, stirring often. Reduce heat. Cover. Simmer for 10 to 12 minutes until zucchini is tender. Cool slightly. Transfer to blender. Process, in 2 batches, until smooth. Return to saucepan. Bring to a boil.

Stir in evaporated milk. Heat and stir until heated through. Do not boil.

Sprinkle individual servings with grated zucchini. Makes 6 cups (1.5 L).

1 cup (250 mL): 76 Calories; 2.5 g Total Fat; 882 mg Sodium; 4 g Protein; 11 g Carbohydrate; 2 g Dietary Fiber

Pictured on page 99.

Top: Borscht, page 97
Center Left: Cheesy Asparagus Chowder, page 96
Center Right: Minestrone, this page
Bottom: Zucchini Cream Soup, above

Thanksgiving Dinner

It's a time to look back with thanks,
and to look forward with family
and friends as everyone comes together
for a traditional thanksgiving feast.
As cool winds blow outside,
this classic menu, with new twists
on old favorites, is certain to bring
a little warmth to your gathering.

Acorn Squash Soup
Apple Cheese Salad

Roast Turkey
Stuffing Balls

Potato And Turnip Medley
Broccoli Meringue
Marinated Carrots
Melon Pickles

Apple Pumpkin Pie
Bread Cornucopia

Acorn Squash Soup

Lovely autumn color and great flavor.

Medium acorn squash, peeled, seeded and cubed (about 6 cups, 1.5 L)	1	1
Chopped onion	1/2 cup	125 mL
Garlic cloves, minced (or 3/4 tsp., 4 mL, powder)	3	3
Salt	1/2 tsp.	2 mL
Pepper	1/8 tsp.	0.5 mL
Bay leaf	1	1
Butter (not margarine)	1/4 cup	60 mL
Can of evaporated milk	13 1/2 oz.	385 mL
Water	2 cups	500 mL
Whipping cream, for garnish	1 tbsp.	15 mL
Chopped chives (or green onion), for garnish	1 tbsp.	15 mL

Combine first 7 ingredients in large pot or Dutch oven. Heat on medium for 5 minutes, stirring occasionally.

Add evaporated milk and water. Stir. Bring to a boil. Reduce heat. Cover. Simmer for about 25 minutes, stirring occasionally, until squash is very tender. Remove and discard bay leaf. Transfer soup to blender. Process, in 2 batches, until puréed. Return to pot to keep warm.

Garnish individual servings with swirl of 1/2 tsp. (2 mL) whipping cream or sprinkle with chives. Makes 6 cups (1.5 L).

1 cup (250 mL): 190 Calories; 8.5 g Total Fat; 366 mg Sodium; 7 g Protein; 24 g Carbohydrate; 3 g Dietary Fiber

Pictured on page 107.

Roast Turkey

The traditional turkey dinner. Great with Stuffing Balls, page 104, and Potato And Turnip Medley, page 104.

Medium onion, quartered	1	1
Turkey, thawed if frozen	12 - 15 lbs.	5.4 - 6.8 kg
GRAVY		
All-purpose flour	3/4 cup	175 mL
Salt	1 tsp.	5 mL
Pepper	1/4 tsp.	1 mL
Water		
Liquid gravy browner (optional)	1-1 1/2 tsp.	5-7 mL
Salt, to taste		

Place onion in cavity of turkey. Tie wings with string to body or tuck under body. Tie legs to tail. Set on rack in large roasting pan. Loosely cover with foil or roasting pan lid. Roast in 325°F (160°C) oven for about 4 hours until meat thermometer inserted deep into thigh, but not touching bone, reads 190°F (88°C) or when thick part of thigh is pierced, juices run clear. Remove cover for last 15 minutes to brown. Remove turkey. Remove drippings, including fat, to 4 cup (1 L) liquid measure.

Gravy: Measure 3/4 cup (175 mL) drippings with fat back into roasting pan. Stir in flour until smooth. Add salt and pepper.

Skim fat from remaining drippings. Add water to equal 4 cups (1L). Stir into flour mixture. Heat and stir on medium-high until boiling and thickened. Add gravy browner. Stir. Add more salt if necessary. Makes 5 cups (1.25 L) gravy. Serves 12.

1 serving: 774 Calories; 33.1 g Total Fat; 559 mg Sodium; 103 g Protein; 8 g Carbohydrate; trace Dietary Fiber

Pictured on page 102/103.

Variation: To roast turkey uncovered, baste several times during cooking time. To roast turkey with stuffing in cavity, allow about 30 minutes longer cooking time, until meat thermometer reads 165°F (74°C) when inserted into center of stuffing.

Apple Cheese Salad

Apples and cheese—a natural combination. A pretty salad when served on shredded lettuce or in lettuce cups.

Light salad dressing (or mayonnaise)	1/2 cup	125 mL
Milk	1 tbsp.	15 mL
Granulated sugar	1 tsp.	5 mL
Medium cooking apples (such as McIntosh), with peel, diced	2	2
Grated light medium Cheddar cheese	1 cup	250 mL
Grated cabbage	1 cup	250 mL
Chopped celery	1/2 cup	125 mL
Finely chopped dates	1/2 cup	125 mL

Mix salad dressing, milk and sugar in medium bowl.

Immediately stir apple into salad dressing mixture to prevent apple from darkening. Add cheese, cabbage, celery and dates. Stir until well coated. Makes 4 1/2 cups (1.1 L).

1/2 cup (125 mL): 115 Calories; 4.7 g Total Fat; 196 mg Sodium; 4 g Protein; 16 g Carbohydrate; 2 g Dietary Fiber

Pictured on page 105.

Tip *Wash apples thoroughly to remove any chemicals, especially if not peeling before using in a recipe.*

Photo Legend next page:

1. Roast Turkey, this page
2. Stuffing Balls, page 104
3. Apple Pumpkin Pie, page 106
4. Melon Pickles, page 106
5. Potato And Turnip Medley, page 104
6. (Gravy, this page)

Stuffing Balls

Colorful, chewy and sweet. Excellent.
Can be made ahead, chilled and baked the next day.
Serve with Roast Turkey, page 101.

Medium onion, chopped	1	1
Chopped celery	1/2 cup	125 mL
Cooking oil	1 tbsp.	15 mL
Package of sweetened dried cranberries (1 1/2 cups, 375 mL)	6 oz.	170 g
Coarse dry bread crumbs	6 cups	1.5 L
Parsley flakes	2 tsp.	10 mL
Poultry seasoning	2 – 3 tsp.	10 – 15 mL
Salt	1 tsp.	5 mL
Pepper	1/4 tsp.	1 mL
Large eggs, fork-beaten	3	3
Water	3/4 cup	175 mL
Hard margarine (or butter), melted	1/3 cup	75 mL

Sauté onion and celery in cooking oil in frying pan until onion is soft and clear.

Combine next 6 ingredients in large bowl.

Add eggs and water. Stir. Add onion mixture. Mix well. Shape into 10 balls using 1/2 cup (125 mL) mixture each. Arrange in single layer in small greased roasting pan.

Drizzle with margarine. Cover. Bake in 350°F (175°C) oven for about 25 minutes until golden. Makes 10 stuffing balls.

1 stuffing ball: 403 Calories; 13.2 g Total Fat; 928 mg Sodium; 11 g Protein; 60 g Carbohydrate; 6 g Dietary Fiber

Pictured on page 102 and on page 103.

Potato And Turnip Medley

Browned onion and butter give a mellow flavor
to both for pairing with Roast Turkey, page 101.
Some people often mash turnip and potato together.

Yellow turnip (about 1 1/2 lbs., 680 g), diced	1	1
Water	2 cups	500 mL
Salt	1 tsp.	5 mL
Medium red potatoes, diced	8	8
Medium onions, thinly sliced	3	3
Butter (not margarine)	1/4 cup	60 mL
Freshly ground pepper, sprinkle		

Cook turnip in water and salt in large pot or Dutch oven for 5 minutes.

Increase heat to keep water boiling. Add potato. Reduce heat. Simmer for 15 minutes until turnip and potato are tender but firm. Drain. Stir gently. Cook on low for 2 minutes, gently lifting and moving potato mixture to allow moisture to evaporate. Turn into serving bowl or casserole. Cover. Keep warm. Makes 8 cups (2 L).

Sauté onion in butter in large frying pan for about 15 minutes, stirring frequently, until onion is caramelized. Spoon over potato mixture.

Sprinkle with pepper. Serves 8.

1 serving: 200 Calories; 6.4 g Total Fat; 77 mg Sodium; 3 g Protein; 34 g Carbohydrate; 3 g Dietary Fiber

Pictured on page 102.

Broccoli Meringue

If you want to dress up your broccoli without using
cream sauce, here's the answer.

Fresh broccoli, cut up	1 1/2 lbs.	680 g
Water	4 cups	1 L
Salt	1 tsp.	5 mL
Egg whites (large), room temperature	4	4
Light mayonnaise (not salad dressing)	1/3 cup	75 mL
Onion powder	1/8 tsp.	0.5 mL
Grated Parmesan cheese	2 tsp.	10 mL

Cook broccoli in water and salt in large saucepan for about 6 minutes until tender-crisp. Drain. Place in ungreased 9 x 13 inch (22 x 33 cm) dish.

Beat egg whites in medium bowl until stiff peaks form. Fold in mayonnaise and onion powder. Spread over broccoli.

Sprinkle with Parmesan cheese. Bake, uncovered, on center rack in 350°F (175°C) oven for about 20 minutes until lightly browned. Makes 8 cups (2 L). Serves 6 to 8.

1 serving: 89 Calories; 4.9 g Total Fat; 172 mg Sodium; 6 g Protein; 7 g Carbohydrate; 3 g Dietary Fiber

Pictured on page 105.

Left: Marinated Carrots, below   Top Center: Apple Cheese Salad, page 101   Right: Broccoli Meringue, page 104

Marinated Carrots

Attractive and colorful, these have a mild, sweet pickled flavor. Will keep for up to one week in the refrigerator.

Carrots, sliced into coins (about 6 cups, 1.5 L)	2 lbs.	900 g
Boiling water		
Salt	1/2 tsp.	2 mL
Granulated sugar	3/4 cup	175 mL
White vinegar	1/2 cup	125 mL
Cooking oil	1/4 cup	60 mL
Worcestershire sauce	1 tsp.	5 mL
Prepared mustard	1 tsp.	5 mL
Salt	1/2 tsp.	2 mL
Pepper	1/4 tsp.	1 mL
Large onion, thinly sliced and separated into rings	1	1
Medium green pepper, cut into short strips	1	1

Cook carrot in boiling water and salt in large saucepan for about 6 minutes until tender-crisp. They should be firm. Drain well.

Combine next 7 ingredients in large bowl. Stir until sugar is dissolved. Add carrot. Combine well.

Add onion and green pepper. Mix well. Cover. Chill for 24 hours, stirring several times to coat all vegetables. Makes 8 cups (2 L).

1/2 cup (125 mL): 103 Calories; 3.8 g Total Fat; 103 mg Sodium; 1 g Protein; 18 g Carbohydrate; 2 g Dietary Fiber

Pictured above.

Melon Pickles

A mild and very attractive "pickle" that goes with anything.

Salt	2 tbsp.	30 mL
Water	8 cups	2 L
Cantaloupe balls (or cubes)	2 1/4 lbs.	1 kg
Honeydew melon balls (or cubes)	2 1/4 lbs.	1 kg
Water	3 1/2 cups	875 mL
Granulated sugar	2 cups	500 mL
White vinegar	1/2 cup	125 mL
Cinnamon sticks (6 inch, 15 cm, length, each)	2	2
Whole cloves	1 tsp.	5 mL
Jar of maraschino cherries, drained	9 oz.	250 mL

Dissolve salt in first amount of water in large pot or Dutch oven.

Add cantaloupe and honeydew. Cover. Let stand overnight in refrigerator. Drain. Remove melon mixture to large bowl. Set aside.

Put second amount of water into same large pot or Dutch oven. Add sugar, vinegar, cinnamon sticks and cloves. Bring to a boil. Boil, stirring often, until sugar is dissolved.

Add cherries and melon mixture. Bring to a boil. Reduce heat. Cover. Simmer for 35 minutes until melon is clear and tender. Fill hot sterilized jars to within 1/2 inch (12 mm) of top. Place sterilized metal lids on jars and screw metal bands on securely. Process in boiling water bath for 15 minutes. Cool. Makes 4 pint (2 cup, 500 mL) jars.

1/4 cup (60 mL): 58 Calories; trace Total Fat; 112 mg Sodium; trace Protein; 15 g Carbohydrate; trace Dietary Fiber

Pictured on page 102/103.

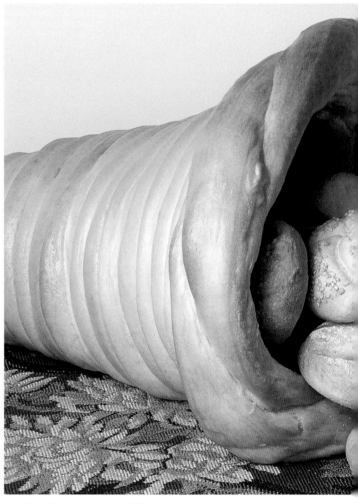

Left: Bread Cornucopia, page 108

Apple Pumpkin Pie

Delicious with ice cream, whipped cream or Maple Cream Sauce, page 122. Recipe may be halved if only one pie is desired. This will become a favorite dessert, especially for the holidays.

Pastry for two 9 inch (22 cm) single crust pies, your own or a mix		
Brown sugar, packed	1/2 cup	125 mL
Vanilla custard powder	1/4 cup	60 mL
Peeled, cored and chopped cooking apple (such as McIntosh)	4 cups	1 L
Brown sugar, packed	2/3 cup	150 mL
Ground cinnamon	1 tsp.	5 mL
Ground ginger	1 tsp.	5 mL
Ground nutmeg	1/2 tsp.	2 mL
Ground allspice	1/2 tsp.	2 mL
Salt	1/2 tsp.	2 mL

Right: Acorn Squash Soup, page 100

Large eggs	4	4
Can of pure pumpkin (not filling) (or 1 3/4 cups, 425 mL, puréed pumpkin)	14 oz.	398 mL
Can of skim evaporated milk	13 1/2 oz.	385 mL

Milk (optional)

Roll out pastry and line two 9 inch (22 cm) glass pie plates. Flute edges or use scraps of dough to create decorative edges, such as leaf cut-outs.

Combine first amount of brown sugar and custard powder in large bowl. Add apple. Mix well. Divide between pie shells. Evenly pat down.

Combine next 6 ingredients in same bowl.

Beat in eggs, pumpkin and evaporated milk until smooth. Divide over apple. Set any cut-outs on top of pastry edge.

Brush pastry edges with milk. Bake on bottom rack in 375°F (190°C) oven for about 45 minutes until knife inserted near center comes out moist but clean. Makes 2 pies, each cutting into 8 wedges, for a total of 16 wedges.

1 wedge: 307 Calories; 12.1 g Total Fat; 357 mg Sodium; 6 g Protein; 45 g Carbohydrate; 1 g Dietary Fiber

Pictured on page 103.

How To

Bread Cornucopia

Use this as a centerpiece or display piece, filled with fall flowers, dried gourds or fancy breads and buns (shown on page 106/107). If you wish to preserve the cornucopia indefinitely, dry completely and then spray with shellac.

Materials: Wire cutters, chicken wire, heavy-duty foil.

Form for Cornucopia: You will need to make cone slightly longer than you want final cornucopia to be as you need some uncovered form to support dough and to prevent dough from sagging over front edge. Cut large triangular piece of 24 inch (60 cm) wide chicken wire. Shape to form cone. Carefully fold cut edges of wire to inside of form. Form a slight curve in tip end of cone. Once form is shaped, cover with 1 or 2 layers of heavy-duty foil.

Frozen white bread dough loaves (1 lb., 454 g, each)	3	3
Large egg	1	1
Water	1 tbsp.	15 mL
Salt		

Place loaves on baking sheet. Cover with greased plastic wrap. Thaw overnight at room temperature. Roll out 2 1/2 loaves, 1 portion at a time, to 1/4 inch (6 mm) thickness and about 15 inches (38 cm) in length. Cut into 1 inch (2.5 cm) lengthwise strips. Cover and set aside remaining dough.

Generously spray form with cooking spray. Place on baking sheet. Starting at narrow end, wrap dough strips around form, slightly overlapping each previous row. Continue up form. Join ends of strips together as necessary, being sure to keep seams on underside for smooth finish on top. Trim off any excess dough. As you progress up form, you will find strips will only go around once. As you are working, cover dough on form with damp tea towel to prevent drying out.

Roll out remaining dough to 1/2 inch (12 mm) thick. Divide into 2 equal lengthwise pieces. Twist around each other to form loose "coil." Place coil on form to create rim of cornucopia. Cover with dry tea towel. Let stand in oven with light on and door closed for 30 minutes. Dough may sag a little as it rises. Gently tuck any excess dough underneath for a rounder finished product.

Stir egg, water and salt together in small bowl. Remove cornucopia from oven. Brush outer surface with egg mixture. Bake in 325°F (160°C) oven for 25 to 30 minutes until golden brown. Place on wire rack to cool completely. Gently, but firmly, remove form from bread.

Roasted Vegetable Stew

One way to keep your vegetables tender-crisp is to cook them separately from the long-cooking beef. Serve with couscous or noodles.

Lean beef stew meat (or inside round steak, cubed)	1 1/2 lbs.	680 g
Olive (or cooking) oil	1 tbsp.	15 mL
Garlic cloves, minced (or 3/4 tsp., 4 mL, powder)	3	3
Pepper	1/2 tsp.	2 mL
Can of condensed beef broth	10 oz.	284 mL
Water	2 cups	500 mL
Bay leaf	1	1
Dried thyme	1 1/2 tsp.	7 mL
Cold water	2 tbsp.	30 ml
Cornstarch	1 tbsp.	15 mL
Halved baby potatoes	2 cups	500 mL
Halved baby carrots	1 cup	250 mL
Small tomatoes, quartered	6	6
Fresh medium mushrooms	12	12
Small onions, cut lengthwise into quarters	3	3
Medium red or yellow pepper, slivered	1	1
Olive (or cooking) oil	2 tbsp.	30 mL
Balsamic vinegar	2 tbsp.	30 mL

Brown beef in first amount of olive oil in large pot or Dutch oven. Add garlic and pepper. Sauté for 1 minute. Stir in beef broth, water, bay leaf and thyme. Cover. Bring to a boil. Reduce heat. Simmer for 1 1/2 hours until beef is tender.

Stir cold water into cornstarch in small cup until smooth. Stir into beef mixture for 1 to 2 minutes until sauce is boiling and slightly thickened. Remove and discard bay leaf.

Place next 6 ingredients on large greased 11 × 17 inch (28 × 43 cm) baking sheet. Drizzle with olive oil and vinegar. Toss until well coated. Bake in 425°F (220°C) oven for 20 minutes. Turn broiler on. Broil, turning frequently, until skins of vegetables are blistered and blackened. Add vegetables to beef mixture. Gently stir. Makes 4 cups (1 L).

1 cup (250 mL): 433 Calories; 16.9 g Total Fat; 565 mg Sodium; 34 g Protein; 39 g Carbohydrate; 7 g Dietary Fiber

Pictured on front cover and on page 111.

Smothered Meatballs

Soft, dark meatballs underneath a
golden brown pastry-like topping.

Large egg	1	1
Milk	1/3 cup	75 mL
Soda cracker crumbs	1/3 cup	75 mL
Dried thyme	1/8 tsp.	0.5 mL
Envelope of dry onion soup mix	1 1/4 oz.	38 g
Chili sauce	1/2 cup	125 mL
Pepper	1/4 tsp.	1 mL
Lean ground beef	1 1/2 lbs.	680 g
TOPPING		
Large eggs	4	4
Milk	1 1/2 cups	375 mL
Hard margarine (or butter), melted	1/4 cup	60 mL
All-purpose flour	1 1/2 cups	375 mL
Baking powder	1 1/2 tsp.	7 mL
Salt	3/4 tsp.	4 mL

Beat egg in large bowl. Add next 6 ingredients. Stir.

Add ground beef. Mix well. Shape into 25 meatballs. Arrange in single layer in greased 9 x 13 inch (22 x 33 cm) pan.

Topping: Beat eggs in medium bowl until frothy. Add milk and margarine. Beat slowly until mixed.

Add flour, baking powder and salt all at once. Stir until just moistened. Pour over meatballs. Bake, uncovered, in 350°F (175°C) oven for 1 1/4 hours. Serves 6 to 8.

1 serving: 597 Calories; 31.5 g Total Fat; 1601 mg Sodium; 34 g Protein; 43 g Carbohydrate; 3 g Dietary Fiber

Pictured on pages 110/111.

 Tip *To prevent meat sticking to your hands when forming meatballs, coat palms with cooking oil first.*

Bottom Left: Smothered Meatballs, this page

Short Ribs

Tender beef with a sweet and savory sauce.
Serve with white rice and steamed vegetables.

Boneless beef short ribs, cut into serving-size pieces	2 lbs.	900 g
Chili sauce	1/2 cup	125 mL
Grape jelly	1/3 cup	75 mL
Medium onion, chopped	1	1
Brown sugar, packed	1 tbsp.	15 mL
Prepared mustard	1 tbsp.	15 mL
Dried rosemary, crushed	1/2 tsp.	2 mL
Lemon juice	1 tbsp.	15 mL
Liquid gravy browner	1/2 tsp.	2 mL
Salt	1 tsp.	5 mL
Pepper	1/2 tsp.	2 mL

Arrange ribs in small roasting pan.

Combine remaining 10 ingredients in small bowl. Spoon over ribs. Cover. Bake in 300°F (150°C) oven for about 4 hours until tender. Remove ribs to serving plate. Skim off fat in pan and discard. Pour remaining sauce over ribs. Serves 4 to 6.

1 serving: 534 Calories; 23.5 g Total Fat; 1387 mg Sodium; 47 g Protein; 34 g Carbohydrate; 3 g Dietary Fiber

Pictured on page 111.

Top Left: Cheesy Sloppy Joes, below   Top Right: Roasted Vegetable Stew, page 109   Bottom Right: Short Ribs, page 110

Cheesy Sloppy Joes

Beef and veggies are visible in this bright rust-colored sauce with a robust taste.

Lean ground beef	1 lb.	454 g
Medium onion, chopped	1	1
Finely chopped celery	1/4 cup	60 mL
Finely chopped green pepper	1/4 cup	60 mL
Can of tomato sauce	7 1/2 oz.	213 mL
Chili sauce	1/2 cup	125 mL
Brown sugar, packed	1 tbsp.	15 mL
Barbecue sauce	1 tbsp.	15 mL
Seasoned salt	1/2 tsp.	2 mL
Pepper	1/4 tsp.	1 mL
Process cheese spread	2/3 cup	150 mL
Water		
Hamburger buns, split (buttered and toasted, optional)	4	4

Scramble-fry ground beef, onion, celery and green pepper in frying pan until beef is no longer pink and onion is soft.

Combine next 6 ingredients in large saucepan. Add beef mixture. Heat, stirring occasionally, until simmering. Simmer, uncovered, for 25 minutes.

Add cheese. Stir until melted. If necessary, add a bit of water if mixture is too thick. Makes 3 1/2 cups (875 mL) beef mixture.

Arrange 2 bun halves, split side up, on each plate. Spoon 3/4 cup (175 mL) beef mixture over top. Repeat with remaining buns and beef mixture. Serves 4.

1 serving: 583 Calories; 29.1 g Total Fat; 2046 mg Sodium; 34 g Protein; 46 g Carbohydrate; 4 g Dietary Fiber

Pictured on pages 110/111.

Top: Wild Rice Medley, below
Bottom: Chicken Pecan, this page

Chicken Pecan

For a special meal anytime. This is delectable.
Serve with Wild Rice Medley, this page.

Large egg	1	1
Water	1 tbsp.	15 mL
All-purpose flour	1/4 cup	60 mL
Ground pecans	1/4 cup	60 mL
Dried rosemary, crushed	1/8 tsp.	0.5 mL
Salt	1/2 tsp.	2 mL
Pepper	1/8 tsp.	0.5 mL
Paprika	1/2 tsp.	2 mL
All-purpose flour	1/4 cup	60 mL
Boneless, skinless chicken breast halves (about 1 lb., 454 g)	4	4
Hard margarine (or butter), melted	2 tbsp.	30 mL

Fork-beat egg and water together in shallow dish.

Combine next 6 ingredients in separate shallow dish or on waxed paper.

Place second amount of flour in separate shallow dish or on waxed paper. Press chicken into flour to coat completely. Dip in egg mixture. Press firmly into pecan mixture to coat completely. Place on greased foil-lined baking sheet.

Drizzle margarine over chicken. Bake in 350°F (175°C) oven for about 1 hour until chicken is tender and no longer pink. Serves 4.

1 serving: 340 Calories; 14.9 g Total Fat; 381 mg Sodium; 35 g Protein; 15 g Carbohydrate; 1 g Dietary Fiber

Pictured on this page.

Wild Rice Medley

Such a nice blend of flavors. Enjoy this as a side dish
or as a stuffing. Serve with Chicken Pecan, this page.

Wild rice	1 cup	250 mL
Boiling water	4 cups	1 L
Salt	1 1/2 tsp.	7 mL
Medium onion, diced (about 1 2/3 cups, 400 mL)	1	1
Thinly sliced celery	1/2 cup	125 mL
Hard margarine (or butter)	2 tbsp.	30 mL
Can of sliced mushrooms, drained	10 oz.	284 mL
Ground sage	1/2 tsp.	2 mL
Salt	1/2 tsp.	2 mL
Pepper	1/8 tsp.	0.5 mL

Cook rice in boiling water and salt in medium saucepan for about 70 minutes until tender. Drain. Turn into large bowl.

Sauté onion and celery in margarine in frying pan until soft. Add to rice along with any drippings.

Add mushrooms, sage, salt and pepper. Stir. Makes 4 1/2 cups (1.1 L).

1/2 cup (125 mL): 100 Calories; 2.9 g Total Fat; 434 mg Sodium; 3 g Protein; 16 g Carbohydrate; 2 g Dietary Fiber

Pictured above.

Top: Pasta Tuna, this page Bottom: Pork Chop Bake, below

Pasta Tuna

Strong tuna, cheese and dill flavors.

Elbow macaroni	2 cups	500 mL
Chopped onion	1/2 cup	125 mL
Boiling water	8 cups	2 L
Cooking oil (optional)	1 tbsp.	15 mL
Salt	2 tsp.	10 mL
All-purpose flour	1/3 cup	75 mL
Dill weed	1/2 tsp.	2 mL
Salt	1/2 tsp.	2 mL
Pepper	1/4 tsp.	1 mL
Milk	2 1/2 cups	625 mL
Grated sharp Cheddar cheese	1 cup	250 mL
Can of white tuna, drained and flaked	6 1/2 oz.	184 g
Grated Parmesan cheese	2 tbsp.	30 mL

Cook macaroni and onion in boiling water, cooking oil and salt in large uncovered pot or Dutch oven for 5 to 7 minutes until macaroni is tender but firm. Drain. Turn into ungreased 2 quart (2 L) casserole.

Combine flour, dill weed, salt and pepper in medium saucepan. Gradually stir in milk until smooth. Heat and stir until boiling and thickened.

Stir in Cheddar cheese until melted.

Add tuna. Stir gently. Pour tuna mixture over macaroni mixture. Stir gently until well coated.

Sprinkle with Parmesan cheese. Bake, uncovered, in 350°F (175°C) oven for 30 minutes. Serves 4.

1 serving: 506 Calories; 14.7 g Total Fat; 772 mg Sodium; 32 g Protein; 60 g Carbohydrate; 2 g Dietary Fiber

Pictured on this page.

Pork Chop Bake

Interesting color and texture. Tender and moist pork.

Pork chops, trimmed of fat (about 2 1/2 lbs., 1.1 kg)	6	6
White bread cubes, 3/4 inch (2 cm) size	3 cups	750 mL
Salt	1/4 tsp.	1 mL
Pepper	1/8-1/4 tsp.	0.5-1 mL
Poultry seasoning	3/4-1 tsp.	4-5 mL
Medium onion, chopped	1	1
Small red pepper, chopped	1	1
Parsley flakes	1 tsp.	5 mL
Water, approximately	1/4 cup	60 mL

Arrange pork chops in single layer in small roasting pan.

Combine next 7 ingredients in medium bowl. Stir well.

Add enough water to make soft, moist mixture. Spoon around and over pork chops. Cover. Bake in 350°F (175°C) oven for about 50 minutes until pork chops are tender. Serves 6.

1 serving: 201 Calories; 5.7 g Total Fat; 264 mg Sodium; 24 g Protein; 12 g Carbohydrate; 1 g Dietary Fiber

Pictured above.

Preserves

When the harvest is in, the preserving begins. Join in the fun. Sample some of these delectable recipes and you'll be well stocked for the long winter ahead. And don't forget, a decorative bow is all you need to turn a simple jar of preserves into a welcome gift at Christmas time.

Canned Coleslaw

Fresh Fall Salsa

Mixed Pickles

Pear Ginger Spread

Spiced Plums

Tomato Marmalade

Canned Coleslaw

It's so convenient to have salad on hand.
No one will believe it's canned.

Medium head of cabbage, grated (about 10 cups, 2.5 L)	1	1
Chopped onion	1 cup	250 mL
Medium carrots, grated	3	3
Celery seed	1 tsp.	5 mL
Coarse (pickling) salt	1/2 tsp.	2 mL
Granulated sugar	2 cups	500 mL
White vinegar	1/2 cup	125 mL
Apple cider vinegar	1/2 cup	125 mL

Measure all 8 ingredients into large bowl. Stir well. Let stand for 5 hours. Turn into large pot or Dutch oven. Bring to a boil. Boil for 5 minutes, stirring frequently. Fill hot sterilized jars to within 1/2 inch (12 mm) of top. Place sterilized metal lids on jars and screw metal bands on securely. Process in boiling water bath for 10 minutes. Makes 4 pint (2 cup, 500 mL) jars.

1/4 cup (60 mL): 65 Calories; 0.1 g Total Fat; 46 mg Sodium; 1 g Protein; 17 g Carbohydrate; 1 g Dietary Fiber

Pictured on page 117.

Tomato Marmalade

A surprisingly tart marmalade containing tomatoes.
Oranges give a flavor boost.

Apple cider vinegar	1/4 cup	60 mL
Chopped ripe tomato	4 cups	1 L
Granulated sugar	2 cups	500 mL
Medium oranges, with peel, finely chopped	2	2
Ground cinnamon	1 tsp.	5 mL

Pour vinegar over tomato in large saucepan. Let stand overnight. Drain well.

Add sugar, orange and cinnamon. Cook slowly for about 2 hours, stirring occasionally, until thickened. Fill hot sterilized jars to within 1/2 inch (12 mm) of top. Place sterilized metal lids on jars and screw metal bands on securely. Process in boiling water bath for 15 minutes. Makes 3 half pint (1 cup, 250 mL) jars.

1 tbsp. (15 mL): 38 Calories; 0.1 g Total Fat; 1 mg Sodium; trace Protein; 10 g Carbohydrate; trace Dietary Fiber

Pictured on page 116 and on page 117.

Mixed Pickles

Sweet and sour tasting brightly colored vegetables.

Large carrots, cut up	6	6
Large head of cauliflower, cut bite size	1/2	1/2
Pickling cucumbers, coarsely chopped	6	6
Hot banana peppers, coarsely chopped	4	4
Pickling onions, skin removed	2 cups	500 mL
Garlic cloves	12	12
BRINE		
Salt	2 tbsp.	30 mL
Granulated sugar	6 cups	1.5 L
White vinegar	3 1/2 cups	875 mL
Celery seed	1 tbsp.	15 mL
Mustard seed	1 tbsp.	15 mL
Turmeric	2 tsp.	10 mL

Firmly pack first 6 ingredients into hot sterilized jars.

Brine: Combine all 6 ingredients in large pot or Dutch oven. Bring to a boil. Pour brine over vegetables to within 1/2 inch (12 mm) of top. Place sterilized metal lids on jars and screw metal bands on securely. Process in boiling water bath for 5 minutes. Makes about 6 pint (2 cup, 500 mL) jars.

2 tbsp. (30 mL): 59 Calories; 0.1 g Total Fat; 146 mg Sodium; trace Protein; 15 g Carbohydrate; trace Dietary Fiber

Pictured on page 117.

Spiced Plums

This condiment is actually meant for cold meat but it's a good go-with for meatloaves and meatballs.

Prune plums, pitted and chopped (pitted weight)	6 lbs.	2.7 kg
Granulated sugar	12 cups	3 L
Ground cinnamon	1 tbsp.	15 mL
Ground cloves	1 tbsp.	15 mL
Salt, approximately	1 tsp.	5 mL
White vinegar	3 cups	750 mL

Combine first 5 ingredients in large pot or Dutch oven. Stir. Bring to a boil. Reduce heat to low. Simmer, stirring occasionally, until pulp settles.

Add vinegar. Stir. Taste and add more salt if you think it needs it. Bring to a boil. Reduce heat to low. Simmer for about 1 1/4 hours, stirring occasionally, until thickened. Fill hot sterilized jars to within 1/2 inch (12 mm) of top. Place sterilized metal lids on jars and screw metal bands on securely. Process in boiling water bath for 10 minutes. Makes 6 pint (2 cup, 500 mL) jars.

2 tbsp. (30 mL): 114 Calories; 0.2 g Total Fat; 24 mg Sodium; trace Protein; 29 g Carbohydrate; trace Dietary Fiber

Pictured on page 116.

Fresh Fall Salsa

This retains a very fresh flavor. One would think tomatoes were created just for this great salsa. Calls for special hot peppers.

Ripe medium tomatoes	6 lbs.	2.7 kg
Boiling water		
Cold water		
Chopped onion	2 cups	500 mL
Large green pepper, chopped	1	1
Large red pepper, chopped	1	1
Chopped celery	1/2 cup	125 mL
Garlic cloves, chopped (or 1 1/2 tsp., 7 mL, powder)	6	6
Jalapeño peppers, chopped (see Note)	2	2
Chipotle chili peppers, chopped	2	2
Can of tomato sauce	7 1/2 oz.	213 mL
Apple cider vinegar	1/4 cup	60 mL
Chopped fresh cilantro (or fresh parsley)	1/2 cup	125 mL
Salt	2 tsp.	10 mL
Granulated sugar	1 tsp.	5 mL

Dip tomatoes, in batches, in boiling water in large saucepan for 1 minute. Immediately plunge into cold water. Remove. Peel. Chop. Put into large pot or Dutch oven.

Add remaining 12 ingredients. Stir. Bring to a boil. Reduce heat. Simmer gently, uncovered, for about 30 minutes, stirring occasionally, until salsa reaches desired consistency. Fill hot sterilized jars to within 1/2 inch (12 mm) of top. Place sterilized metal lids on jars and screw metal bands on securely. Process in boiling water bath for 20 minutes for pint jars and 30 minutes for quart jars. Makes 6 pint (2 cup, 500 mL) jars or 3 quart (4 cup, 1 L) jars.

2 tbsp. (30 mL): 10 Calories; 0.1 g Total Fat; 64 mg Sodium; trace Protein; 2 g Carbohydrate; trace Dietary Fiber

Pictured on page 117.

Note: Wear gloves when chopping jalapeño peppers and avoid touching your eyes.

Pear Ginger Spread

Sunshine yellow. Fresh pear flavor. Easy to make.

Fresh pears, peeled, cored and chopped	12	12
Medium orange, peeled and chopped	1	1
Medium orange, with peel, chopped	1	1
Can of crushed pineapple, with juice	19 oz.	540 mL
Granulated sugar	3 cups	750 mL
Minced crystallized ginger	3 tbsp.	50 mL
Pouches of liquid pectin (3 oz., 85 mL, each)	2	2

Put pears and oranges into food processor. Process until smooth. Turn into large pot or Dutch oven.

Add pineapple with juice, sugar and ginger. Heat and stir on medium-high until boiling. Reduce heat to medium. Boil, quite rapidly, for about 25 minutes until thickened to marmalade consistency.

Add pectin. Stir. Bring to a boil. Fill hot sterilized jars to within 1/2 inch (12 mm) of top. Place sterilized metal lids on jars and screw metal bands on securely. Process in boiling water bath for 10 minutes. Makes 4 pint (2 cup, 500 mL) jars.

2 tbsp. (30 mL): 65 Calories; 0.1 g Total Fat; 2 mg Sodium; trace Protein; 17 g Carbohydrate; 1 g Dietary Fiber

Pictured on this page.

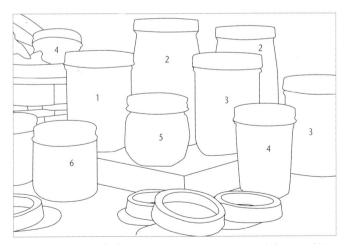

1. Pear Ginger Spread, above
2. Fresh Fall Salsa, page 115
3. Mixed Pickles, page 115
4. Tomato Marmalade, page 114
5. Canned Coleslaw, page 114
6. Spiced Plums, page 115

Baked Stuffed Tomatoes

The fresher the tomatoes, the more flavorful this will be.

Ripe medium tomatoes	6	6
Fine dry bread crumbs	1/4 cup	60 mL
Grated sharp Cheddar cheese	1/2 cup	125 mL
Granulated sugar	1 tsp.	5 mL
Salt	1/2 tsp.	2 mL
Pepper	1/16 tsp.	0.5 mL
Dried sweet basil	1/4 tsp.	1 mL
Dried whole oregano	1/4 tsp.	1 mL
Tomato paste	1/4 cup	60 mL
Cooked long grain white rice (1/3 cup, 75 mL, uncooked)	1 cup	250 mL

Cut 1/4 inch (6 mm) slice from stem end of each tomato. Scoop out pulp. Coarsely chop pulp. Strain, discarding juice. Put pulp into medium bowl.

Add next 8 ingredients. Stir.

Add rice. Mix well. Makes 3 1/3 cups (825 mL) filling. Fill tomato shells with about 1/2 cup (125 mL) filling each. Place tomatoes in greased 9 x 9 inch (22 x 22 cm) pan. Bake, uncovered, in 350°F (175°C) oven for 30 to 35 minutes until filling is heated through and tomatoes are tender. Serves 6.

1 serving: 145 Calories; 4.2 g Total Fat; 320 mg Sodium; 6 g Protein; 22 g Carbohydrate; 2 g Dietary Fiber

Pictured on page 119.

Honeyed Carrots

Short and sweet. A simple glaze.

Medium carrots, cut diagonally into 1 inch (2.5 cm) pieces (about 6 cups, 1.5 L)	2 lbs.	900 g
Boiling water	1 cup	250 mL
Salt	1/2 tsp.	2 mL
Liquid honey	2 tbsp.	30 mL
Ground cinnamon, sprinkle		

Cook carrot in boiling water and salt in large saucepan on medium until tender. Drain well. Return to saucepan.

Drizzle honey over carrot. Sprinkle with cinnamon. Heat and stir on medium for 5 to 6 minutes until carrot is glazed and liquid has evaporated. Makes 4 cups (1 L).

1/2 cup (125 mL): 72 Calories; 0.2 g Total Fat; 82 mg Sodium; 1 g Protein; 17 g Carbohydrate; 3 g Dietary Fiber

Pictured on page 119.

Mushroomed Potatoes

Wonderful mushroom and garlic flavor in these potatoes.

Medium potatoes (about 2 lbs., 900 g), peeled and cut up	4	4
Water		
Salt	1 tsp.	5 mL
Milk	1/4 cup	60 mL
Garlic cloves, minced (or 1/2 tsp., 2 mL, powder)	2	2
Minced onion flakes	1 tbsp.	15 mL
Hard margarine (or butter)	2 tbsp.	30 mL
Chopped fresh brown mushrooms (about 7 oz., 200 g)	2 cups	500 mL
Freshly ground pepper, sprinkle		
Grated Swiss cheese	3/4 cup	175 mL

Cook potato in water and salt in large saucepan for 15 to 20 minutes until tender. Drain.

Add milk. Mash until light and fluffy. Keep warm.

Sauté garlic and onion flakes in margarine for 1 minute. Add mushrooms. Sauté until liquid has evaporated and mushrooms are golden.

Sprinkle with pepper. Add to potato. Add cheese. Mix well. Makes 5 cups (1.25 L).

1/2 cup (125 mL): 139 Calories; 4.9 g Total Fat; 58 mg Sodium; 5 g Protein; 20 g Carbohydrate; 2 g Dietary Fiber

Pictured on page 119.

Top Center: Mushroomed Potatoes, page 118
Bottom Left: Greek Stuffed Zucchini, below

Bottom Right: Honeyed Carrots, page 118
Bottom Center: Baked Stuffed Tomatoes, page 118

Greek Stuffed Zucchini

*Tomato filling with mild flavoring from
cinnamon, onion and basil.*

Medium zucchini, with peel	4	4
Lean ground beef	1 lb.	454 g
Medium onion, chopped	1	1
Garlic cloves, minced (or 1/2 tsp., 2 mL, powder)	2	2
Chopped fresh sweet basil (or 3/4 tsp., 4 mL, dried)	1 tbsp.	15 mL
Ground cinnamon	1/2 tsp.	2 mL
Can of tomato sauce	7 1/2 oz.	213 mL
Feta cheese, crumbled	1/2 cup	125 mL

Cut ends off of zucchini. Slice in half lengthwise. Scoop out flesh, leaving 1/4 inch (6 mm) thick shell. Chop flesh. Set aside. Lay zucchini, cut sides up, in ungreased shallow pan. Bake, uncovered, in 375°F (190°C) oven for 15 minutes until tender-crisp. Drain any liquid.

Scramble-fry ground beef, reserved zucchini flesh, onion and garlic in non-stick frying pan until beef is no longer pink and liquid has evaporated.

Add basil and cinnamon. Stir. Add tomato sauce. Stir. Bring to a boil. Reduce heat. Cover. Simmer for 5 minutes. Makes 3 1/4 cups (800 mL) filling. Fill zucchini shells. Bake in 350°F (175°C) oven for about 10 minutes until heated through.

Sprinkle with cheese. Let stand for 2 minutes before serving. Serves 8.

1 serving: 177 Calories; 10.9 g Total Fat; 322 mg Sodium; 14 g Protein; 7 g Carbohydrate; 2 g Dietary Fiber

Pictured above.

Company Carrots

A deliciously different serving of carrots. A great make-ahead.

Carrots, sliced into 1/4 inch (6 mm) coins (about 5 cups, 1.25 L)	1 1/2 lbs.	680 g
Water		
Salt	1/2 tsp.	2 mL
Finely chopped red onion	1/2 cup	125 mL
Light mayonnaise (not salad dressing)	1/2 cup	125 mL
Prepared horseradish	1 tbsp.	15 mL
Canned French fried onions, lightly crushed	1/2 cup	125 mL

Cook carrot in water and salt in large saucepan for about 7 minutes until tender-crisp. Drain well, reserving 1/4 cup (60 mL) cooking liquid. Turn carrot into ungreased shallow 1 1/2 quart (1.5 L) casserole.

Combine red onion, mayonnaise, horseradish and reserved cooking liquid in small dish. Spoon evenly over carrot.

Sprinkle with French fried onions. Bake, uncovered, in 350°F (175°C) oven for about 30 minutes until lightly browned. Serves 6 to 8.

1 serving: 178 Calories; 9.3 g Total Fat; 304 mg Sodium; 2 g Protein; 23 g Carbohydrate; 4 g Dietary Fiber

Pictured on page 121.

Baked Broccoli

Although fresh broccoli is almost always available in our stores — the frozen product can sure come in handy. About 1 1/2 lbs. (680 g) of fresh cut broccoli can be substituted for the frozen. It will just have to be cooked tender-crisp first.

Frozen cut broccoli, chopped smaller	7 cups	1.75 L
Water		
Salt	1/2 tsp.	2 mL
Hard margarine (or butter)	1/4 cup	60 mL
Grated medium Cheddar cheese	2 cups	500 mL
Salt	1/8 tsp.	0.5 mL
Pepper, sprinkle		
Hard margarine (or butter)	2 tbsp.	30 mL
Fine dry bread crumbs	1/2 cup	125 mL

Cook broccoli in water and first amount of salt in large saucepan for about 5 minutes until tender-crisp. Drain well.

Add first amount of margarine, cheese, second amount of salt and pepper. Stir. Turn into ungreased 1 1/2 quart (1.5 L) casserole.

Melt second amount of margarine in small saucepan. Stir in bread crumbs. Sprinkle over top of broccoli mixture. Bake, uncovered, in 350°F (175°C) oven for 25 to 30 minutes until crumbs are golden. Serves 6.

1 serving: 368 Calories; 25.9 g Total Fat; 575 mg Sodium; 18 g Protein; 20 g Carbohydrate; 6 g Dietary Fiber

Pictured on page 121.

Apple-Cran Squash

A very different appearance to this side dish. A real conversation piece.

Small butternut squash	2	2
Fresh (or frozen, thawed) cranberries	1/3 cup	75 mL
Medium cooking apple (such as McIntosh), peeled and chopped	1	1
Chopped pecans	1/4 cup	60 mL
Prepared orange juice	1 1/2 tbsp.	25 mL
Brown sugar, packed	1 1/2 tbsp.	25 mL
Hard margarine (or butter), softened	1 tbsp.	15 mL
Grated lemon peel	1/4 tsp.	1 mL
Ground cinnamon	1/2 tsp.	2 mL

Cut squash in half lengthwise. Scrape out and discard seeds. Arrange squash, cut side down, on baking sheet. Bake in 350°F (175°C) oven for 25 minutes.

Combine remaining 8 ingredients in small bowl. Makes 2 1/3 cups (575 mL) filling. Turn squash over, cut side up. Divide and fill cavities with filling. Bake in 350°F (175°C) oven for about 20 minutes until squash is tender. Serves 4.

1 serving: 214 Calories; 8.5 g Total Fat; 45 mg Sodium; 3 g Protein; 37 g Carbohydrate; 5 g Dietary Fiber

Pictured on page 121.

Top Left: Baked Broccoli, page 120
Bottom Left: Apple-Cran Squash, page 120

Top Center: Company Potatoes, below

Top Right: Pink-Sauced Beets, below
Bottom Right: Company Carrots, page 120

Company Potatoes

These are creamy and satisfying.

Potatoes, peeled and quartered	4 lbs.	1.8 kg
Water		
Hard margarine (or butter)	2 tbsp.	30 mL
Milk	1/2 cup	125 mL
Salad dressing (or mayonnaise)	1/2 cup	125 mL
Sour cream	1/2 cup	125 mL
Salt	1/2 tsp.	2 mL
Pepper	1/4 tsp.	1 mL
Chopped chives, for garnish	2 tbsp.	30 mL

Cook potato in water in large pot or Dutch oven until tender. Drain. Mash until no lumps remain.

Combine remaining 6 ingredients in small saucepan. Heat and stir until hot. Add to potato. Mash until light and fluffy.

Turn into serving bowl. Sprinkle with chives. Makes 8 cups (2 L).

1 cup (250 mL): 312 Calories; 13 g Total Fat; 307 mg Sodium; 6 g Protein; 44 g Carbohydrate; 3 g Dietary Fiber

Pictured above.

Pink-Sauced Beets

Adding sour cream to beets makes a pretty pink-colored sauce. The flavor will be enjoyed by all.

Cans of sliced beets (14 oz., 398 mL, each), drained (or 3 cups, 750 mL, cooked beets)	2	2
Light sour cream	1/2 cup	125 mL
Green onion, thinly sliced	1	1
Granulated sugar	1 tbsp.	15 mL
White vinegar	1 tbsp.	15 mL
Salt	1/2 tsp.	2 mL
Pepper	1/8 tsp.	0.5 mL
Prepared horseradish	1/2 tsp.	2 mL
Chopped walnuts (optional)	1/2 cup	125 mL

Combine first 8 ingredients in large saucepan. Heat, stirring occasionally, until heated through. Turn into serving bowl.

Sprinkle with walnuts. Makes 3 cups (750 mL).

1/2 cup (125 mL): 55 Calories; 1.6 g Total Fat; 453 mg Sodium; 1 g Protein; 10 g Carbohydrate; 2 g Dietary Fiber

Pictured above.

Dutch Apple Cream Pie

Both eye appeal and taste are rated tops for this dessert.
Apples retain their shape in the custard-like sauce.
Serve drizzled with Maple Cream Sauce, below.

Pastry for 9 inch (22 cm) pie shell, your own or a mix	1	1
Granulated sugar	1/2 cup	125 mL
All-purpose flour	3 tbsp.	50 mL
Cornstarch	2 tbsp.	30 mL
Medium cooking apples (such as McIntosh) peeled, cored and cut into wedges (about 6 cups, 1.5 L)	2 lbs.	900 g
Large egg	1	1
Sour cream	1 cup	250 mL
Granulated sugar	1/4 cup	60 mL
Ground cinnamon	1/2 tsp.	2 mL

Roll out pastry and line 9 inch (22 cm) glass pie plate. Flute edge if desired.

Combine first amount of sugar, flour and cornstarch in large bowl. Add apple. Stir until coated. Turn into pie shell. Spread evenly.

Mix egg and sour cream in small bowl. Spoon evenly over apple mixture.

Combine second amount of sugar and cinnamon in small dish. Sprinkle over sour cream mixture. Bake on bottom rack in 350°F (175°C) oven for about 1 1/4 hours until crust is golden and apples are tender-crisp. Cool to room temperature before cutting. Cuts into 8 wedges.

1 wedge: 282 Calories; 10.4 g Total Fat; 124 mg Sodium; 3 g Protein; 46 g Carbohydrate; 2 g Dietary Fiber

Pictured on page 123.

Maple Cream Sauce

A mild maple flavor adds richness when drizzled over
Dutch Apple Cream Pie, above. Also good over ice cream.
Serve warm or at room temperature.

Can of evaporated milk	13 1/2 oz.	385 mL
Golden corn syrup	1/2 cup	125 mL
Maple flavoring	1 tsp.	5 mL

Measure evaporated milk and corn syrup into small heavy saucepan. Bring to a boil. Reduce heat to medium-low. Simmer, uncovered, for 50 to 60 minutes, stirring occasionally, until reduced and slightly thickened.

Stir in maple flavoring. Makes about 1 cup (250 mL).

2 tbsp. (30 mL): 126 Calories; 3.8 g Total Fat; 84 mg Sodium; 3 g Protein; 21 g Carbohydrate; 0 g Dietary Fiber

Pictured on page 123.

Vanilla Custard Sauce

A rich sauce that tastes so good when
drizzled on Fall Fruit Pudding, page 124.

Granulated sugar	1/3 cup	75 mL
Cornstarch	2 tsp.	10 mL
All-purpose flour	2 tsp.	10 mL
Salt, just a pinch		
Homogenized milk (or half-and-half cream)	1 1/2 cups	375 mL
Egg yolks (large), fork-beaten	2	2
Hard margarine (or butter)	2 tsp.	10 mL
Vanilla	1 1/2 tsp.	7 mL

Combine sugar, cornstarch, flour and salt in medium saucepan. Slowly stir in milk until smooth. Heat and stir on medium until boiling and slightly thickened. Remove from heat.

Stir tablespoonful of hot milk mixture into egg yolks in small bowl. Gradually stir egg yolk mixture into milk mixture. Heat and stir over medium-low for about 1 minute until boiling and slightly thickened. Remove from heat.

Stir in margarine and vanilla. Cover to prevent skin forming. Serve warm or at room temperature. Makes 1 2/3 cups (400 mL).

2 tbsp. (30 mL): 54 Calories; 2.2 g Total Fat; 21 mg Sodium; 1 g Protein; 7 g Carbohydrate; trace Dietary Fiber

Pictured on page 123.

Top Left: Vanilla Custard Sauce, above
Top Right: Deep Plum Pie, page 124
Center Left: Fall Fruit Pudding, page 124
Center Right: Maple Cream Sauce, this page
Bottom: Dutch Apple Cream Pie, this page

Fall Fruit Pudding

This makes a delicious and beautiful presentation at Thanksgiving. Uses both carrots and beets. Serve with Vanilla Custard Sauce or Maple Cream Sauce, both on page 122.

Chopped glazed cherries	3/4 cup	175 mL
Diced dried apricots	3/4 cup	175 mL
Chopped pecans	3/4 cup	175 mL
All-purpose flour	1/2 cup	125 mL
Hard margarine (or butter), softened	3/4 cup	175 mL
Brown sugar, packed	1 cup	250 mL
Vanilla	1 1/2 tsp.	7 mL
Large eggs	3	3
All-purpose flour	1 1/2 cups	375 mL
Baking powder	1 1/2 tsp.	7 mL
Ground cinnamon	1/2 tsp.	2 mL
Ground nutmeg	1/4 tsp.	1 mL
Ground allspice	1/4 tsp.	1 mL
Salt	1/2 tsp.	2 mL
Grated carrot	1 cup	250 mL
Frozen concentrated orange juice, thawed	1/2 cup	125 mL
Finely grated beets (about 1 medium), see Note	1 cup	250 mL
Water	1/4 cup	60 mL

Toss first 4 ingredients together in medium bowl until well coated. Set aside.

Beat margarine and brown sugar together in large bowl until light and fluffy. Beat in vanilla. Add eggs, 1 at a time, beating well after each addition.

Combine next 6 ingredients in small bowl. Add 1/3 of flour mixture to margarine mixture. Beat.

Beat in carrot and orange juice concentrate. Beat in another 1/3 of flour mixture. Beat in beets and water. Beat in remaining 1/3 of flour mixture. Stir in cherry mixture until flour is incorporated and fruit is well coated. Spoon into well greased 10 x 4 1/2 inch (25 x 11 cm) angel food tube pan. Smooth top. Bake on bottom rack in 325°F (160°C) oven for about 1 1/4 hours until wooden pick inserted near center comes out clean. Cool in pan on wire rack for 20 minutes. Serve warm or turn out to cool completely. Serves 12 to 14.

1 serving: 414 Calories; 19 g Total Fat; 321 mg Sodium; 5 g Protein; 58 g Carbohydrate; 2 g Dietary Fiber

Pictured on page 123.

Note: To prevent hands from staining, wear rubber gloves while handling beets.

Deep Plum Pie

During the short plum season this becomes an extra special treat.

Minute tapioca	1/3 cup	75 mL
Granulated sugar	1 1/2 cups	375 mL
Prune plums, halved and pitted (about 20 large)	3 lbs.	1.4 kg
PASTRY		
All-purpose flour	1 1/2 cups	375 mL
Salt	1/4 tsp.	1 mL
Butter (not margarine), chilled	1/2 cup	125 mL
Ice water	4 1/2 tbsp.	67 mL
Granulated sugar	2 tsp.	10 mL

Combine tapioca, sugar and plums in large bowl. Turn into greased 9 x 13 inch (22 x 33 cm) dish. Let stand.

Pastry: Combine flour and salt in separate large bowl. Cut in butter until mixture is crumbly. Drizzle water, a little at a time, over flour mixture, tossing and stirring with fork until all liquid is absorbed. Shape into ball. Press into flattened circle. Cover with plastic wrap. Chill for 1 hour. Roll dough between sheets of waxed paper to 10 x 14 inch (25 x 35 cm) rectangle. Remove top sheet of waxed paper. If dough sticks to waxed paper, chill dough with waxed paper for a few minutes. Turn, pastry side down, over plums. Peel back waxed paper. Tuck crust into sides or flute decoratively around inside edge. Cut slits here and there in top of crust.

Sprinkle crust with sugar. Bake in 350°F (175°C) oven for about 1 hour until plums are soft and bubbling and crust is golden. Serves 12 to 15.

1 serving: 312 Calories; 9 g Total Fat; 133 mg Sodium; 3 g Protein; 58 g Carbohydrate; 2 g Dietary Fiber

Pictured on page 123.

Winter

Winter

December Shhhhh—perennials are resting, soil is restoring and nature is dark and quiet.

January Some people migrate to warmer climates and old man winter takes over.

February Seed catalogues arrive and planning of dream gardens begins.

Long, dark winter nights inspire in us a need for comfort foods and cozy evenings around a fireplace. Hunkering under blankets to watch a movie or gathering at the kitchen table for a game of cards become favorite pastimes.

Soon, the hustle and bustle of the holiday season will have our complete attention—but let's not forget about the other amusements this wondrous season has to offer. Tobogganing, ice skating, hockey, skiing and crisp winter walks beckon us into the winter wonderland, bringing rosy cheeks and a surge of energy to young and old alike. And what better way to build an appetite than with an afternoon of snowball fights, snowmen and snow forts?

December

December is a festive but busy month as we begin preparations for the holidays. Faced with crowded stores and shorter tempers, we sometimes find ourselves struggling to remember that this is a holiday of cheer.

Why not turn some of the chores of the Christmas season into a fun event—invite people over to help with tree decorating, and serve hot apple cider, shortbread cookies and chocolate chip squares. Have a cookie exchange where at least six people bring six dozen cookies of their favorite recipe. Or get together with a fellow cookie baker or two for an afternoon of baking. The same can be done with homemade chocolates or appetizers since both can be frozen and reheated when company comes visiting. After all, December should be a time to indulge as we attend numerous parties and entertain friends and family.

Some people choose to celebrate the spirit of the Christmas season by attending children's pageants, choral performances and Christmas Eve church services. It's a perfect opportunity to invite family or friends to your home afterwards to enjoy a late supper with plenty of make-ahead dishes. Don't feel you have to prepare everything yourself: many people will ask if they can bring something and you should be prepared to suggest something.

Christmas is a good time to remember people who have helped you out during the year, and those jars of preserves you tucked away in fall months will make wonderful gifts. Homemade jelly, flavored vinegar or

pickles are inexpensive and unique presents for a teacher, postal worker or personal trainer. A newspaper delivery person or secretary may enjoy a prettily wrapped package of cookies. Keep it simple and that way you'll get as much enjoyment from giving these items as those receiving them.

Between Christmas and New Year's is a week of unbridled energy for children and adults alike. New toboggans, skates and skis are put to the test along with stacks of games and toys. School remains out, and for many businesses doors remain closed—creating a perfect opportunity for the whole family to have a little fun. Organize a tobogganing party, and end it off with pizza and hot chocolate in front of a roaring fire. Pull on your skates and have a game of tag at the local rink with your children, or make a day trip to the mountains to enjoy fresh air on the ski slopes.

Here is a good opportunity too to host a neighborhood party, an afternoon open house where everyone brings an appetizer or dessert. Fill the punch bowl, lay out the food, then relax and enjoy the fellowship.

January

As New Year's Eve rolls into January, we gather our resolve and vow to make changes. Even for those who don't believe in resolutions, this first month of the New Year is when we look for a break from the whirlwind of activities of the past month. We yearn for less indulgent foods that are lower in fat—a change from the heavy sauces and extravagant desserts of December—foods with the clean and crisp tastes of citrusy, vinegar-spiked dressings and leaner cuts of meat.

February

February is perhaps the hardest month of all to endure when bone-rattling cold shows no signs of dissipating. Energy levels drop. Cabin fever strikes when the daytime highs aren't warm enough for even a walk outdoors with the dog. Now is the time to break out of the winter doldrums with a costume party. Pair it up with a murder mystery where everyone can dress in character and play act. Serve food and drinks appropriate to the plot. Many murder mystery games contain lots of decorating and entertaining tips.

One bright light in the midst of February's chill is the celebration of love on Valentine's Day. Make homemade valentines and adorn them with ribbons and lace, or buy children's valentines for adults to enjoy a bit of nostalgia. Make heart-shaped cookies or cake for the special people in your life. Or cook a romantic dinner to share by the fireplace with seafood and rice, finishing with a decadent dessert.

The days are not yet brighter, nor the winds warmer, but as February draws to a close, a new energy is felt while everyone waits, impatiently, for spring to arrive.

Top Left: Tortilla Pizza Wedges, this page   Center: Creamy Beef Appetizer Pie, this page   Top Right: Pacific Meatballs, page 129

Creamy Beef Appetizer Pie

Cream cheese and sour cream base complemented with a pleasant nutty flavor. Serve warm with assorted crackers.

Light cream cheese, softened	8 oz.	250 g
Milk	2 tbsp.	30 mL
Light sour cream	1/2 cup	125 mL
Finely chopped cooked (or deli) beef	1 1/2 cups	375 mL
Finely chopped green pepper	3 tbsp.	50 mL
Finely chopped onion	2 tbsp.	30 mL
Salt	1/4 tsp.	1 mL
Freshly ground pepper	1/8 tsp.	0.5 mL
Chopped walnuts	1/4 cup	60 mL

Beat cream cheese, milk and sour cream together in medium bowl until smooth.

Stir in beef, green pepper, onion, salt and pepper. Spread in ungreased 9 inch (22 cm) pie plate.

Sprinkle with walnuts. Bake in 350°F (175°C) oven for 20 minutes. Makes 3 cups (750 mL).

2 tbsp. (30 mL): 55 Calories; 3.8 g Total Fat; 101 mg Sodium; 4 g Protein; 1 g Carbohydrate; trace Dietary Fiber

Pictured above.

Tortilla Pizza Wedges

Perfect to serve as finger food on New Year's Eve.

TOPPING

Sausage meat	13 oz.	370 g
Chopped onion	1 cup	250 mL
Sliced fresh mushrooms	2 cups	500 mL

CRUST

Flour tortillas (8 inch, 20 cm, size)	3	3
Ketchup	3 tbsp.	50 mL
Grated part-skim mozzarella (or Monterey Jack) cheese	3/4 cup	175 mL
Grated medium Cheddar cheese	3/4 cup	175 mL

Topping: Scramble-fry sausage meat, onion and mushrooms in frying pan until no pink remains in sausage and onion is soft.

Crust: Arrange tortillas in single layer on ungreased baking sheets. Spread 1 tbsp. (15 mL) ketchup over each. Divide and scatter sausage mixture over ketchup.

Toss both cheeses together in small bowl. Sprinkle 1/2 cup (125 mL) over each tortilla. Bake in 375°F (190°C) oven for 8 minutes. Each pizza cuts into 8 wedges, for a total of 24 wedges.

1 wedge: 100 Calories; 7 g Total Fat; 198 mg Sodium; 4 g Protein; 5 g Carbohydrate; trace Dietary Fiber

Pictured above.

Pacific Meatballs

These meatballs are cooked in a sweet and savory dark brown sauce.

Deviled Eggs, below

MEATBALLS

Large eggs	2	2
Finely chopped onion	1/2 cup	125 mL
Garlic powder	1/4 tsp.	1 mL
Salt	1/4 tsp.	1 mL
Pepper	1/4 tsp.	1 mL
Crushed chow mein noodles	1/2 cup	125 mL
Lean ground beef	1 lb.	454 g

SWEET AND SAVORY SAUCE

Pineapple juice	1/2 cup	125 mL
Brown sugar, packed	1/3 cup	75 mL
Soy sauce	1/4 cup	60 mL
Ketchup	1/3 cup	75 mL
Ground ginger	1/4 tsp.	1 mL

Meatballs: Beat eggs in large bowl. Add onion, garlic powder, salt and pepper. Stir.

Add noodles and ground beef. Mix well. Shape into 1 inch (2.5 cm) balls. Cook in large non-stick frying pan until browned. Drain.

Sweet And Savory Sauce: Combine all 5 ingredients in small bowl. Makes about 1 cup (250 mL) sauce. Add to meatballs. Cover. Simmer for 15 minutes. Makes 40 meatballs. Serves 6.

1 serving: 251 Calories; 9.5 g Total Fat; 1079 mg Sodium; 17 g Protein; 24 g Carbohydrate; 1 g Dietary Fiber

Pictured on page 128.

Deviled Eggs

An all-season favorite.

Hard-boiled eggs	6	6
Salad dressing (or mayonnaise)	2 tbsp.	30 mL
Sweet pickle relish	2 tbsp.	30 mL
Onion powder	1/4 - 1/2 tsp.	1 - 2 mL

Paprika, sprinkle

Cut eggs in half lengthwise. Remove yolks to small bowl. Place egg whites on large plate.

Add salad dressing, relish and onion powder to egg yolks. Mash together well with fork. Spoon or pipe into egg white halves.

Sprinkle with paprika. Makes 12 deviled eggs.

1 deviled egg: 54 Calories; 3.9 g Total Fat; 67 mg Sodium; 3 g Protein; 2 g Carbohydrate; 0 g Dietary Fiber

Pictured above.

Holiday Baking

If the results are always so delicious, then baking should never be a chore! Take a moment and look through some of the great recipes that have been assembled. You'll find everything you need to create a stunning assortment of goodies. There's something to please everyone!

Pistachio Shortbread

Chocolate Butter Tarts

Gingerbread Cookie Cutouts

Pecan Squares

Orange Cookies

Chocolate Peanut Squares

Pistachio Shortbread

This makes a pretty and less sweet-tasting cookie for your next cookie exchange. Purchase already shelled pistachios in the Asian section of the grocery store or East Indian food store.

Butter (not margarine), softened	1 cup	250 mL
Granulated sugar	2/3 cup	150 mL
Almond flavoring	1/2 tsp.	2 mL
Drops of green food coloring (optional)	3 - 4	3 - 4
All-purpose flour	2 1/4 cups	550 mL
Ground cardamom	1/2 tsp.	2 mL
Shelled pistachios, finely chopped	1/2 cup	125 mL
Shelled pistachios, finely chopped	1/2 cup	125 mL
Melted white (or dark) chocolate, for decorating		

Cream butter and sugar in large bowl.

Add almond flavoring and food coloring. Stir. Add flour, cardamom and 1/2 cup (125 mL) pistachios. Dough will be dry and crumbly and may require use of your hands to mix until no visible flour remains. Pack and form into 2 rolls, about 1 1/2 inches (3.8 cm) in diameter each.

Spread second amount of pistachios over 12 × 12 inch (30 × 30 cm) sheet of waxed paper. Roll dough in pistachios to coat completely. Wrap in waxed paper. Cover with plastic wrap. Chill for several hours or overnight. Cut into 1/4 inch (6 mm) thick slices. Arrange about 1 inch (2.5 cm) apart on ungreased cookie sheets. Bake on center rack in 325°F (160°C) oven for about 15 minutes until edges are golden. Let stand on sheet for 2 minutes. Remove to wire racks to cool.

Drizzle with chocolate. Makes about 7 dozen cookies.

1 cookie: 50 Calories; 3.2 g Total Fat; 36 mg Sodium; 1 g Protein; 5 g Carbohydrate; trace Dietary Fiber

Pictured on page 132/133.

Chocolate Butter Tarts

Mmm! A favorite. Golden brown filling full of nuts and raisins. Moist but not gooey.

Hard margarine (or butter)	3 tbsp.	50 mL
Golden corn syrup	1/3 cup	75 mL
Brown sugar, packed	1/3 cup	75 mL
Cocoa, sifted if lumpy	2 tsp.	10 mL
Large egg	1	1
Vanilla	1/2 tsp.	2 mL
Lemon juice	1/2 tsp.	2 mL
Raisins	1/2 cup	125 mL
Chopped walnuts (optional)	1/2 cup	125 mL
Unbaked tart shells	12	12

Melt margarine in medium saucepan. Remove from heat.

Add next 6 ingredients. Stir well. Heat and stir for about 1 minute until bubbly. Remove from heat.

Add raisins and walnuts. Stir. Makes about 1 1/2 cups (375 mL) filling.

Divide filling evenly among tart shells. Bake in 375°F (190°C) oven for 15 to 17 minutes until set. Makes 12 tarts.

1 tart: 172 Calories; 7.5 g Total Fat; 139 mg Sodium; 1 g Protein; 26 g Carbohydrate; trace Dietary Fiber

Pictured on page 133.

Gingerbread Cookie Cutouts

Decorating makes these special cookies extra special. Let the kids help!

Fancy (mild) molasses	1/2 cup	125 mL
Granulated sugar	1/3 cup	75 mL
Hard margarine (or butter), softened	1/2 cup	125 mL
Large egg	1	1
All-purpose flour	2 1/2 cups	625 mL
Baking powder	1 tsp.	5 mL
Ground ginger	1/2 tsp.	2 mL
Ground cloves	1/2 tsp.	2 mL
Ground nutmeg	1/2 tsp.	2 mL
Ground cinnamon	1/2 tsp.	2 mL
Salt	1/2 tsp.	2 mL

Place molasses, sugar and margarine in large bowl. Beat until well mixed. Add egg. Beat.

Combine remaining 7 ingredients in medium bowl. Add in small additions to molasses mixture, beating well after each addition, until all flour mixture is mixed in. Shape into a ball. Cover with plastic wrap. Chill for at least 1 hour. Divide dough into 2 equal portions. Roll out 1 portion on generously floured surface to about 1/8 inch (3 mm) thick. Cut out, using cookie cutters. Place on lightly greased cookie sheets. Repeat with second portion until all dough is used. Bake in 350°F (175°C) oven for about 12 minutes until cookie springs back when lightly pressed. Makes about 3 dozen cookies.

1 cookie: 80 Calories; 2.9 g Total Fat; 79 mg Sodium; 1 g Protein; 12 g Carbohydrate; trace Dietary Fiber

Pictured on page 133.

Pecan Squares

A thin square with a nutty top over a tender shortbread base. Sugar bubbles up through the top.

Hard margarine (or butter), softened	1/2 cup	125 mL
Brown sugar, packed	1/2 cup	125 mL
Large egg, fork-beaten	1	1
All-purpose flour	1 cup	250 mL
Brown sugar, packed	1/4 cup	60 mL
Chopped pecans	1/2 cup	125 mL
Brown sugar, packed	1/4 cup	60 mL

Cream margarine and first amount of brown sugar in large bowl. Beat in 1/2 of egg. Mix in flour. Press into greased 9 x 9 inch (22 x 22 cm) pan. Layer will be thin. Brush remaining egg over top.

Sprinkle with second amount of brown sugar and pecans.

Sprinkle third amount of brown sugar over top. Bake in 350°F (175°C) oven for 20 to 25 minutes until wooden pick inserted in center comes out clean. Cut into squares while still warm. Makes 36 squares.

1 square: 75 Calories; 4 g Total Fat; 36 mg Sodium; 1 g Protein; 9 g Carbohydrate; trace Dietary Fiber

Pictured on page 132/133.

Orange Cookies

Light and delicate. Orange flavor is just right.

Hard margarine (or butter), softened	1/2 cup	125 mL
Granulated sugar	1 cup	250 mL
Large egg	1	1
Plain yogurt	1/2 cup	125 mL
Freshly squeezed orange juice	1 tbsp.	15 mL
Vanilla	1/4 tsp.	1 mL
All-purpose flour	2 cups	500 mL
Ground almonds	1/4 cup	60 mL
Freshly grated orange peel	1 tbsp.	15 mL
Baking powder	2 tsp.	10 mL
Baking soda	1/2 tsp.	2 mL
Salt	1/2 tsp.	2 mL

Cream margarine and sugar in large bowl until fluffy. Add egg, yogurt, orange juice and vanilla. Beat.

Add remaining 6 ingredients. Stir until well mixed. Drop by heaping teaspoonfuls 1 inch (2.5 cm) apart onto lightly greased cookie sheets. Bake in 375°F (190°C) oven for about 10 minutes until lightly golden. Do not overbake. Makes about 4 dozen cookies.

1 cookie: 60 Calories; 2.5 g Total Fat; 77 mg Sodium; 1 g Protein; 9 g Carbohydrate; trace Dietary Fiber

Pictured on this page.

Photo Legend:

1. Orange Cookies, above
2. Gingerbread Cookie Cutouts, page 131
3. Chocolate Butter Tarts, page 131
4. Pecan Squares, page 131
5. Pistachio Shortbread, page 130
6. Chocolate Peanut Squares, page 134

Chocolate Peanut Squares

*These cut best when chilled but hold up well
at room temperature for serving.*

All-purpose flour	1 1/4 cups	300 mL
Graham cracker crumbs	3/4 cup	175 mL
Brown sugar, packed	1/3 cup	75 mL
Baking powder	1/2 tsp.	2 mL
Large egg, fork-beaten	1	1
Hard margarine (or butter), melted	1/2 cup	125 mL
Miniature colored marshmallows	3 cups	750 mL
TOPPING		
Hard margarine (or butter)	1/4 cup	60 mL
Golden corn syrup	2/3 cup	150 mL
Milk (or semisweet) chocolate chips	1 1/3 cups	325 mL
Crisp rice cereal	2 cups	500 mL
Roasted salted peanuts, coarsely chopped	1 cup	250 mL

Combine flour, graham crumbs, brown sugar and baking powder in large bowl. Make a well in center.

Add egg and margarine to well. Mix until no visible flour remains. Pack into bottom of foil-lined and greased 9 x 13 inch (22 x 33 cm) pan. Bake in 350°F (175°C) oven for about 12 minutes until firm.

Scatter marshmallows over crust. Bake in oven for 1 1/2 to 2 minutes until just puffy.

Topping: Melt margarine in large heavy saucepan. Add corn syrup and chocolate chips. Heat and stir on low for about 5 minutes until chocolate chips are melted and smooth.

Quickly stir in cereal and peanuts. Immediately spoon over marshmallows. Spread with a fork as best you can. Chill before cutting. Cuts into 54 pieces.

1 piece: 110 Calories; 5.6 g Total Fat; 90 mg Sodium; 2 g Protein; 14 g Carbohydrate; 1 g Dietary Fiber

Pictured on page 132/133.

Apple Cider Punch

*Tangy, red, sweet punch that looks pretty as is,
or garnish mug rim with a slice of fresh orange.*

Cran-apple juice	8 cups	2 L
Granulated sugar	1/2 cup	125 mL
Orange slices	4	4
Cinnamon sticks (6 inch, 15 cm, each)	2	2

Combine all 4 ingredients in large saucepan. Simmer, uncovered, for 15 minutes to blend flavors. Makes 7 1/2 cups (1.9 L).

1 cup (250 mL): 244 Calories; trace Total Fat; 6 mg Sodium; trace Protein; 62 g Carbohydrate; trace Dietary Fiber

Pictured on page 135.

Apple Spiced Tea

Rich amber color with strong apple aroma.

Apple juice	4 1/2 cups	1.1 L
Cinnamon stick (3 inch, 7.5 cm), broken up	1	1
Granulated sugar	1 tsp.	5 mL
Orange pekoe tea bags	2	2

Combine apple juice, cinnamon and sugar in medium saucepan. Bring to a boil. Remove from heat.

Add tea bags. Cover. Steep for 5 minutes. Remove and discard tea bags. Strain liquid into glasses. Discard solids. Makes 4 1/2 cups (1.1 L).

1 cup (250 mL): 135 Calories; 0.3 g Total Fat; 12 mg Sodium; 1 g Protein; 33 g Carbohydrate; trace Dietary Fiber

Pictured on page 135.

Hot Irish Chocolate

Packs a pleasant punch!

Milk	2 1/2 cups	625 mL
Milk chocolate chips	1/2 cup	125 mL
Irish whiskey	1/2 cup	125 mL
Granulated sugar	1 tbsp.	15 mL
Whipped cream (optional)	1/4 cup	60 mL
Chocolate shavings, sprinkle (optional)		

Heat milk in medium saucepan. Add chocolate chips. Heat and stir until chips are melted.

Add whiskey and sugar. Stir. Pour into 4 heavy glasses or mugs.

Top each with 1 tbsp. (15 mL) whipped cream. Sprinkle chocolate shavings over top. Makes 3 1/2 cups (875 mL).

1 cup (250 mL): 299 Calories; 9.7 g Total Fat; 113 mg Sodium; 8 g Protein; 27 g Carbohydrate; 1 g Dietary Fiber

Pictured on page 135.

Top Left: Rum Toddy Tempest, page 136
Top Right: Hot Irish Chocolate, above
Bottom Left: Apple Spiced Tea, above
Bottom Right Apple Cider Punch, this page

Rum Toddy Tempest

Spicy orange and rum flavor. Great on a cold winter's night or after a skating party.

Prepared orange juice	2 cups	500 mL
Cranberry cocktail	1 cup	250 mL
Spiced rum	1 cup	250 mL
Granulated sugar	1/4 cup	60 mL
Whole cloves	2	2
Cinnamon sticks (6 inch, 15 cm, each), broken into thirds	2	2
Whole allspice	1	1
Butter (not margarine)	4 tsp.	20 mL

Ground nutmeg, sprinkle

Combine first 8 ingredients in medium saucepan. Bring to a boil. Reduce heat. Simmer, uncovered, for 5 minutes. Strain liquid into heavy glasses or mugs. Discard solids.

Sprinkle nutmeg over individual servings. Makes 4 cups (1 L).

1 cup (250 mL): 320 Calories; 4 g Total Fat; 44 mg Sodium; 1 g Protein; 37 g Carbohydrate; trace Dietary Fiber

Pictured on page 135.

Banana Bread Ring

Moist with a rich banana flavor. A must for that huge brunch gathering. Bananas and peanut butter go together so well.

Hard margarine (or butter), softened	3/4 cup	175 mL
Granulated sugar	1 1/2 cups	375 mL
Large eggs	3	3
Mashed banana (about 3 large)	1 1/2 cups	375 mL
Vanilla	1 tsp.	5 mL
All-purpose flour	2 2/3 cups	650 mL
Baking powder	1 tsp.	5 mL
Baking soda	1 1/2 tsp.	7 mL
Salt	3/4 tsp.	4 mL
Chopped walnuts (or pecans), optional	1 cup	250 mL
PEANUT BUTTER GLAZE		
Smooth peanut butter	1/4 cup	60 mL
Hot water	2 tbsp.	30 mL
Vanilla	1 tsp.	5 mL
Icing (confectioner's) sugar, sifted	2/3 cup	150 mL

Cream margarine and sugar in large bowl. Beat in eggs, 1 at a time. Add banana and vanilla. Beat until well combined.

Add next 5 ingredients. Stir until just moistened. Turn into greased 10 x 4 1/2 inch (25 x 11 cm) angel food tube pan. Bake in 350°F (175°C) oven for 50 to 60 minutes until wooden pick inserted in center comes out clean. Let stand in pan for 20 minutes. Turn out onto wire rack to cool completely.

Peanut Butter Glaze: Stir peanut butter and hot water together in liquid measure until smooth.

Stir in vanilla. Slowly add icing sugar, stirring well, until barely pourable consistency. Makes 1/2 cup (125 mL) glaze. Drizzle over cake. Cuts into 24 pieces.

1 piece with 1 tsp. (5 mL) glaze: 211 Calories; 8.4 g Total Fat; 263 mg Sodium; 3 g Protein; 32 g Carbohydrate; 1 g Dietary Fiber

Pictured on page 137.

Strawberry Loaf

Spread with butter or cream cheese or serve plain. Very moist.

Mashed frozen whole strawberries (or fresh)	1 cup	250 mL
Hard margarine (or butter), softened	6 tbsp.	100 mL
Granulated sugar	1 cup	250 mL
Large eggs	2	2
Water	1/3 cup	75 mL
Vanilla	1/2 tsp.	2 mL
All-purpose flour	1 3/4 cups	425 mL
Baking soda	1 tsp.	5 mL
Baking powder	1/2 tsp.	2 mL
Salt	3/4 tsp.	4 mL
Ground cinnamon	1/2 tsp.	2 mL
Chopped walnuts (optional)	1/2 cup	125 mL

Bring strawberries to a boil in small saucepan, stirring often. Reduce heat. Simmer for 1 minute. Cool.

Cream margarine and sugar in large bowl. Beat in eggs, 1 at a time. Add water and vanilla. Mix. Stir in strawberries.

Measure remaining 6 ingredients into medium bowl. Stir well. Add to batter. Stir until just moistened. Turn into greased 9 x 5 x 3 inch (22 x 12.5 x 7.5 cm) loaf pan. Bake in 350°F (175°C) oven for 60 to 65 minutes until wooden pick inserted in center comes out clean. Let stand in pan for 15 minutes. Turn out onto wire rack to cool. Cuts into 18 slices.

1 slice: 139 Calories; 4.6 g Total Fat; 233 mg Sodium; 2 g Protein; 22 g Carbohydrate; 1 g Dietary Fiber

Pictured on page 137.

Left: Strawberry Loaf, page 136   Center: Chippy Date Bread, below   Right: Banana Bread Ring, page 136

Chippy Date Bread

Moist and chocolaty. Not too sweet and very good.

Granulated sugar	1/3 cup	75 mL
Brown sugar, packed	1/2 cup	125 mL
Cooking oil	1/4 cup	60 mL
Large eggs	2	2
Cold prepared strong coffee	1 1/2 cups	375 mL
All-purpose flour	3 cups	750 mL
Baking powder	1 tbsp.	15 mL
Baking soda	1/4 tsp.	1 mL
Salt	1 tsp.	5 mL
Chopped dates	3/4 cup	175 mL
Semisweet chocolate chips	1 cup	250 mL

Beat both sugars, cooking oil and eggs together in large bowl. Slowly beat in coffee.

Combine flour, baking powder, baking soda and salt in medium bowl. Add to egg mixture. Stir until moistened.

Add dates and chocolate chips to batter. Stir. Turn into greased 9 x 5 x 3 inch (22 x 12.5 x 7.5 cm) loaf pan. Bake in 350°F (175°C) oven for about 1 hour until wooden pick inserted in center comes out clean. Let stand in pan for 15 minutes. Turn out onto wire rack to cool. Cuts into 16 slices.

1 slice: 255 Calories; 7.9 g Total Fat; 252 mg Sodium; 4 g Protein; 44 g Carbohydrate; 2 g Dietary Fiber

Pictured above.

Fudge Mini Muffins

Cute little brownie-like muffins.

Hard margarine (or butter)	1/2 cup	125 mL
Semisweet chocolate baking squares (1 oz., 28 g, each), cut up	2	2
All-purpose flour	1/2 cup	125 mL
Granulated sugar	3/4 cup	175 mL
Salt	1/16 tsp.	0.5 mL
Cocoa	2 tbsp.	30 mL
Large eggs, fork-beaten	2	2
Vanilla	1/2 tsp.	2 mL
Chopped walnuts (or pecans)	1/2 cup	125 mL

Melt margarine and chocolate in large heavy saucepan on low, stirring often, until smooth.

Add next 4 ingredients. Beat well.

Stir in eggs, vanilla and walnuts. Fill greased mini-muffin cups with about 4 tsp. (20 mL) batter. Bake in 325°F (160°C) oven for about 20 minutes until wooden pick inserted in center comes out clean. Let stand in pan for 5 minutes. Turn out onto wire racks to cool. Makes 2 dozen muffins.

1 muffin: 107 Calories; 6.8 g Total Fat; 59 mg Sodium; 2 g Protein; 11 g Carbohydrate; trace Dietary Fiber

Pictured on page 139.

Ever-Ready Bran Muffins

So handy to have this batter in the refrigerator.
Bake a few at a time for a nutritious breakfast.

All-bran cereal	4 cups	1 L
Natural wheat bran	2 cups	500 mL
Boiling water	2 cups	500 mL
Hard margarine (or butter), softened	1 cup	250 mL
Granulated sugar	2 3/4 cups	675 mL
Large eggs	4	4
Fancy (mild) molasses	3 tbsp.	50 mL
Buttermilk (or reconstituted from powder)	4 cups	1 L
All-purpose flour	5 cups	1.25 L
Baking soda	1 1/2 tbsp.	25 mL
Salt	1 tsp.	5 mL
Dark raisins	2 cups	500 mL

Combine cereal, bran and boiling water in medium bowl. Set aside.

Cream margarine and sugar in large bowl. Beat in eggs, 1 at a time. Add molasses and buttermilk. Mix well.

Combine flour, baking soda and salt in separate large bowl. Add to buttermilk mixture. Add bran mixture. Stir until just combined.

Add raisins. Stir. Makes 16 cups (4 L) batter. Turn into 16 cup (4 L) container. Cover. Chill. Store in refrigerator for up to 4 weeks. To bake, fill greased muffin cups 3/4 full. Bake in 400°F (205°C) oven for about 18 minutes until wooden pick inserted in center comes out clean. Let stand in pan for 5 minutes. Turn out onto wire racks to cool. Makes 4 dozen.

1 muffin: 191 Calories; 5 g Total Fat; 313 mg Sodium; 4 g Protein; 36 g Carbohydrate; 4 g Dietary Fiber

Pictured on page 139.

Pumpkin Chip Muffins

Spicy pumpkin and chocolate chips.

Hard margarine (or butter), softened	6 tbsp.	100 mL
Brown sugar, packed	1 cup	250 mL
Large egg	1	1
Vanilla	1 tsp.	5 mL
Canned pumpkin (not filling)	1 cup	250 mL
Milk	1/2 cup	125 mL
All-purpose flour	2 cups	500 mL
Semisweet chocolate chips	1/2 cup	125 mL
Baking powder	1 tbsp.	15 mL
Ground cinnamon	1 tsp.	5 mL
Ground ginger	3/4 tsp.	4 mL
Ground nutmeg	1/2 tsp.	2 mL
Ground cloves	1/8 tsp.	0.5 mL
Salt	1/2 tsp.	2 mL

Cream margarine, brown sugar and egg in large bowl until smooth. Beat in vanilla, pumpkin and milk.

Combine remaining 8 ingredients in medium bowl. Add to pumpkin mixture. Mix until just moistened. Fill greased muffin cups 3/4 full. Bake in 375°F (190°C) oven for about 25 minutes until wooden pick inserted in center comes out clean. Let stand in pan for 5 minutes. Turn out onto wire rack to cool. Makes 12 muffins.

1 muffin: 261 Calories; 8.9 g Total Fat; 280 mg Sodium; 4 g Protein; 43 g Carbohydrate; 2 g Dietary Fiber

Pictured on page 139.

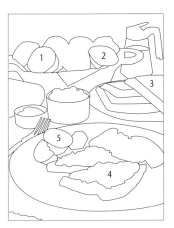

Creamed Eggs On Toast

Chopped eggs in a tasty sauce that
makes a nice topping for toast.

All-purpose flour	3 tbsp.	50 mL
Onion powder	1/4 tsp.	1 mL
Chicken bouillon powder	1 tsp.	5 mL
Salt	1/2 tsp.	2 mL
Pepper	1/8 tsp.	0.5 mL
Milk	1 1/2 cups	375 mL
Hard margarine (or butter)	1 tbsp.	15 mL
Hard-boiled eggs, sliced both ways in egg slicer (or chopped)	6	6
Bread slices, toasted (buttered, optional)	6	6
Chives (or green onion), for garnish		

Combine flour, onion powder, bouillon powder, salt and pepper in medium saucepan. Gradually add milk, a bit at a time, stirring after each addition until smooth.

Add margarine. Heat and stir until boiling and thickened.

Add eggs. Stir until heated through. Makes 2 1/2 cups (625 mL).

Place 1 1/2 pieces of toast on each of 4 luncheon plates. Spoon egg mixture over toast. Sprinkle chives over top. Serves 4.

1 serving: 307 Calories; 13.4 g Total Fat; 837 mg Sodium; 17 g Protein; 29 g Carbohydrate; 1 g Dietary Fiber

Pictured on page 139.

Variation: Lay 1 slice of ham or cooked Canadian back bacon on toast before spooning egg mixture over top.

Southern Waffles

A touch of molasses and cornmeal
makes these waffles special.

Large eggs	2	2
Milk	1 cup	250 mL
Fancy (mild) molasses	1 1/2 tbsp.	25 mL
Salt	1 tsp.	5 mL
All-purpose flour	1 1/2 cups	375 mL
Yellow cornmeal	4 tsp.	20 mL
Milk	1 cup	250 mL
Cooking oil	1/3 cup	75 mL
All-purpose flour	1 cup	250 mL
Baking powder	2 1/2 tbsp.	37 mL

Beat eggs in medium bowl. Add first amount of milk, molasses and salt. Stir.

Add first amount of flour and cornmeal. Mix.

Add second amount of milk and cooking oil. Mix.

Mix second amount of flour and baking powder in small bowl. Stir into batter. Batter will still be lumpy. Cook 1/2 cup (125 mL) batter in hot waffle iron until golden. Repeat with remaining batter. Makes ten 4 x 4 1/2 inch (10 x 11 cm) waffles.

1 waffle: 239 Calories; 9.5 g Total Fat; 555 mg Sodium; 6 g Protein; 32 g Carbohydrate; 1 g Dietary Fiber

Pictured on page 139.

Popover With Eggs

Yorkshire pudding base topped with scrambled eggs.

Large eggs	2	2
Milk	1 cup	250 mL
Cooking oil	1 tbsp.	15 mL
All-purpose flour	1 cup	250 mL
Salt	1/4 tsp.	1 mL
Large eggs	6	6
Milk (or water)	1/4 cup	60 mL
Hard margarine (or butter)	1 tbsp.	15 mL
Salt	1/2 tsp.	2 mL
Pepper	1/8 tsp.	0.5 mL

Beat eggs in large bowl until light and fluffy.

Add remaining 4 ingredients. Beat until smooth. Preheat greased 9 inch (22 cm) pie plate in 400°F (205°C) oven for 3 to 4 minutes until heated. Pour batter into hot pie plate. Bake for 30 minutes. Reduce heat to 350°F (175°C). Bake for 10 to 15 minutes until center is cooked. Cut popover into 6 wedges.

Fork-beat eggs and milk in medium bowl.

Melt margarine in frying pan on medium. Add eggs, salt and pepper. Cook, stirring frequently, until eggs are set. Serve eggs over wedges. Makes 6 wedges.

1 wedge: 143 Calories; 4.6 g Total Fat; 142 mg Sodium; 6 g Protein; 19 g Carbohydrate; 1 g Dietary Fiber

Pictured on page 141.

Top Left: Crustless Salmon Quiche, below   Bottom Center: Cheesy French Toast, below   Right: Popover With Eggs, page 140

Crustless Salmon Quiche

Convenient and easy to prepare.
Forms its own crust while baking.

Chopped onion	1 cup	250 mL
Hard margarine (or butter)	2 tsp.	10 mL
Large eggs	6	6
Skim evaporated milk	1/2 cup	125 mL
Can of red salmon, drained, flaked, skin and round bones removed	7 3/4 oz.	220 g
Grated Dofino (or Havarti) cheese	1 cup	250 mL
Parsley flakes (or 2 tbsp., 30 mL, chopped fresh parsley)	1 1/2 tsp.	7 mL
Salt	1/2 tsp.	2 mL
Pepper	1/4 tsp.	1 mL

Sauté onion in margarine in frying pan until soft.

Beat eggs in medium bowl. Add remaining 6 ingredients. Stir. Add onion. Turn into greased 9 inch (22 cm) pie plate. Bake in 350°F (175°C) oven for about 45 minutes until knife inserted near center comes out clean. Serves 6.

1 serving: 234 Calories; 13.6 g Total Fat; 631 mg Sodium; 21 g Protein; 6 g Carbohydrate; trace Dietary Fiber

Pictured above.

Cheesy French Toast

A more moist French toast than the usual. Use only a small amount of syrup to allow cream cheese flavor to be tasted.

Cream cheese, softened	1/4 cup	60 mL
Day-old bread slices (see Note)	6	6
Ground cinnamon	1/4 – 1/2 tsp.	1 – 2 mL
Large eggs	3	3
Milk	2/3 cup	150 mL
Hard margarine (or butter), melted	2 tbsp.	30 mL
Vanilla	3/4 tsp.	4 mL
Salt	1/16 tsp.	0.5 mL

Spread 2 tsp. (10 mL) cream cheese on 1 side of each bread slice. Arrange slices, cream cheese side up, in well greased 9 x 13 inch (22 x 33 cm) pan. Sprinkle cinnamon over cream cheese.

Beat eggs lightly in medium bowl. Add milk, margarine, vanilla and salt. Mix. Slowly pour over bread slices. Bake, uncovered, on center rack in 400°F (205°C) oven for 20 to 25 minutes until set. Makes 6 slices.

1 slice: 218 Calories; 11.2 g Total Fat; 283 mg Sodium; 7 g Protein; 16 g Carbohydrate; 1 g Dietary Fiber

Pictured above.

Note: Use whatever type of bread you like, but Texas toast fits best in the 9 x 13 inch (22 x 33 cm) pan.

Broccoli Cauliflower Salad, this page   Walnut And Green Leaf Salad, below

Walnut And Green Leaf Salad

Bright green lettuce with fresh basil and crunchy nut topping.

Hard margarine (or butter)	1 tbsp.	15 mL
Coarsely chopped walnuts	1/2 cup	125 mL
Large head of green leaf lettuce, cut or torn	1	1
Medium red pepper, slivered	1	1
Medium tomato, diced	1	1
Olive (or cooking) oil	3 tbsp.	50 mL
Walnut (or cooking) oil	2 tbsp.	30 mL
Lemon juice	3 tbsp.	50 mL
Honey Dijon mustard	1 tsp.	5 mL
Chopped fresh sweet basil	1/4 cup	60 mL
Granulated sugar	1/2 tsp.	2 mL
Salt	1/4 tsp.	1 mL
Freshly ground pepper	1/4 tsp.	1 mL
Freshly grated Parmesan cheese, sprinkle		

Melt margarine in small frying pan. Add walnuts. Stir for about 2 minutes until fragrant. Cool.

Put lettuce into large salad bowl. Add red pepper and tomato.

Combine next 8 ingredients in small bowl. Drizzle over salad. Toss until well coated.

Sprinkle with walnuts and Parmesan cheese. Makes 10 cups (2.5 L).

1 cup (250 mL): 129 Calories; 12 g Total Fat; 86 mg Sodium; 3 g Protein; 5 g Carbohydrate; 1 g Dietary Fiber

Pictured above.

Broccoli Cauliflower Salad

Red, white and green—great for Christmas!

Medium bow pasta	1 1/2 cups	375 mL
Boiling water	12 cups	3 L
Cooking oil (optional)	1 tbsp.	15 mL
Salt	2 tsp.	10 mL
Broccoli, cut bite size	3 cups	750 mL
Cauliflower, cut bite size	3 cups	750 mL
Cherry tomatoes, cut in half	15	15
CREAMY DRESSING		
Light mayonnaise	1/2 cup	125 mL
Light sour cream	1/2 cup	125 mL
Apple cider vinegar	2 tbsp.	30 mL
Prepared mustard	1 tbsp.	15 mL
Liquid honey	1 1/2 tsp.	7 mL
Granulated sugar	1 tsp.	5 mL
Dill weed	1/4 tsp.	1 mL
Salt	1/4 tsp.	1 mL
Freshly ground pepper, sprinkle		

Cook pasta in boiling water, cooking oil and salt in large uncovered pot or Dutch oven for 10 to 12 minutes until tender but firm. Drain. Rinse with cold water. Drain well. Turn into large bowl.

Add broccoli, cauliflower and tomatoes. Toss.

Creamy Dressing: Stir all 9 ingredients together in small bowl. Add to pasta mixture. Gently toss until coated. Makes 9 cups (2.25 L).

1/2 cup (125 mL): 70 Calories; 2.9 g Total Fat; 105 mg Sodium; 2 g Protein; 10 g Carbohydrate; 1 g Dietary Fiber

Pictured on this page.

Potato Corn Chowder

A meal in itself. Has a hint of bacon with the sweetness of creamed corn.

Bacon slices, diced	4	4
Large onion, diced	1	1
Medium potatoes, grated	4	4
All-purpose flour	2 tbsp.	30 mL
Chicken bouillon powder	2 tsp.	10 mL
Milk	4 cups	1 L
Cans of cream-style corn (14 oz., 398 mL, each)	2	2
Salt	1/2 tsp.	2 mL
Pepper	1/4 – 1/2 tsp.	1 – 2 mL

Real bacon bits, for garnish
Paprika, sprinkle, for garnish

Fry bacon in large saucepan until half cooked. Add onion. Sauté until onion is golden.

Add potato. Stir well. Add flour and bouillon powder. Stir. Gradually stir in milk. Simmer, uncovered, for about 20 minutes, stirring occasionally, until potato is tender.

Add corn, salt and pepper. Stir.

Top individual servings with bacon bits and paprika. Makes 9 cups (2.25 L).

1 cup (250 mL): 188 Calories; 3.2 g Total Fat; 655 mg Sodium; 8 g Protein; 35 g Carbohydrate; 2 g Dietary Fiber

Pictured on page 145.

Cream Of Onion Soup

Creamy and satisfying. Delicate onion flavor.

Medium Spanish onions, cut in half lengthwise and very thinly sliced	3	3
Hard margarine (or butter)	1/4 cup	60 mL
All-purpose flour	1/4 cup	60 mL
Salt	1 tsp.	5 mL
Pepper	1/4 tsp.	1 mL
Ground thyme	1/4 tsp.	1 mL
Chicken stock	2 cups	500 mL
Milk	2 cups	500 mL

Grated medium Cheddar cheese, for garnish
Chopped chives, for garnish

Sauté onion in margarine in large pot or Dutch oven, stirring occasionally, until clear and soft.

Add flour, salt, pepper and thyme. Stir until well combined. Add chicken stock and milk. Heat and stir until boiling and thickened.

Sprinkle individual servings with cheese and chives. Makes about 8 cups (2 L).

1 cup (250 mL): 123 Calories; 7.3 g Total Fat; 606 mg Sodium; 4 g Protein; 10 g Carbohydrate; 1 g Dietary Fiber

Pictured on page 145.

Vegetable Beef And Bean Soup

A load of taste in one bowl. Only 25 minutes from start to finish.

Lean ground beef	3/4 lb.	340 g
Large onion, chopped	1	1
Envelope of dry vegetable soup mix	1 1/4 oz.	40 g
Chopped celery	1/2 cup	125 mL
Baby carrots, cut into 1/4 inch (6 mm) slices	6	6
Water	3 cups	750 mL
Beef bouillon powder	1 tbsp.	15 mL
Tomato juice	1 1/2 cups	375 mL
Can of baked beans in tomato sauce	14 oz.	398 mL

Scramble-fry ground beef and onion in large saucepan until beef is no longer pink.

Add next 5 ingredients. Stir. Cover. Cook for about 15 minutes until carrots are tender.

Add tomato juice and beans. Stir until heated through. Makes 8 1/2 cups (2.1 L).

1 cup (250 mL): 171 Calories; 6.8 g Total Fat; 913 mg Sodium; 12 g Protein; 17 g Carbohydrate; 5 g Dietary Fiber

Pictured on page 145.

Fish Chowder

Pleasantly chunky with fish, potato, bacon and onion.

Fish fillets (your favorite), cut into chunks	1 lb.	454 g
Boiling water	2 cups	500 mL
Diced potato	3 cups	750 mL
Salt	1 1/2 tsp.	7 mL
Pepper	1/4 tsp.	1 mL
Bacon slices, diced	4	4
Chopped onion	1 1/2 cups	375 mL
All-purpose flour	1 tbsp.	15 mL
Can of skim evaporated milk	13 1/2 oz.	385 mL
Milk	1 cup	250 mL
Fish-shaped crackers (optional)	3/4 cup	175 mL

Place fish in large saucepan. Add boiling water. Bring to a boil. Reduce heat. Simmer, uncovered, until fish flakes easily with fork. Do not drain. Transfer fish to large plate. Flake, removing any bones.

Add potato, salt and pepper to fish water in same saucepan. Cook until tender. Do not drain. Coarsely mash potatoes while still in saucepan.

Sauté bacon in frying pan for 2 minutes. Add onion. Cook until bacon is crisp and onion is lightly browned.

Stir in flour until well blended. Add evaporated milk and milk. Heat and stir, scraping up any browned bits from pan, until boiling and thickened. Add to potato mixture. Add fish. Stir until heated through.

Top individual servings with fish-shaped crackers. Makes 8 cups (2 L).

1 cup (250 mL): 214 Calories; 6 g Total Fat; 636 mg Sodium; 18 g Protein; 22 g Carbohydrate; 1 g Dietary Fiber

Pictured on page 145.

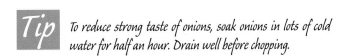

Tip *To reduce strong taste of onions, soak onions in lots of cold water for half an hour. Drain well before chopping.*

Ham And Pea Soup

Veggies make this good soup colorful and tasty.

Smoked pork hock (or meaty ham bone)	1	1
Yellow split peas	1 2/3 cups	400 mL
Water	10 cups	2.5 L
Chopped onion	1 cup	250 mL
Sliced carrot	1 cup	250 mL
Diced yellow turnip	1/2 cup	125 mL
Sliced celery	1 cup	250 mL
Grated potato	1 cup	250 mL
Salt	2 tsp.	10 mL
Pepper	1/8 tsp.	0.5 mL

Put pork hock, peas and water into large pot or Dutch oven. Stir. Bring to a boil. Reduce heat. Simmer for about 1 hour, stirring occasionally, until peas are mushy.

Add remaining 7 ingredients. Bring to a boil. Reduce heat. Simmer, uncovered, for about 20 minutes until vegetables are tender. Remove pork hock. Cut off meat. Dice. Return meat to pot. Makes about 10 cups (2.5 L).

1 cup (250 mL): 186 Calories; 3.4 g Total Fat; 515 mg Sodium; 12 g Protein; 28 g Carbohydrate; 4 g Dietary Fiber

Pictured on page 145.

Top Left: Ham And Pea Soup, above
Top Right: Potato Corn Chowder, page 143
Center Left: Fish Chowder, this page
Center Right: Cream Of Onion Soup, page 143
Bottom: Vegetable Beef And Bean Soup, page 143

New Year's Day Buffet

It's the last great feast of the
holiday season—why not end it in style?
Offer weary family and friends
a crowd-pleasing selection of food
in the relaxed atmosphere of a buffet.
Don't forget to raise a toast to
the first day of the New Year!

Antipasto Clock
Beef Turnovers
Nutty Ham Canapés
Sauced Mini Smokies
Smoked Salmon Rolls

Cranberry Bowl

Chorizo Chili
Polenta
Pumpernickel Bread

Cran-Raisin Pie
Blueberry Pecan Cake

Beef Turnovers

An excellent blend of flavors in a golden pastry.

FILLING

Lean ground beef	1/4 lb.	113 g
Garlic clove, minced (or 1/4 tsp., 1 mL, powder)	1	1
Salt	1/4 tsp.	1 mL
Chopped sun-dried tomatoes, softened in boiling water for 5 minutes before chopping	1/4 cup	60 mL
Chopped green onion	2 tbsp.	30 mL
Chopped fresh sweet basil	1 1/2 tsp.	7 mL
Part-skim ricotta cheese	1/4 cup	60 mL

DOUGH

All-purpose flour	2 cups	500 mL
Baking powder	4 tsp.	20 mL
Ground oregano	1/2 tsp.	2 mL
Salt	3/4 tsp.	4 mL
Garlic oil (or cooking oil and 1/8 tsp., 0.5 mL, garlic powder)	1/4 cup	60 mL
Milk	3/4 cup	175 mL
Egg white (large), fork-beaten	1	1

Filling: Scramble-fry ground beef, garlic and salt in non-stick frying pan for 4 to 5 minutes until beef is no longer pink.

Add tomatoes, green onion, basil and cheese. Mix well. Cool. Makes 3/4 cup (175 mL) filling.

Dough: Combine flour, baking powder, oregano and salt in large bowl. Add garlic oil. Stir in milk with fork until just combined. Turn out onto lightly floured surface. Knead 8 to 10 times. Do not over knead. Roll out to 1/8 inch (3 mm) thickness. Cut into 3 inch (7.5 cm) circles. Place about 1 tsp. (5 mL) filling in center of each circle. Brush edges with water. Fold dough over. Press with fork to seal.

Cut 2 to 3 slits in tops with sharp knife. Brush with egg white. Arrange in single layer on greased baking sheet. Bake in 400°F (205°C) oven for 15 to 20 minutes until golden. Makes about 36 turnovers.

1 turnover: 54 Calories; 2.4 g Total Fat; 124 mg Sodium; 2 g Protein; 6 g Carbohydrate; trace Dietary Fiber

Pictured on page 148 and on page 149.

Nutty Ham Canapés

A really nutty-flavored ham spread for your favorite bread.

Can of ham flakes, drained	6 1/2 oz.	184 g
Light sour cream	1/4 cup	60 mL
Light mayonnaise	1/4 cup	60 mL
Prepared mustard	1 tsp.	5 mL
Curry powder	1/2 tsp.	2 mL
Parsley flakes	1 tsp.	5 mL
Onion powder	1/4 tsp.	1 mL
Finely chopped walnuts (or your favorite nuts)	1/3 cup	75 mL
Bread slices, crusts removed and bread quartered	12	12

Mix first 8 ingredients in medium bowl.

Place bread on ungreased baking sheet. Spread 1 1/2 tsp. (7 mL) ham mixture on each piece. Bake, uncovered, in 400°F (205°C) oven for 10 minutes until topping is golden. Makes 48 appetizers.

1 appetizer: 31 Calories; 1.5 g Total Fat; 81 mg Sodium; 1 g Protein; 3 g Carbohydrate; trace Dietary Fiber

Pictured on page 148 and on page 149.

Sauced Mini Smokies

Sweet and sour sauce goes well with cocktail-size smokies.

Cornstarch	2 tbsp.	30 mL
Brown sugar, packed	1 1/2 cups	375 mL
White vinegar	1/2 cup	125 mL
Water	1/2 cup	125 mL
Pineapple juice	1 cup	250 mL
Soy sauce	3 tbsp.	50 mL
Package of precooked mini smokies (or small sausages)	2 lbs.	900 g

Stir cornstarch, brown sugar and vinegar in large saucepan until smooth.

Stir in water, pineapple juice and soy sauce. Heat and stir on medium until boiling and thickened. Makes 2 1/2 cups (625 mL) sauce.

Add smokies. Heat through. Serves 8.

1 serving: 510 Calories; 28.4 g Total Fat; 1481 mg Sodium; 12 g Protein; 52 g Carbohydrate; trace Dietary Fiber

Pictured on page 148.

Smoked Salmon Rolls

Striking white and pink rolls with a creamy taste that won't disappoint.

Light cream cheese, softened	4 oz.	125 g
Salad dressing (or mayonnaise)	1/4 cup	60 mL
White vinegar	1 tsp.	5 mL
Dill weed	1/2 tsp.	2 mL
Parsley flakes	1/2 tsp.	2 mL
Onion powder	1/4 tsp.	1 mL
Flour tortillas (8 inch, 20 cm, size)	4	4
Thinly sliced smoked salmon	8 oz.	225 g

Mash first 6 ingredients together well with fork in small bowl. Makes 3/4 cup (175 mL) filling.

Spread about 3 tbsp. (50 mL) filling over each tortilla.

Lay smoked salmon over top, being sure to cover all across center of tortilla. Fill in here and there with remaining salmon. Snugly roll up, jelly roll-style. Wrap each roll in plastic wrap. Chill for at least 1 hour. Trim ends. Cut into 3/4 inch (2 cm) slices. Each roll cuts into about 10 slices, for a total of 40.

1 slice: 37 Calories; 2.4 g Total Fat; 80 mg Sodium; 2 g Protein; 2 g Carbohydrate; trace Dietary Fiber

Pictured on page 148 and on page 149.

Photo Legend next page:

1. Sauced Mini Smokies, this page
2. Cranberry Bowl, page 150
3. Nutty Ham Canapés, this page
4. Smoked Salmon Rolls, above
5. Beef Turnovers, page 146
6. Antipasto Clock, page 154

Cranberry Bowl

*Refreshing, sweet and fizzy rose-colored punch.
Instead of ice cubes, chill this punch with
frozen cranberries or frozen pineapple rings.*

Can of frozen concentrated orange juice (12 1/2 oz., 355 mL, size)	1/2	1/2
Cranberry cocktail	6 cups	1.5 L
Pineapple juice	2 cups	500 mL
Ginger ale	8 cups	2 L

Combine orange juice, cranberry cocktail and pineapple juice in punch bowl. Chill.

Add ginger ale just before serving. Makes 16 cups (4 L).

1 cup (250 mL): 141 Calories; 0.1 g Total Fat; 14 mg Sodium; trace Protein; 36 g Carbohydrate; trace Dietary Fiber

Pictured on page 149.

Chorizo Chili

*Garnish individual servings with a dollop of sour cream and
finely diced red onion. Spicy hot flavors are perfect with
cold beer for your next casual get-together.*

Chopped onion	1 cup	250 mL
Medium red pepper, diced	1	1
Garlic clove, minced (or 1/4 tsp., 1 mL, powder)	1	1
Cooking oil	2 tsp.	10 mL
Lean ground beef	1 lb.	454 g
Chili sauce	3/4 cup	175 mL
Chili powder	1 tbsp.	15 mL
Beef bouillon powder	1 tbsp.	15 mL
Paprika	1 tbsp.	15 mL
Dried whole oregano	1 tbsp.	15 mL
Ground cumin	1 tsp.	5 mL
Cayenne pepper	1/4 tsp.	1 mL
Pepper	1 tsp.	5 mL
Liquid smoke	1/2 tsp.	2 mL
Cans of diced tomatoes, with juice (14 oz., 398 mL, each)	2	2
Beer	1 cup	250 mL
Can of tomato paste	5 1/2 oz.	156 mL
Bay leaf	1	1
Cooked chorizo sausage, cut into 1/4 inch (6 mm) slices (about 3 cups, 750 mL)	1 lb.	454 g
Can of black beans, drained and rinsed	19 oz.	540 mL
Currants	1/3 cup	75 mL

Sauté onion, red pepper and garlic in cooking oil in large pot or Dutch oven until onion is soft.

Add ground beef. Scramble-fry for about 5 minutes until beef is no longer pink. Drain.

Add next 9 ingredients. Stir. Cook for 3 minutes to blend flavors.

Add tomatoes, beer, tomato paste and bay leaf. Stir. Bring to a boil. Reduce heat. Cover. Simmer for 1 1/2 hours, stirring occasionally. Remove and discard bay leaf.

Add sausage, beans and currants. Stir. Simmer, uncovered, for about 30 minutes until thickened. Makes 8 cups (2 L).

1 cup (250 mL): 434 Calories; 21.9 g Total Fat; 1408 mg Sodium; 28 g Protein; 31 g Carbohydrate; 6 g Dietary Fiber

Pictured on page 151.

Tip *To save time and effort when cooking chili, make a double or triple batch and freeze the leftovers in serving-sized containers. For variety, try chili served inside bread bowls, spooned over hot dogs, slathered onto burgers, folded into omelets or even topped over spaghetti.*

Left: Pumpernickel Bread, page 152   Top Center: Polenta, below   Bottom Right: Chorizo Chili, page 150

Polenta

So good served with chili or stew.
Great blend of chicken broth, herb and cheese flavors.

Can of condensed chicken broth	10 oz.	284 mL
Water	1 cup	250 mL
Finely grated carrot	1/2 cup	125 mL
Cayenne pepper	1/8 tsp.	0.5 mL
Cold water	3/4 cup	175 mL
Yellow cornmeal	1 cup	250 mL
Grated Parmesan cheese	2 tbsp.	30 mL
Parsley flakes	1/2 tsp.	2 mL
Italian no-salt seasoning (such as Mrs. Dash)	1/2 tsp.	2 mL
Salt	1/2 tsp.	2 mL

Combine chicken broth, first amount of water, carrot and cayenne pepper in large non-stick frying pan. Bring to a boil.

Combine second amount of water and cornmeal in small bowl. Gradually stir into chicken broth mixture. Heat and stir on medium-low for about 15 minutes until boiling and very thick.

Add Parmesan cheese, parsley, seasoning and salt. Pour into greased 9 inch (22 cm) round cake pan. Cover. Chill for at least 2 hours until firm. Turn out onto cutting board. Cut into 12 wedges. Place wedges 1 inch (2.5 cm) apart on greased baking sheet. Bake in 400°F (205°C) oven for about 30 minutes, turning once, until edges are golden and crisp. Makes 12 wedges.

1 wedge: 60 Calories; 0.8 g Total Fat; 278 mg Sodium; 3 g Protein; 10 g Carbohydrate; 1 g Dietary Fiber

Pictured above.

Variation: Fry polenta wedges in 2 tsp. (10 mL) olive (or cooking) oil in non-stick frying pan until golden.

Pumpernickel Bread

*Excellent for making sandwiches with
a distinctive caraway seed taste.*

Fancy (mild) molasses	1 tsp.	5 mL
Warm water	1/4 cup	60 mL
Active dry yeast	2 tbsp.	30 mL
Warm water	1 cup	250 mL
Fancy (mild) molasses	3 tbsp.	50 mL
All-purpose flour	2 cups	500 mL
Cocoa	2 tbsp.	30 mL
Caraway seeds	2 tsp.	10 mL
Salt	2 tsp.	10 mL
Rye flour	1 cup	250 mL
Whole wheat flour	1/2 cup	125 mL

Combine first amounts of molasses and water in medium bowl. Stir until smooth. Sprinkle yeast over top. Let stand for 10 minutes. Stir to dissolve yeast.

Food Processor Method: Put remaining 8 ingredients into food processor fitted with dough or knife blade. With motor running, slowly add yeast mixture through feed chute. Process for about 2 minutes until dough pulls away from sides of food processor.

Hand Method: Transfer yeast mixture to large bowl. Add next 6 ingredients. Stir until sticky dough forms. Work in rye and whole wheat flours for about 10 minutes until dough is smooth and firm.

To Complete: Place dough in greased bowl, turning once to grease top. Cover with tea towel. Let stand in oven with light on and door closed for about 1 hour until doubled in bulk. Punch dough down. Divide into 2 equal portions. Shape each portion into a ball. Arrange 2 inches (5 cm) apart on greased baking sheet. Grease surface of dough. Cover with tea towel. Let stand in oven with light on and door closed for about 1 1/2 hours until doubled in size. Cut tic-tac-toe design on top of dough with very sharp knife. Bake in center of 375°F (190°C) oven for 20 minutes until browned and hollow-sounding when tapped. Makes 2 loaves, each cutting into 16 slices, for a total of 32 slices.

1 slice: 57 Calories; 0.3 g Total Fat; 150 mg Sodium; 2 g Protein; 12 g Carbohydrate; 1 g Dietary Fiber

Pictured on page 151.

Cran-Raisin Pie

*Real whipping cream is a must to mellow
the tangy sweet flavor of this delicious pie.*

Granulated sugar	2 1/4 cups	550 mL
All-purpose flour	1/3 cup	75 mL
Salt	3/4 tsp.	4 mL
Boiling water	1 1/2 cups	375 mL
Raisins	3 cups	750 mL
Fresh (or frozen, thawed) cranberries	4 1/2 cups	1.1 L
Vanilla	1 1/2 tsp.	7 mL
Unbaked 9 inch (22 cm) pie shells, your own or a mix	2	2
Whipping cream	2 cups	500 mL
Granulated sugar	4 tsp.	20 mL
Vanilla	1 tsp.	5 mL

Mix sugar, flour and salt in large bowl. Stir in boiling water.

Put raisins and cranberries into food processor. Process with on/off pulsing motion until finely chopped. Do not purée. Stir into sugar mixture. Add vanilla. Stir.

Turn cranberry mixture into pie shells. Bake on bottom rack in 350°F (175°C) oven for about 1 hour until crust is golden and filling is set. Cool.

Beat whipping cream, sugar and vanilla in small bowl until soft peaks form. Divide equally over both pies. Makes 2 pies, each cutting into 8 wedges, for a total of 16 wedges.

1 wedge: 407 Calories; 15.5 g Total Fat; 229 mg Sodium; 3 g Protein; 68 g Carbohydrate; 2 g Dietary Fiber

Pictured on page 153.

Left: Cran-Raisin Pie, page 152

Right: Blueberry Pecan Cake, below

Blueberry Pecan Cake

So many blueberries in this moist, tender cake.

CRUMB TOPPING

All-purpose flour	1 cup	250 mL
Hard margarine (or butter), softened	1/2 cup	125 mL
Brown sugar, packed	1/3 cup	75 mL
Medium coconut	1/4 cup	60 mL
Lemon zest	1 tsp.	5 mL

CAKE

Granulated sugar	3/4 cup	175 mL
Hard margarine (or butter), softened	1/4 cup	60 mL
Large egg	1	1
Sour cream	1/2 cup	125 mL
All-purpose flour	1 1/2 cups	375 mL
Baking powder	2 tsp.	10 mL
Salt	1 tsp.	5 mL
Frozen blueberries, thawed and drained (or fresh)	2 cups	500 mL
Coarsely chopped pecans	1/2 cup	125 mL
Whipped cream (optional)	2 cups	500 mL

Crumb Topping: Combine first 5 ingredients in small bowl. Mix until crumbly. Set aside.

Cake: Cream sugar and margarine in large bowl until smooth. Beat in egg and sour cream.

Gradually stir in flour, baking powder and salt until just combined.

Fold in blueberries and pecans. Turn into greased 8 x 8 inch (20 x 20 cm) pan. Sprinkle with topping. Bake in 350°F (175°C) oven for 50 to 60 minutes until wooden pick inserted in center comes out clean.

Serve with whipped cream. Cuts into 9 pieces.

1 piece: 490 Calories; 25.4 g Total Fat; 555 mg Sodium; 6 g Protein; 62 g Carbohydrate; 3 g Dietary Fiber

Pictured above.

How To

Antipasto Clock

Ring in the first day of the new year with this edible clock! We've created an easy and fun appetizer tray that will draw attention and conversation to your New Year's Day buffet table. Although our Antipasto Clock features Italian meats and olives, feel free to create your own variation using deli meats, vegetable chunks, pickles and crackers. Just remember to keep the arrangement fairly flat so that the face of the clock is obvious.

Materials: 12 inch (30 cm) platter, sharp knife, brown paper (or other heavier paper), cutting board, utility knife.

Sliced Genoa salami	1/3 lb.	150 g
Sliced mortadella sausage	1/3 lb.	150 g
Sliced prosciutto	2 oz.	57 g
Kalamata olives	10 - 12	10 - 12
Pimiento-stuffed olives	6 - 8	6 - 8
Slices of smoked Gouda cheese (or your choice)	3 - 4	3 - 4
Pickled asparagus spears (see Note)	2	2

Fold salami slices into quarters. Arrange, overlapping, around outside of 12 inch (30 cm) platter.

Cut mortadella slices into quarters. Arrange, overlapping, around platter on inside of salami.

Cut prosciutto slices in half. Arrange overlapping, in center of platter. Place kalamata and pimiento-stuffed olives in mound in center of prosciutto. Serves 4.

To make numbers out of cheese, copy pattern, below, onto brown paper. Cut out numbers from cheese. Place cheese on cutting board. Set number patterns on cheese. Using utility knife, carefully trace and cut out numbers. Place cheese numbers around face of clock in the 1 through 12 positions.

Cut asparagus spears to make long and short hands of clock. Position between olives and over prosciutto to indicate desired time of day.

1 serving: 306 Calories; 23.2 g Total Fat; 1426 mg Sodium; 19 g Protein; 5 g Carbohydrate; 1 g Dietary Fiber

Pictured on page 148 and on page 155.

Note: Clocks hands can also be cut from cheese slices using the pattern below.

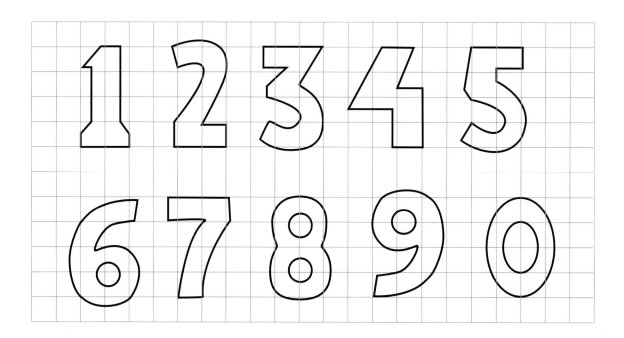

Antipasto Clock, this page

Fruity Chili Mole

Many very different flavors—from garlic to cocoa—blend to make this full-bodied chili.

Lean ground beef	1 1/2 lbs.	680 g
Chopped onion	2 cups	500 mL
Garlic cloves, minced (or 3/4 tsp., 4 mL, powder)	3	3
Curry paste	2 tsp.	10 mL
Can of diced tomatoes, with juice	28 oz.	796 mL
Can of crushed tomatoes	14 oz.	398 mL
Can of condensed chicken broth	10 oz.	284 mL
Cans of diced green chilies (4 oz., 113 mL, each), drained	2	2
Tart cooking apples (such as Granny Smith), peeled, cored and chopped	3	3
Medium green peppers, chopped	3	3
Chili powder	2 tbsp.	30 mL
Cocoa, sifted if lumpy	2 tbsp.	30 mL
Ground cinnamon	1 tsp.	5 mL
Can of red kidney beans, drained and rinsed	19 oz.	540 mL
Slivered almonds, toasted (see Tip, page 28)	2/3 cup	150 mL
Dark raisins	1/2 cup	125 mL
Grated medium Cheddar cheese (optional)		
Plain yogurt (or sour cream), optional		

Sauté ground beef, onion and garlic in large pot or Dutch oven until beef in no longer pink. Drain.

Add curry paste. Stir. Cook for 1 minute. Add next 9 ingredients. Stir. Bring to a boil. Reduce heat. Cover. Simmer for 1 hour, stirring occasionally.

Add beans, almonds and raisins. Stir. Cook, uncovered, for 30 minutes, stirring occasionally.

Sprinkle cheese over individual servings. Add dollop of yogurt to each. Makes 16 cups (4 L).

1 cup (250 mL): 193 Calories; 7.7 g Total Fat; 361 mg Sodium; 13 g Protein; 21 g Carbohydrate; 4 g Dietary Fiber

Pictured on page 157.

Stove-Top Lasagne

Great flavor in a one-dish meal!

Lean ground beef	3/4 lb.	340 g
Finely chopped onion	1/3 cup	75 mL
Chopped green pepper	1/3 cup	75 mL
Chopped mushrooms	1 cup	250 mL
Can of stewed tomatoes, with juice, chopped	28 oz.	796 mL
Italian no-salt seasoning (such as Mrs. Dash)	1 tbsp.	15 mL
Seasoned salt	1/2 tsp.	2 mL
Freshly ground pepper, sprinkle		
Broad egg noodles, uncooked	8 oz.	225 g
Part-skim ricotta cheese	1/2 cup	125 mL
Grated part-skim mozzarella cheese	1/2 cup	125 mL
Grated light Parmesan cheese	2 tbsp.	30 mL
Parsley flakes	2 tsp.	10 mL

Scramble-fry first 4 ingredients in frying pan until onion is soft and ground beef is no longer pink.

Add next 4 ingredients. Bring to a boil.

Add noodles. Stir. Reduce heat. Cover. Simmer for 12 minutes, stirring occasionally, until noodles are tender but firm.

Stir remaining 4 ingredients into noodle mixture. Heat for about 4 minutes on medium-high until cheese is melted. Makes about 8 cups (2 L). Serves 6.

1 serving: 378 Calories; 14.1 g Total Fat; 621 mg Sodium; 24 g Protein; 40 g Carbohydrate; 3 g Dietary Fiber

Pictured on page 157.

Top Left: Stove-Top Lasagne, page 156

Center: Fruity Chili Mole, page 156

Porcupine Meatballs

Spiky meatballs cooked in a flavorful tomato sauce.

MEATBALLS

Water	1/3 cup	75 mL
Long grain white rice, uncooked	1/2 cup	125 mL
Beef bouillon powder	1 tsp.	5 mL
Dried sweet basil	1/4 tsp.	1 mL
Dried whole oregano	1/4 tsp.	1 mL
Chili powder	1/4 tsp.	1 mL
Salt	1/2 tsp.	2 mL
Pepper	1/4 tsp.	1 mL
Lean ground beef	1 lb.	454 g

TOMATO SAUCE

Can of condensed tomato soup	10 oz.	284 mL
Can of diced tomatoes, with juice	14 oz.	398 mL
Medium onion, chopped	1	1
Celery salt	1/4 tsp.	1 mL
Garlic powder	1/4 tsp.	1 mL
Salt	1/2 tsp.	2 mL
Pepper	1/8 tsp.	0.5 mL

Meatballs: Combine first 8 ingredients in medium bowl.

Add ground beef. Mix. Shape into 25 meatballs. Arrange in single layer in ungreased 2 quart (2 L) shallow casserole.

Tomato Sauce: Combine all 7 ingredients in medium bowl. Pour over meatballs. Cover. Bake in 350°F (175°C) oven for about 70 minutes until rice is tender. Serves 4.

1 serving: 447 Calories; 18.6 g Total Fat; 1591 mg Sodium; 34 g Protein; 36 g Carbohydrate; 3 g Dietary Fiber

Pictured on page 159.

Mushroom-Stuffed Meatloaf

A tunnel of creamy mushroom filling
encased in meatloaf walls.

FILLING
Chopped fresh mushrooms	3 cups	750 mL
Chopped onion	1 cup	250 mL
Hard margarine (or butter)	1 tbsp.	15 mL
All-purpose flour	3 tbsp.	50 mL
Salt	1/2 tsp.	2 mL
Pepper	1/4 tsp.	1 mL
Dried thyme	1/2 tsp.	2 mL
Light cream cheese, cut into chunks	4 oz.	125 g

MEAT LAYER
Large egg, fork-beaten	1	1
Low-sodium soy sauce	3 tbsp.	50 mL
Ground ginger	1/2 tsp.	2 mL
Garlic powder	1/4 tsp.	1 mL
Worcestershire sauce	1/2 tsp.	2 mL
Milk	1/4 cup	60 mL
Fine dry bread crumbs	2/3 cup	150 mL
Lean ground beef	1 1/2 lbs.	680 g

Filling: Sauté mushrooms and onion in margarine in frying pan until onion is soft and liquid from mushrooms has evaporated. Reduce heat to medium.

Add flour, salt, pepper and thyme. Stir quickly until well combined. Add cream cheese. Stir until blended. Cool.

Meat Layer: Combine first 7 ingredients in large bowl.

Mix in ground beef. Place about 2/3 of beef mixture in greased 9 x 5 x 3 inch (22 x 12.5 x 7.5 cm) loaf pan. Pack mixture into bottom and 2 inches (5 cm) up sides of pan. Add mushroom mixture to cavity. Spread evenly. Flatten remaining 1/3 of beef mixture to fit in pan. Place on top, smoothing and sealing sides. Bake, uncovered, in 325°F (160°C) oven for 1 hour. Serves 6.

1 serving: 416 Calories; 24.9 g Total Fat; 819 mg Sodium; 28 g Protein; 19 g Carbohydrate; 2 g Dietary Fiber

Pictured on page 159.

Chili In Potato Skins

Quick-to-make chili made with canned corned beef
is a filling meal when served in potato skins.

Large baking potatoes	6	6
Diced celery	1 cup	250 mL
Diced onion	1 cup	250 mL
Cooking oil	2 tsp.	10 mL
Can of tomato sauce	7 1/2 oz.	213 mL
Ketchup	1/3 cup	75 mL
Worcestershire sauce	1 tbsp.	15 mL
Brown sugar, packed	2 tbsp.	30 mL
White vinegar	1 tbsp.	15 mL
Chili powder	1 1/2 tsp.	7 mL
Can of corned beef, broken into small pieces	11 oz.	310 g
Grated medium Cheddar cheese	3/4 cup	175 mL

Pierce potatoes all over. Bake on center rack in 400°F (205°C) oven for 1 hour until tender. Cool enough to handle. Slice off tops lengthwise. Scoop out potato flesh, leaving 1/4 inch (6 mm) edge to make shell. Reserve potato flesh for another use.

Sauté celery and onion in cooking oil in large frying pan until soft.

Add next 7 ingredients. Stir. Bring to a boil. Reduce heat. Simmer, uncovered, for 20 minutes, stirring occasionally, until boiling and thickened. Fill potato shells.

Sprinkle 2 tbsp. (30 mL) cheese over each filled shell. Bake in 350°F (175°C) oven for 15 minutes until hot and cheese is melted. Makes 6 potato skins.

1 potato skin: 397 Calories; 14.7 g Total Fat; 1072 mg Sodium; 23 g Protein; 45 g Carbohydrate; 5 g Dietary Fiber

Pictured on page 159.

Top Left: Chili In Potato Skins, above
Top Right: Porcupine Meatballs, page 157
Bottom: Mushroom-Stuffed Meatloaf, this page

Pineapple Chicken, below   Simple Turkey Stew, this page

Pineapple Chicken

Lots of dark brown sauce with chunks of chicken.

SAUCE

Can of pineapple tidbits, with juice	8 oz.	225 mL
Water	1/2 cup	125 mL
Soy sauce	3 tbsp.	50 mL
Granulated sugar	2 tsp.	10 mL
Sherry (or alcohol-free sherry)	2 tsp.	10 mL
Ground ginger	1/4 tsp.	1 mL
Garlic powder	1/4 tsp.	1 mL
Salt	1/4 tsp.	1 mL
Pepper	1/8 tsp.	0.5 mL
Boneless, skinless chicken breast halves (about 8), cut into 3/4 inch (2 cm) cubes	2 lbs.	900 g
Cooking oil	1 tbsp.	15 mL
Water	1 1/2 tbsp.	25 mL
Cornstarch	1 tbsp.	15 mL

Sauce: Combine first 9 ingredients in large saucepan. Heat through without boiling.

Brown chicken in cooking oil in frying pan. Add to sauce. Stir. Bring to a boil. Reduce heat. Cover. Simmer for 25 to 35 minutes, stirring occasionally, until chicken is tender and no longer pink inside.

Stir second amount of water into cornstarch in small cup until smooth. Stir into chicken mixture. Heat and stir until boiling and thickened. Makes 6 cups (1.5 L).

1 cup (250 mL): 229 Calories; 4.9 g Total Fat; 622 mg Sodium; 35 g Protein; 10 g Carbohydrate; trace Dietary Fiber

Pictured above.

Simple Turkey Stew

Generous amount of creamy sauce with chunks of turkey and vegetables.

Bone-in turkey parts (thighs, wings and legs), skin removed	3 1/2 lbs.	1.6 kg
Water	2 cups	500 mL
Chicken bouillon powder	2 tbsp.	30 mL
Parsley flakes	1 tsp.	5 mL
Dried thyme	1/2 tsp.	2 mL
Pepper	1/4 tsp.	1 mL
Medium onions, chopped	2	2
Medium potatoes, peeled and cut into chunks	4	4
Baby carrots	12	12
Large celery ribs, cut diagonally into 1 inch (2.5 cm) pieces	2	2
Skim evaporated milk	2/3 cup	150 mL
All-purpose flour	1/4 cup	60 mL

Place first 10 ingredients in ungreased medium roasting pan or 4 quart (4 L) casserole. Cover. Bake in 300°F (150°C) oven for about 3 1/2 hours until turkey is tender. Remove turkey to cutting board. Pull turkey off in large pieces, discarding bones and cartilage. Cut turkey into bite-size pieces. Remove vegetables from roasting pan with slotted spoon to serving bowl. Add turkey to vegetables. Keep warm. Pour liquid from roasting pan into medium saucepan. Skim off fat, leaving broth.

Stir evaporated milk into flour in small bowl until smooth. Gradually stir into broth. Heat and stir on medium until boiling and thickened. Pour over turkey mixture. Stir. Makes 12 cups (3 L). Serves 6.

1 serving: 351 Calories; 5.9 g Total Fat; 837 mg Sodium; 45 g Protein; 28 g Carbohydrate; 3 g Dietary Fiber

Pictured on this page.

Left: Seasoned Sirloin, below

Right: Baked Chicken, below

Seasoned Sirloin

A delightfully flavored roast to perk up your cold winter night.

Sirloin roast	3 lbs.	1.4 kg
Garlic cloves, minced (or 1 tsp., 5 mL, powder)	4	4
Olive (or cooking) oil	2 tsp.	10 mL
Paprika	1 tsp.	5 mL
Onion powder	1 tsp.	5 mL
Freshly ground pepper	1 tsp.	5 mL

Place roast on rack in medium roasting pan.

Combine remaining 5 ingredients in small bowl. Mix into paste. Spread over entire surface of roast. Roast, uncovered, in 325°F (160°C) oven for 30 to 40 minutes per pound (65 to 85 minutes per kg) until meat thermometer registers 160°F (75°C) for medium doneness. Let roast stand for 10 minutes before carving. Serves 8.

1 serving: 225 Calories; 9.9 g Total Fat; 60 mg Sodium; 31 g Protein; 1 g Carbohydrate; trace Dietary Fiber

Pictured on front cover and above.

Baked Chicken

Golden and crispy. Quick and easy to prepare.

Corn flakes cereal, coarsely crushed	1 cup	250 mL
Grated Parmesan cheese	1/2 cup	125 mL
Sesame seeds, toasted (see Tip, page 28)	1/3 cup	75 mL
Salt	3/4 tsp.	4 mL
Pepper	1/8 tsp.	0.5 mL
Whole chicken, cut up (or chicken parts), skin removed	3 lbs.	1.4 kg
Hard margarine (or butter), melted	3 tbsp.	50 mL

Combine first 5 ingredients in shallow bowl. Stir well.

Brush chicken with margarine. Press chicken into crumb mixture to coat completely. Arrange in single layer on greased foil-lined baking sheet. Sprinkle remaining crumb mixture over top. Bake in 350°F (175°C) oven for about 40 minutes until tender. Serves 4.

1 serving: 509 Calories; 24.2 g Total Fat; 1171 mg Sodium; 46 g Protein; 26 g Carbohydrate; 3 g Dietary Fiber

Pictured above.

Turkey À La King

This can also be made with leftover chicken.
Serve over puff pastry patty shells or rice.

Sliced fresh mushrooms	1 cup	250 mL
Diced red pepper	1/4 cup	60 mL
Hard margarine (or butter)	2 tbsp.	30 mL
Hard margarine (or butter)	2 tbsp.	30 mL
All-purpose flour	1/4 cup	60 mL
Cayenne pepper	1/8 tsp.	0.5 mL
Salt	1/2 tsp.	2 mL
Pepper	1/4 tsp.	1 mL
Milk, room temperature	2 cups	500 mL
White (or alcohol-free) wine	1 tbsp.	15 mL
Frozen peas	3/4 cup	175 mL
Diced cooked turkey	2 cups	500 mL

Sauté mushrooms and red pepper in first amount of margarine in large frying pan until soft.

Add second amount of margarine. Stir until melted. Add flour, cayenne pepper, salt and pepper. Stir until smooth. Gradually stir in milk and wine. Heat and stir until boiling and thickened.

Add peas and turkey. Stir. Heat on low, stirring occasionally, until heated through and peas are cooked. Makes 4 cups (1 L).

1 cup (250 mL): 321 Calories; 13.8 g Total Fat; 569 mg Sodium; 30 g Protein; 18 g Carbohydrate; 2 g Dietary Fiber

Pictured on page 163.

Chicken Cacciatore

Lots of sauce to serve over noodles or rice.
Showy amounts of mushrooms and tomatoes.

Boneless, skinless chicken breast halves (about 1 1/2 lbs., 680 g)	6	6
Cooking oil	1 tbsp.	15 mL
Medium onion, chopped	1	1
Garlic cloves, minced (or 1/2 tsp., 2 mL, powder)	2	2
Sliced fresh mushrooms	2 cups	500 mL
Can of crushed tomatoes	14 oz.	398 mL
Ketchup	2 tbsp.	30 mL
Granulated sugar	1/2 tsp.	2 mL
Dried sweet basil	1/2 tsp.	2 mL
Dried whole oregano	1/2 tsp.	2 mL
Salt	1/2 tsp.	2 mL
Pepper	1/4 tsp.	1 mL
Water	1 tbsp.	15 mL
Cornstarch	1 tbsp.	15 mL

Fry chicken in cooking oil in large frying pan for about 3 minutes per side until browned. Transfer chicken to plate. Keep warm.

Sauté onion and garlic in same frying pan until onion is soft.

Add next 8 ingredients. Stir. Add chicken. Bring to a boil. Reduce heat. Cover. Simmer for 20 to 30 minutes until chicken is tender. Transfer chicken to plate.

Stir water into cornstarch in small cup until smooth. Gradually stir into boiling mixture. Heat and stir until boiling and thickened. Add chicken. Serve immediately. Makes 3 cups (750 mL) sauce. Serves 6.

1 serving: 187 Calories; 4.6 g Total Fat; 369 mg Sodium; 27 g Protein; 9 g Carbohydrate; 1 g Dietary Fiber

Pictured on page 163.

Tip *Chicken and turkey are most easily removed from the bone while still warm. Don't throw away the bones, keep them to make stock.*

Left: Fast Fricassee, below   Center: Chicken Cacciatore, page 162   Right: Turkey À La King, page 162

Fast Fricassee

A delicious way to use up leftover turkey or chicken for a thick, chunky stew.

Coarsely chopped onion	1 1/2 cups	375 mL
Thickly sliced mushrooms	2 cups	500 mL
Small green pepper, diced	1	1
Small red pepper, diced	1	1
Hard margarine (or butter)	1/4 cup	60 mL
All-purpose flour	1/4 cup	60 mL
Can of condensed chicken broth	10 oz.	284 mL
Can of skim evaporated milk	13 1/2 oz.	385 mL
Granulated sugar	1 tsp.	5 mL
Turmeric	1/2 tsp.	2 mL
Salt	1/2 tsp.	2 mL
Pepper	1/4 tsp.	1 mL
Egg yolks (large), fork-beaten	2	2
Cooked turkey (or chicken), cut bite size	3 cups	750 mL

Sauté onion, mushrooms and both peppers in margarine in large pot or Dutch oven for 8 to 10 minutes until onion is soft.

Sprinkle with flour. Stir. Heat and stir for 1 to 2 minutes until well combined.

Gradually stir in chicken broth and evaporated milk. Add sugar, turmeric, salt and pepper. Heat and stir until boiling and thickened.

Slowly add about 1 cup (250 mL) hot milk mixture to egg yolks in small bowl. Gradually stir yolk mixture back into milk mixture. Heat and stir on medium-low until almost boiling. Do not boil as sauce may curdle.

Add turkey. Heat and stir until turkey is hot. Makes 6 1/2 cups (1.6 L).

1 cup (250 mL): 296 Calories; 10.5 g Total Fat; 676 mg Sodium; 30 g Protein; 20 g Carbohydrate; 2 g Dietary Fiber

Pictured above.

Poached Fish, below   Baked Cod, this page

Baked Cod

Still have fish in the freezer from last summer?
Now's the time to have it. Tender and juicy fish
with a crispy crumb coating.

Coarse dry bread crumbs, lightly crushed	1/4 cup	60 mL
Grated Parmesan cheese	2 tbsp.	30 mL
Parsley flakes	1 tsp.	5 mL
Dried sweet basil	1/8 tsp.	0.5 mL
Dried whole oregano	1/8 tsp.	0.5 mL
Garlic powder	1/8 tsp.	0.5 mL
Onion powder	1/8 tsp.	0.5 mL
Paprika	1/8 tsp.	0.5 mL
Salt	1/8 tsp.	0.5 mL
Pepper, just a pinch		
Cod fillets (about 1 1/4 lbs., 560 g)	4 - 6	4 - 6
Lemon wedges	4	4

Combine first 10 ingredients in shallow dish.

Press moist fillets into crumb mixture to coat completely. Arrange in single layer in greased 3 quart (3 L) shallow baking dish. Bake, uncovered, in 375°F (190°C) oven for 15 to 20 minutes until fish flakes easily when tested with fork.

Serve with lemon wedges. Serves 4 to 6.

1 serving: 159 Calories; 2.3 g Total Fat; 274 mg Sodium; 27 g Protein; 6 g Carbohydrate; trace Dietary Fiber

Pictured on this page.

 Tip *To thaw frozen fish quickly and safely, let fish stand covered in cold water.*

Poached Fish

When you need a taste of summer in winter,
serve this tasty fish over steamed rice.

Chopped onion	1 cup	250 mL
Hard margarine (or butter)	1 tbsp.	15 mL
Water	1 1/4 cups	300 mL
Chicken bouillon powder	1 1/2 tsp.	7 mL
Dried marjoram	1/2 tsp.	2 mL
Lemon juice	2 tsp.	10 mL
Fish fillets (about 1 lb., 454 g)	4	4
Small red pepper, slivered (or chopped)	1	1

Sauté onion in margarine in large frying pan until caramelized.

Add water, bouillon powder, marjoram and lemon juice. Bring to a boil.

Measure thickest part of fillets. Add fillets and red pepper to onion mixture. Bring to a gentle boil. Cover. Poach for 10 minutes for every 1 inch (2.5 cm) thickness until fish flakes easily when tested with fork. Remove fish to platter. Strain liquid, reserving onion and red pepper. Top with reserved onion and red pepper. Serves 4.

1 serving: 158 Calories; 4.6 g Total Fat; 372 mg Sodium; 22 g Protein; 6 g Carbohydrate; 1 g Dietary Fiber

Pictured above.

Bow Bolognese

One of the most popular pasta sauces.

BOLOGNESE SAUCE

Medium onion, finely chopped	1	1
Chopped celery	1/4 cup	60 mL
Olive (or cooking) oil	1/2 tbsp.	7 mL
Lean ground beef	1/2 lb.	225 g
Salt	3/4 tsp.	4 mL
Pepper	1/4 tsp.	1 mL
Dried whole oregano	1 tsp.	5 mL
Chili sauce	1/4 cup	60 mL
Apple juice (or white grape juice or white wine)	1/2 cup	125 mL
Medium bow (or other) pasta	12 oz.	340 g
Boiling water	16 cups	4 L
Cooking oil (optional)	1 tbsp.	15 mL
Salt	2 tsp.	10 mL

Grated fresh Parmesan cheese, sprinkle

Bolognese Sauce: Sauté onion and celery in olive oil in large pot or Dutch oven for about 5 minutes until soft.

Add ground beef. Scramble-fry until beef is no longer pink. Drain.

Add next 5 ingredients. Stir. Bring to a boil. Reduce heat. Simmer, uncovered, for 20 to 30 minutes, stirring occasionally, until thickened. Add a bit of water if sauce seems too thick. Makes 1 2/3 cups (400 mL) sauce.

Cook pasta in boiling water, cooking oil and salt in large uncovered pot or Dutch oven for 11 to 13 minutes until tender but firm. Drain. Turn out onto platter. Pour sauce over pasta.

Sprinkle with Parmesan cheese. Serves 4.

1 serving: 464 Calories; 8.1 g Total Fat; 732 mg Sodium; 22 g Protein; 75 g Carbohydrate; 4 g Dietary Fiber

Pictured on this page.

Cheesy Pasta

Perfect comfort food for a cold winter day.

Fusilli pasta	2 2/3 cups	650 mL
Boiling water	10 cups	2.5 L
Cooking oil (optional)	1 tbsp.	15 mL
Salt	2 tsp.	10 mL
Frozen mixed vegetables (such as California or Italian), thawed and coarsely chopped	2 cups	500 mL
All-purpose flour	1/3 cup	75 mL
Salt	3/4 tsp.	4 mL
Pepper	1/4 tsp.	1 mL
Onion salt	1 tsp.	5 mL
Milk	2 1/2 cups	625 mL
Chili sauce (not paste)	1/4 cup	60 mL
Grated sharp Cheddar cheese	1 1/2 cups	375 mL

CRUMB TOPPING

Soda cracker crumbs	1/2 cup	125 mL
Hard margarine (or butter), melted	1 tbsp.	15 mL

Cook pasta in boiling water, cooking oil and salt in large uncovered pot or Dutch oven for 5 minutes.

Add vegetables. Stir. Bring to a boil. Boil for 2 to 3 minutes until pasta is tender. Drain. Turn into ungreased 2 quart (2 L) casserole.

Combine flour, salt, pepper and onion salt in large saucepan. Gradually stir in milk until smooth. Heat and stir until boiling and thickened. Remove from heat.

Add chili sauce and cheese. Stir until melted. Pour over pasta and vegetables. Stir until well coated.

Crumb Topping: Sauté cracker crumbs in margarine in frying pan until golden. Sprinkle over pasta mixture. Bake, uncovered, in 350°F (175°C) oven for about 30 minutes until bubbly and hot. Makes about 7 cups. Serves 4.

1 serving: 711 Calories; 22.2 g Total Fat; 1554 mg Sodium; 31 g Protein; 97 g Carbohydrate; 7 g Dietary Fiber

Pictured below.

Bow Bolognese, this page   Cheesy Pasta, this page

Creamy Noodle Bake

Lots of beef in a sweet tomato sauce.
All you need is a salad for a complete meal.

Medium egg noodles	8 oz.	225 g
Boiling water	12 cups	3 L
Cooking oil (optional)	1 tbsp.	15 mL
Salt	2 tsp.	10 mL
Lean ground beef	1 1/2 lbs.	680 g
Medium onion, chopped	1	1
Can of tomato paste	5 1/2 oz.	156 mL
Can of water	5 1/2 oz.	156 mL
Worcestershire sauce	2 tsp.	10 mL
Granulated sugar	1 1/2 tsp.	7 mL
Salt	1 tsp.	5 mL
Garlic salt	1/2 tsp.	2 mL
Pepper	1/4 tsp.	1 mL
Light sour cream	1 cup	250 mL
Light creamed cottage cheese	1 cup	250 mL
Grated medium Cheddar cheese (optional)	1 cup	250 mL

Cook noodles in boiling water, cooking oil and salt in large uncovered pot or Dutch oven for 5 to 7 minutes until tender but firm. Drain. Return to pot.

Scramble-fry ground beef and onion in frying pan until beef is no longer pink. Drain.

Add next 7 ingredients to beef mixture. Stir.

Add sour cream and cottage cheese to noodles. Stir. Put 1/2 of noodle mixture into ungreased 3 quart (3 L) casserole. Cover with all of beef mixture. Top with remaining noodle mixture. Bake, uncovered, in 350°F (175°C) oven for about 40 minutes until bubbly hot.

Sprinkle with Cheddar cheese. Bake until cheese is melted. Serves 6.

1 serving: 454 Calories; 16.2 g Total Fat; 905 mg Sodium; 38 g Protein; 38 g Carbohydrate; 3 g Dietary Fiber

Pictured on page 167.

Mushroom Pasta Wedges

Sets well. Cuts well. The pasta makes a nice crust.
Nice contrast of vegetables and pasta.

Capellini (or angel hair or vermicelli pasta, broken in half)	8 oz.	225 g
Boiling water	10 cups	2.5 L
Cooking oil (optional)	1 tbsp.	15 mL
Salt	2 tsp.	10 mL
Large eggs	4	4
Creamed cottage cheese	1/2 cup	125 mL
Grated light Parmesan cheese	1/4 cup	60 mL
Chopped fresh sweet basil (or 3/4 tsp., 4 mL, dried)	1 tbsp.	15 mL
Chopped fresh parsley (or 3/4 tsp., 4 mL, flakes)	1 tbsp.	15 mL
Sliced fresh mushrooms	3 cups	750 mL
Olive (or cooking) oil	2 tsp.	10 mL
Green onions, sliced	2	2
Freshly ground pepper, sprinkle		
Spaghetti sauce	2 cups	500 mL

Cook pasta in boiling water, cooking oil and salt in large uncovered pot or Dutch oven for 5 to 7 minutes until tender but firm. Drain well. Transfer to large bowl.

Combine next 5 ingredients in blender. Process until quite smooth. Add to pasta. Toss until well coated.

Sauté mushrooms in olive oil in frying pan until golden and liquid from mushrooms has evaporated. Reserve 1/2 cup (125 mL). Add remaining mushrooms to pasta mixture.

Add green onion. Toss. Place pasta mixture in greased 10 inch (25 cm) glass pie plate. Firmly press down with lightly greased hands until evenly packed. Arrange reserved mushrooms over top. Sprinkle with pepper. Bake, uncovered, in 375°F (190°C) oven for 35 to 40 minutes until pasta is turning golden on edges and egg is set. Let stand for 10 minutes before cutting.

Heat spaghetti sauce in small saucepan until heated through. Spoon over individual servings. Cuts into 8 wedges.

1 wedge with 1/4 cup (60 mL) sauce: 261 Calories; 9 g Total Fat; 479 mg Sodium; 12 g Protein; 34 g Carbohydrate; 2 g Dietary Fiber

Pictured on page 167.

Left: Cheesy Veggie Pizza, below   Top Right: Creamy Noodle Bake, page 166   Bottom Right: Mushroom Pasta Wedges, page 166

Cheesy Veggie Pizza

Prominent tomato and green pepper flavors.
Colorful and attractive.

Unbaked pizza crust (12 inch, 30 cm, size), see Note	1	1
Medium green pepper, chopped	1	1
Chopped onion	1 cup	250 mL
Chopped fresh mushrooms	1 cup	250 mL
Cooking oil	2 tsp.	10 mL
Pizza sauce	1/2 cup	125 mL
Grated Edam (or mozzarella) cheese	3/4 cup	175 mL
Roma (plum) tomatoes, sliced	2	2
Grated part-skim mozzarella cheese	3/4 cup	175 mL

Place pizza crust in greased 12 inch (30 cm) pizza pan.

Sauté green pepper, onion and mushrooms in cooking oil in frying pan until onion is soft.

Spread pizza sauce over crust. Layer vegetable mixture, Edam cheese, tomato and mozzarella cheese over sauce. Bake on bottom rack in 425°F (220°C) oven for 13 to 15 minutes until cheese is melted and crust is golden. Cuts into 8 wedges.

1 wedge: 222 Calories; 8.7 g Total Fat; 395 mg Sodium; 9 g Protein; 27 g Carbohydrate; 1 g Dietary Fiber

Pictured above.

Note: If using a partially baked pizza crust, reduce baking time to 8 minutes.

Spaghetti Frittata

A great way to use leftover spaghetti.

Chopped green onion	1/3 cup	75 mL
Garlic clove, minced (or 1/4 tsp., 1 mL, powder)	1	1
Finely chopped roma (plum) tomato	3/4 cup	175 mL
Olive (or cooking) oil	2 tsp.	10 mL
Salt	1/2 tsp.	2 mL
Dried sweet basil	1/4 tsp.	1 mL
Freshly ground pepper, sprinkle		
Large eggs	2	2
Egg whites (large)	4	4
Cooked spaghetti (or other pasta)	2 cups	500 mL
Salt	3/4 tsp.	4 mL
Olive (or cooking) oil	1 tsp.	5 mL
Grated medium Cheddar cheese (optional)	1/4 cup	60 mL

Sauté green onion, garlic and tomato in first amount of olive oil in large ovenproof frying pan for about 3 minutes until tomato is soft.

Add first amount of salt, basil and pepper. Stir.

Beat eggs and egg whites together in medium bowl until frothy. Add tomato mixture. Stir.

Add spaghetti and second amount of salt. Stir.

Heat second amount of olive oil in same frying pan on medium. Add spaghetti mixture. Distribute evenly on bottom of frying pan. Cover. Cook for 5 minutes. Top will not be completely set.

Sprinkle with cheese. Place frying pan under broiler for 1 to 2 minutes until cheese is melted and egg is set. Cuts into 4 wedges.

1 wedge: 212 Calories; 7.1 g Total Fat; 878 mg Sodium; 12 g Protein; 24 g Carbohydrate; 2 g Dietary Fiber

Pictured on page 169.

Vegetables And Pasta

Cooked beef, pork, chicken or turkey could be added for a complete meal.

Cauliflower, cut into florets (about 7 1/2 cups, 1.9 L)	1 1/2 lbs.	680 g
Broccoli, cut into florets (about 5 cups, 1.25 L)	1 lb.	454 g
Water		
Salt	1 tsp.	5 mL
Sliced mushrooms	6 cups	1.5 L
Hard margarine (or butter)	1/4 cup	60 mL
Salt	1 tsp.	5 mL
Garlic powder	1/4 tsp.	1 mL
Cayenne pepper	1/8 tsp.	0.5 mL
Linguine (or other) pasta	8 oz.	225 g
Boiling water	12 cups	3 L
Cooking oil (optional)	1 tbsp.	15 mL
Salt	2 tsp.	10 mL
Grated Parmesan (or Romano) cheese, sprinkle		

Cook cauliflower and broccoli in first amount of water and salt in large saucepan until barely tender. Drain. Keep hot.

Sauté mushrooms in margarine in frying pan until golden and liquid has evaporated.

Add salt, garlic powder and cayenne pepper. Stir.

Cook pasta in boiling water, cooking oil and salt in large uncovered pot or Dutch oven for 7 to 9 minutes until tender but firm. Drain. Return to pot. Add cauliflower mixture and mushrooms. Toss. Arrange on serving platter.

Sprinkle with Parmesan cheese. Serves 12.

1 serving: 140 Calories; 4.8 g Total Fat; 275 mg Sodium; 5 g Protein; 21 g Carbohydrate; 3 g Dietary Fiber

Pictured on page 169.

Top: Quick Pasta-In-A-Pot, page 170
Center Left: Vegetables And Pasta, above
Center Right: Pasta And Sauce, page 170
Bottom: Spaghetti Frittata, this page

Quick Pasta-In-A-Pot

Lots of ham and veggies in this appealing, creamy dish.

Linguine pasta	8 oz.	225 g
Boiling water	12 cups	3 L
Cooking oil (optional)	1 tbsp.	15 mL
Salt	2 tsp.	10 mL
Frozen California vegetable mix (or broccoli and cauliflower mix)	2 cups	500 mL
Skim evaporated milk	1 cup	250 mL
Milk	1/2 cup	125 mL
All-purpose flour	1 tbsp.	15 mL
Grated light sharp Cheddar cheese	1/2 cup	125 mL
Grated light Parmesan cheese	2 tbsp.	30 mL
Garlic and herb no-salt seasoning (such as Mrs. Dash)	1 tsp.	5 mL
Chopped Canadian back bacon (or ham), cooked	1 1/2 cups	375 mL

Cook pasta in boiling water, cooking oil and salt in large uncovered pot or Dutch oven for 7 minutes.

Add vegetable mix. Bring to a boil. Cook for 2 to 3 minutes until pasta is tender but firm. Drain. Transfer to bowl. Keep warm.

Combine both milks and flour in same pot until smooth. Bring to a boil. Reduce heat.

Add both cheeses and seasoning. Stir until cheese is melted. Add bacon. Stir. Add pasta mixture. Toss until well coated. Makes 6 1/2 cups (1.6 L). Serves 6.

1 serving: 309 Calories; 4.5 g Total Fat; 541 mg Sodium; 22 g Protein; 45 g Carbohydrate; 3 g Dietary Fiber

Pictured on page 169.

Pasta And Sauce

A nice chunky sauce rounds out this spaghetti plate. Works with pasta such as penne or radiatore as well.

Lean ground beef	1 lb.	454 g
Finely chopped onion	1/2 cup	125 mL
Diced green pepper	3/4 cup	175 mL
Olive (or cooking) oil	1 tsp.	5 mL
Can of diced tomatoes, with juice	14 oz.	398 mL
Can of spaghetti sauce	24 oz.	680 mL
Can of sliced mushrooms, drained	10 oz.	284 mL
Granulated sugar	1 1/2 tsp.	7 mL
Salt	1/2 tsp.	2 mL
Pepper	1/4 tsp.	1 mL
Dried sweet basil	1/2 tsp.	2 mL
Dried whole oregano	1/2 tsp.	2 mL
Worcestershire sauce	1 tsp.	5 mL
Tortiglioni (or other spiral) pasta	1 lb.	454 g
Boiling water	20 cups	5 L
Cooking oil (optional)	1 tbsp.	15 mL
Salt	1 tbsp.	15 mL

Scramble-fry ground beef, onion and green pepper in olive oil in large pot or Dutch oven until beef is no longer pink and onion is soft.

Add next 9 ingredients. Stir. Bring to a boil. Reduce heat to medium-low. Simmer, uncovered, for 20 to 30 minutes, stirring occasionally, until thickened. Makes 6 3/4 cups (1.7 L) sauce.

Cook pasta in boiling water, cooking oil and salt in large uncovered pot or Dutch oven for 11 to 13 minutes until tender but firm. Drain. Serve with sauce. Serves 6.

1 serving: 603 Calories; 18.8 g Total Fat; 1021 mg Sodium; 27 g Protein; 82 g Carbohydrate; 5 g Dietary Fiber

Pictured on page 169.

Tip To make perfect pasta every time, put pasta into rapidly boiling water. Use at least 4 cups (1 L) water for every 4 oz. (113 g) uncooked pasta.

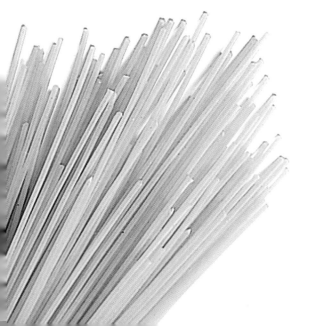

Sweet And Sour Pineapple Pork

Makes lots of tangy sauce to serve over steamed rice.
An attractive dish with colorful red pepper
and pineapple pieces.

Can of condensed chicken broth	10 oz.	284 mL
White vinegar	1/4 cup	60 mL
Brown sugar, packed	1/4 cup	60 mL
Reserved pineapple juice		
Chili sauce	2 tbsp.	30 mL
Cooking oil	1 tbsp.	15 mL
Pork loin, cut into 3/4 inch (2 cm) cubes	1 1/2 lbs.	680 g
Freshly ground pepper, generous sprinkle		
Large onion, cut lengthwise into wedges	1	1
Large red pepper, cut into 1/2 inch (12 mm) slivers	1	1
Soy sauce	1/4 cup	60 mL
Cornstarch	3 tbsp.	50 mL
Can of pineapple tidbits, drained and juice reserved	14 oz.	398 mL

Combine broth, vinegar, brown sugar, pineapple juice and chili sauce in large saucepan. Heat and stir until brown sugar is dissolved.

Heat cooking oil in large frying pan until hot. Add pork cubes and pepper. Stir-fry for 5 to 10 minutes until pork is well browned. Add to broth mixture.

Add onion and red pepper. Reduce heat. Cover. Simmer for 30 minutes, stirring occasionally.

Stir soy sauce into cornstarch in small dish until smooth. Gradually stir into pork mixture until boiling and thickened.

Add pineapple. Cover. Simmer for about 20 minutes, stirring occasionally, until pork is tender. Makes 8 cups (2 L).

1 cup (250 mL): 280 Calories; 11.5 g Total Fat; 883 mg Sodium; 21 g Protein; 24 g Carbohydrate; 1 g Dietary Fiber

Pictured on this page.

Sweet And Sour Pineapple Pork, this page   Pork Noodle Bake, below

Pork Noodle Bake

A very pretty dish with the red tomatoes on top.
Easy to prepare.

Medium egg noodles, uncooked	8 oz.	225 g
Lean ground pork	1 lb.	454 g
Chopped onion	1 cup	250 mL
Chopped celery	1 cup	250 mL
Medium green pepper, chopped	1	1
Cans of tomatoes (14 oz., 398 mL, each), with juice, broken up	2	2
Frozen kernel corn	1 1/2 cups	375 mL
Granulated sugar	1 tsp.	5 mL
Dried whole oregano	1/2 tsp.	2 mL
Salt	1/2 tsp.	2 mL
Pepper	1/8 tsp.	0.5 mL

Arrange noodles in ungreased 3 quart (3 L) casserole.

Scramble-fry ground pork, onion, celery and green pepper in non-stick frying pan until pork is no longer pink. Drain. Spoon over noodles.

Put tomatoes with juice into same frying pan. Heat and stir to loosen any brown bits. Add corn, sugar, oregano, salt and pepper. Stir. Bring to a boil. Pour over pork mixture. Cover. Bake in 350°F (175°C) oven for 1 to 1 1/2 hours until noodles are tender. Serves 4.

1 serving: 581 Calories; 19.8 g Total Fat; 726 mg Sodium; 33 g Protein; 71 g Carbohydrate; 6 g Dietary Fiber

Pictured above.

Ham And Cheese Pizza, below   Chops And Pasta, this page

Ham And Cheese Pizza

This pizza will remind you of a ham and cheese sandwich.

Unbaked pizza crust (12 inch, 30 cm, size), see Note	1	1
Prepared mustard	3 tbsp.	50 mL
Diced cooked smoked ham slice (1/4 inch, 6 mm, thick)	1 1/4 cups	300 mL
Grated medium Cheddar cheese	3/4 cup	175 mL
Grated Monterey Jack cheese	3/4 cup	175 mL

Place pizza crust in greased 12 inch (30 cm) pizza pan. Spread mustard over crust. Sprinkle with ham. Sprinkle both cheeses over top. Bake on bottom rack in 425°F (220°C) oven for 13 to 15 minutes until cheese is melted and crust is golden. Cuts into 8 wedges.

1 wedge: 250 Calories; 12.3 g Total Fat; 740 mg Sodium; 15 g Protein; 20 g Carbohydrate; 0 g Dietary Fiber

Pictured above.

Note: If using a partially baked pizza crust, reduce baking time to 8 minutes.

Chops And Pasta

Colored pasta and chops make for an attractive plate.

Wagon wheel pasta, uncooked	8 oz.	225 g
Pork loin chops, 3/4 inch (2 cm) thick, trimmed of fat	1 1/2 lbs.	680 g
Cooking oil	2 tsp.	10 mL
Salt, sprinkle		
Pepper, sprinkle		
Can of condensed chicken broth	10 oz.	284 mL
Can of condensed cream of mushroom soup	10 oz.	284 mL
Chili sauce	1/2 cup	125 mL
Chili powder	1/2 tsp.	2 mL
Dried whole oregano	1 tsp.	5 mL
Dried sweet basil	1 tsp.	5 mL
Minced onion flakes	1 tbsp.	15 mL
Water	1 1/2 cups	375 mL

Arrange pasta in ungreased 9 x 13 inch (22 x 33 cm) baking pan.

Fry pork chops in cooking oil in frying pan until browned. Sprinkle with salt and pepper. Lay chops over pasta.

Combine remaining 8 ingredients in large saucepan. Heat and stir until boiling. Pour over chops. Cover. Bake in 350°F (175°C) oven for about 1 hour until pork and pasta are tender. Serves 4.

1 serving: 527 Calories; 15.2 g Total Fat; 1666 mg Sodium; 37 g Protein; 59 g Carbohydrate; 5 g Dietary Fiber

Pictured on this page.

Tip *To brown pork chops, do them in smaller batches rather than all at once. Having too much meat in the frying pan will cause it to steam rather than brown.*

Creamed Pork And Cabbage Stew

Real comfort food. Serve with mashed potatoes.

Boneless pork loin, cut into thin strips	1 lb.	454 g
Cooking oil	1 tbsp.	15 mL
Large onion, cut in half lengthwise and sliced	1	1
Water	2 1/2 cups	625 mL
Beef bouillon powder	1 tbsp.	15 mL
Apple juice	1/2 cup	125 mL
Dry mustard	1/4 tsp.	1 mL
Ground nutmeg	1/4 tsp.	1 mL
Medium carrots, cut into 1/4 inch (6 mm) slices	4	4
Celery rib, sliced	1	1
Coarsely chopped cabbage	4 cups	1 L
Whipping cream	1 cup	250 mL
All-purpose flour	1/4 cup	60 mL

Fry pork in cooking oil in large pot or Dutch oven until browned.

Add onion. Cook for 3 to 4 minutes until onion is starting to soften.

Add next 5 ingredients. Stir. Bring to a boil. Reduce heat. Cover. Simmer for about 40 minutes, stirring occasionally, until pork is tender.

Add carrot, celery and cabbage. Stir. Cover. Cook for 15 minutes until vegetables are tender-crisp.

Stir whipping cream into flour in small bowl until smooth. Gradually stir into pork mixture. Heat and stir until boiling and thickened. Makes 8 cups (2 L).

1 cup (250 mL): 252 Calories; 15.3 g Total Fat; 286 mg Sodium; 15 g Protein; 14 g Carbohydrate; 2 g Dietary Fiber

Pictured on page 174.

Mellow Ham Casserole

This colorful, creamy casserole is quick to prepare. Sure to become a family favorite.

Milk	1/2 cup	125 mL
Light cream cheese, softened	4 oz.	125 g
Can of condensed cream of chicken soup (see Note)	10 oz.	284 mL
Frozen kernel corn	1 1/2 cups	375 mL
Frozen peas	1 1/2 cups	375 mL
Pepper	1/4 tsp.	1 mL
Medium egg noodles	8 oz.	225 g
Boiling water	12 cups	3 L
Cooking oil (optional)	1 tbsp.	15 mL
Salt	1 tsp.	5 mL
Ham slice (rind removed), cut into 1/2 - 3/4 inch (1.2 - 2 cm) cubes	1 lb.	454 g

Mash milk and cream cheese together with fork in large bowl.

Add next 4 ingredients. Stir.

Cook noodles in boiling water, cooking oil and salt in large uncovered pot or Dutch oven for 7 to 8 minutes until tender but firm. Drain. Add to soup mixture.

Add ham. Stir well. Turn into ungreased 3 quart (3 L) casserole. Bake, uncovered, in 350°F (175°C) oven for about 1 hour until bubbly around edges. Makes 10 cups (2.5 L).

1 cup (250 mL): 269 Calories; 9.7 g Total Fat; 1043 mg Sodium; 18 g Protein; 28 g Carbohydrate; 2 g Dietary Fiber

Pictured on page 174.

Note: Cream of celery or mushroom soup can be substituted for the chicken soup.

Bottom Left: Creamed Pork And Cabbage Stew, page 173   Center: Mellow Ham Casserole, page 173   Right: Pork Tourtière, below

Pork Tourtière

This is a main course pie that is sure to please.

Lean ground pork	2 lbs.	900 g
Finely chopped onion	1 1/2 cups	375 mL
Water	1 cup	250 mL
Bay leaf	1	1
Poultry seasoning	1/4 – 1/2 tsp.	1 – 2 mL
Garlic powder	1/4 tsp.	1 mL
Ground cloves	1/8 tsp.	0.5 mL
Salt	1 tsp.	5 mL
Pepper	1/2 tsp.	2 mL
Cooked mashed potato	2 cups	500 mL
Unbaked 9 inch (22 cm) pie shells, your own or a mix	4	4
Large egg, fork-beaten	1	1
Water	1 tbsp.	15 mL

Combine first 9 ingredients in large pot or Dutch oven. Bring to a boil. Reduce heat. Simmer, uncovered, for about 15 minutes, stirring occasionally, until pork is no longer pink and liquid has been reduced by half. Remove and discard bay leaf.

Add potato. Stir. Mixture should be moist and thick. Cool completely.

Fill 2 pie shells with potato mixture. Dampen edges with water. Roll out remaining pie shells to fit over top. Cut designs or slits. Place over top. Press and crimp to seal.

Combine egg and water in small bowl. Brush over surface of both pies. Bake in 375°F (190°C) oven for about 50 minutes until golden. Makes 2 pies. Serves 12.

1 serving: 305 Calories; 18.3 g Total Fat; 490 mg Sodium; 16 g Protein; 19 g Carbohydrate; 1 g Dietary Fiber

Pictured above.

Harvard Carrots

*The sweetness of the carrots is nicely
contrasted by the tangy, glaze-like sauce.*

Baby carrots	1 1/2 lbs.	680 g
Water		
HARVARD SAUCE		
Water	1/3 cup	75 mL
Granulated sugar	1/4 cup	60 mL
Cornstarch	1 tbsp.	15 mL
White vinegar	3 tbsp.	50 mL
Salt	1/2 tsp.	2 mL
Pepper	1/8 tsp.	0.5 mL
Hard margarine (or butter)	1 tbsp.	15 mL

Cook carrots in water in medium saucepan until tender. Drain.

Harvard Sauce: Stir water into sugar and cornstarch in small saucepan until no lumps remain. Add vinegar, salt and pepper. Heat and stir until boiling and thickened.

Add margarine. Stir until melted. Makes 3/4 cup (175 mL) sauce. Add to carrots. Toss until coated. Serves 8.

1 serving: 80 Calories; 1.6 g Total Fat; 195 mg Sodium; 1 g Protein;
17 g Carbohydrate; 2 Dietary Fiber

Pictured on page 178.

Brussels Sprouts Polonaise

*Dress up your sprouts with this
different crumb and egg topping.*

Brussels sprouts	1 1/2 lbs.	680 g
Water		
Salt (optional)	1/4 tsp.	1 mL
Hard margarine (or butter)	3 tbsp.	50 mL
Fine dry bread crumbs	1/4 cup	60 mL
Chopped fresh chives	2 tbsp.	30 mL
(or 1 1/2 tsp., 7 mL, dried)		
Parsley flakes	2 tsp.	10 mL
Hard-boiled eggs, grated	2	2
Salt	1/4 tsp.	1 mL
Freshly ground pepper, sprinkle		

Cook brussels sprouts in water and salt in large saucepan until tender. Drain.

Melt margarine in small saucepan. Add remaining 6 ingredients. Stir. Add to brussels sprouts. Toss. Serves 6.

1 serving: 146 Calories; 8.2 g Total Fat; 258 mg Sodium; 7 g Protein;
14 g Carbohydrate; 5 g Dietary Fiber

Pictured on page 177.

Scratch Potato Casserole

*Cheese and onion throughout make this
an attractive and tasty dish.*

Large eggs	3	3
Milk	1 cup	250 mL
Chopped green onion	1/3 cup	75 mL
Grated light sharp Cheddar cheese	1 cup	250 mL
Hard margarine (or butter), melted	2 tbsp.	30 mL
Salt	1 tsp.	5 mL
Pepper	1/4 tsp.	1 mL
Medium potatoes, grated	4	4

Beat eggs in medium bowl until frothy. Add next 6 ingredients. Stir.

Stir in potato. Turn into greased 8 x 8 inch (20 x 20 cm) pan. Bake, uncovered, in 350°F (175°C) oven for 60 to 70 minutes until tender. Serves 6.

1 serving: 185 Calories; 8.3 g Total Fat; 621 mg Sodium; 11 g Protein;
17 g Carbohydrate; 1 g Dietary Fiber

Pictured on page 177.

Onion Rings

Excellent when deep-fried and just as good when baked—you pick! Or try both methods.

Onions, cut into 1/4 inch (6 mm) slices (about 3 medium)	1 1/4 lbs.	560 g
All-purpose flour	1/2 cup	125 mL
Large eggs	3	3
Water	1/4 cup	60 mL
Fine dry bread crumbs	1 1/2 cups	375 mL
Seasoned salt	1 tbsp.	15 mL
Paprika	1 1/2 tsp.	7 mL
Pepper	1/4 tsp.	1 mL
Cooking oil, for deep-frying		

Separate onion slices into rings. Divide into 3 equal portions (see Tip, this page).

Place flour in shallow bowl or on waxed paper.

Lightly beat eggs and water in separate shallow bowl.

Combine next 4 ingredients in medium bowl. Divide into 3 equal portions, about 1/2 cup (125 mL) each. Press onion rings, in 3 batches, into flour to coat completely, removing excess flour. Dip into egg mixture. Roll in crumb mixture to coat completely. Arrange onion rings in single layer on ungreased baking sheet. Chill for least 1 hour to ensure batter is clinging properly.

Deep-fry onion rings, 6 to 8 at a time, in hot (375°F, 190°C) cooking oil for about 1 minute until golden brown. Remove to paper towels to drain. Makes about 75 onion rings.

5 onion rings: 142 Calories; 7.5 g Total Fat; 350 mg Sodium; 4 g Protein; 15 g Carbohydrate; 1 g Dietary Fiber

Pictured on page 177.

Variation: Arrange onion rings in single layer on greased baking sheet. Bake in 400°F (205°C) oven for about 12 minutes until golden.

Sweet Potato Casserole

Kids will love the marshmallows and cereal topping.

Sweet potatoes, peeled and cubed	3 lbs.	1.4 kg
Water		
Salt	1/2 tsp.	2 mL
Large eggs	3	3
Granulated sugar	1/4 cup	60 mL
Vanilla	1 tsp.	5 mL
Hard margarine (or butter), melted	2 tbsp.	30 mL
Salt	1/4 tsp.	1 mL
Miniature marshmallows	2 cups	500 mL
Crushed corn flakes cereal	1/2 cup	125 mL

Cook sweet potatoes in water and first amount of salt in large saucepan for about 5 minutes until tender. Drain. Mash.

Beat eggs, sugar, vanilla, margarine and second amount of salt together in medium bowl. Add sweet potatoes. Stir well. Turn into greased 2 quart (2 L) shallow casserole.

Cover sweet potato mixture with marshmallows. Sprinkle with cereal. Bake, uncovered, in 325°F (160°C) oven for 30 minutes until golden. Serves 8.

1 serving: 323 Calories; 5.3 g Total Fat; 221 mg Sodium; 6 g Protein; 64 g Carbohydrate; 5 g Dietary Fiber

Pictured on page 177.

Tip *To prevent clumping of dry ingredients when preparing onion rings, divide both the onion and flour mixture into three portions each. Evenly coated onion rings will be the end result and well worth the extra effort.*

Top Right: Sweet Potato Casserole, this page
Center Left: Onion Rings, above
Center Right: Scratch Potato Casserole, page 175
Bottom Left: Brussels Sprouts Polonaise, page 175

Cabbage Beef Bake, below   Harvard Carrots, page 175

Cabbage Beef Bake

Slightly creamy but not too thick. Nice homey taste.

Medium head of cabbage, cut into 1 - 1 1/2 inch (2.5 - 3.8 cm) pieces	1	1
Water		
Salt	1/2 tsp.	2 mL
Hard margarine (or butter)	1/4 cup	60 mL
Lean ground beef	1 lb.	454 g
Chopped onion	1 cup	250 mL
Garlic powder	1/4 tsp.	1 mL
Salt	1 tsp.	5 mL
Pepper	1/4 tsp.	1 mL
Can of condensed cream of mushroom soup	10 oz.	284 mL
Cooked long grain white rice (about 1/2 cup, 125 mL, uncooked)	1 cup	250 mL
Hard margarine (or butter)	1 tbsp.	15 mL
Fine dry bread crumbs	1/4 cup	60 mL

Cook cabbage in water and first amount of salt in large pot or Dutch oven for 10 to 15 minutes until tender. Drain.

Scramble-fry next 6 ingredients in large saucepan until ground beef is no longer pink. Drain. Add to cabbage.

Add soup and rice. Stir until well combined. Turn into ungreased 2 quart (2 L) casserole.

Melt second amount of margarine in small frying pan. Add bread crumbs. Heat and stir until lightly toasted. Sprinkle over cabbage mixture. Bake, uncovered, in 350°F (175°C) oven for about 35 minutes until heated through and bubbly around edges. Serves 6.

1 serving: 372 Calories; 21.1 g Total Fat; 1028 mg Sodium; 18 g Protein; 28 g Carbohydrate; 4 g Dietary Fiber

Pictured on this page.

Cauliflower Casserole

Mushroom, cheese and cauliflower flavors go so well together.

Large head of cauliflower, cut into florets	1	1
Water		
Salt	1 tsp.	5 mL
Small green pepper, diced	1	1
Sliced fresh mushrooms (or 10 oz., 284 mL, can, drained)	2 cups	500 mL
Finely chopped onion	1/4 cup	60 mL
Hard margarine (or butter)	1/4 cup	60 mL
All-purpose flour	1/4 cup	60 mL
Salt	1 tsp.	5 mL
Pepper	1/8 tsp.	0.5 mL
Milk	1 3/4 cups	425 mL
Grated sharp Cheddar cheese	1 cup	250 mL
Jar of pimientos, drained and chopped	2 oz.	57 mL

Cook cauliflower in water and salt in large pot or Dutch oven until tender-crisp. Drain.

Sauté green pepper, mushrooms and onion in margarine in frying pan until soft.

Sprinkle flour, salt and pepper over mushroom mixture. Stir. Gradually stir in milk until mixture is boiling and thickened.

Add cheese and pimiento. Stir. Put 1/2 of cauliflower into ungreased 2 quart (2 L) casserole. Pour 1/2 of sauce over top. Top with remaining cauliflower. Pour remaining sauce over top. Bake, uncovered, in 350°F (175°C) oven for 35 to 40 minutes until bubbly hot. Serves 8 to 10.

1 serving: 197 Calories; 12.1 g Total Fat; 528 mg Sodium; 9 g Protein; 15 g Carbohydrate; 3 g Dietary Fiber

Pictured on page 179.

Scalloped Celery With Tomato

*If you are used to having your celery raw,
you will want to try this baked version.*

Sliced celery	5 cups	1.25 L
Can of tomatoes, with juice	14 oz.	398 mL
Finely chopped onion	1 cup	250 mL
Granulated sugar	2 tsp.	10 mL
Salt	1/2 tsp.	2 mL
Pepper	1/4 tsp.	1 mL
Hard margarine (or butter), melted	3 tbsp.	50 mL
All-purpose flour	2 tbsp.	30 mL
Hard margarine (or butter)	3 tbsp.	50 mL
Soda cracker crumbs	1/2 cup	125 mL

Combine first 6 ingredients in large saucepan. Bring to a boil. Reduce heat. Cover. Simmer for 10 minutes.

Stir first amount of margarine into flour in small bowl until smooth. Gradually add to tomato mixture. Heat and stir until boiling and thickened. Pour into ungreased 2 quart (2 L) casserole.

Melt second amount of margarine in small saucepan. Stir in cracker crumbs. Sprinkle over tomato mixture. Bake, uncovered, in 350°F (175°C) oven for 20 to 25 minutes until hot. Serve hot or cold. Serves 4 to 6.

1 serving: 270 Calories; 19.1 g Total Fat; 859 mg Sodium; 3 g Protein; 23 g Carbohydrate; 3 g Dietary Fiber

Pictured below.

Rice Pilaf

*Chicken broth with a bite of onion and
pepper enhances ordinary rice.*

Long grain white rice, uncooked	1 cup	250 mL
Hard margarine (or butter)	2 tbsp.	30 mL
Chopped onion	1 cup	250 mL
Chopped celery	1/2 cup	125 mL
Chicken broth	2 cups	500 mL
Fresh parsley, chopped	2 cups	500 mL
Salt	1/2 tsp.	2 mL
Pepper	1/4 tsp.	1 mL

Sauté rice, margarine, onion and celery in large saucepan until rice is golden.

Add broth, parsley, salt and pepper. Stir. Bring to a boil. Reduce heat. Cover. Cook on low for about 20 minutes until rice is tender. Makes 4 cups (1 L).

1/2 cup (125 mL): 141 Calories; 3.6 g Total Fat; 405 mg Sodium; 4 g Protein; 23 g Carbohydrate; 1 g Dietary Fiber

Pictured below.

Top Left: Cauliflower Casserole, page 178
Top Right: Scalloped Celery With Tomato, this page
Bottom: Rice Pilaf, above

Carrot Coffee Cake

A wonderful orange and cinnamon flavor in this tender, crumb-topped cake. Good warm or cold with whipped cream.

Yellow cake mix (2 layer size)	1	1
Plain yogurt	1 cup	250 mL
Large eggs	3	3
Frozen concentrated orange juice, thawed	1/4 cup	60 mL
Ground cinnamon	1 tsp.	5 mL
Finely grated carrot	2 cups	500 mL
Chopped walnuts	1 cup	250 mL
Brown sugar, packed	1/2 cup	125 mL
Grated orange peel	2 tsp.	10 mL
Ground cinnamon	1/2 tsp.	2 mL
Ground cloves	1/4 tsp.	1 mL

Beat cake mix, yogurt, eggs, orange juice and first amount of cinnamon together in large bowl on low until moistened. Beat on medium for about 2 minutes until smooth.

Add carrot. Mix well. Pour 1/2 of batter into greased 9 x 13 inch (22 x 33 cm) pan. Spread evenly.

Combine next 5 ingredients in small bowl. Evenly sprinkle 1/2 of walnut mixture over batter. Drop dabs of remaining batter here and there over top. Smooth as best you can. Sprinkle remaining walnut mixture over top. Bake in 350°F (175°C) oven for about 40 minutes until wooden pick inserted in center comes out clean. Cuts into 15 pieces.

1 piece: 275 Calories; 10.4 g Total Fat; 263 mg Sodium; 6 g Protein; 41 g Carbohydrate; 1 g Dietary Fiber

Pictured on page 181.

Cranberry Cheesecake

A pretty pink-colored cheesecake perfect for the holiday season. Allow extra time to prepare.

FRESH CRANBERRY TOPPING

Fresh (or frozen) cranberries	2 cups	500 mL
Cranberry cocktail	1 cup	250 mL
Finely grated orange peel	1/2 tsp.	2 mL
Granulated sugar	1/2 cup	125 mL
Cornstarch	1 1/2 tbsp.	25 mL
Ground cinnamon (optional)	1/8 tsp.	0.5 mL
Unflavored gelatin	2 tsp.	10 mL
Orange-flavored liqueur (such as Grand Marnier)	1 tbsp.	15 mL

CRUST

Hard margarine (or butter)	1/3 cup	75 mL
Ground cinnamon	1/4 tsp.	1 mL
Graham cracker crumbs	1 1/2 cups	375 mL

FILLING

Can of sweetened condensed milk	11 oz.	300 mL
Light cream cheese, softened	16 oz.	454 g
Finely grated orange peel	1 tsp.	5 mL
Vanilla	1 tsp.	5 mL
Dry curd cottage cheese	1 1/2 cups	375 mL
Prepared orange juice	2 tbsp.	30 mL
Large eggs	4	4

Fresh Cranberry Topping: Combine cranberries, cranberry cocktail and orange peel in medium saucepan. Cover. Cook for about 2 minutes until some cranberries are starting to split.

Combine sugar, cornstarch and cinnamon in small bowl. Add to cranberries. Heat and stir on medium-low until clear and slightly thickened.

Sprinkle gelatin over liqueur in separate small bowl. Let stand for 1 minute to soften. Add to hot cranberry mixture. Stir to dissolve. Chill. Makes 2 cups (500 mL) topping.

Crust: Melt margarine in small saucepan. Stir in cinnamon and graham crumbs. Mix well. Press into bottom and slightly up sides of greased 10 inch (25 cm) springform pan.

Filling: Beat condensed milk, cream cheese, orange peel and vanilla together in large bowl until mixed.

Process cottage cheese, orange juice and 3/4 cup (175 mL) cranberry topping in food processor using on/off motion until finely textured and smooth. Add to cream cheese mixture. Beat well. Add eggs, 1 at a time, beating on low until just mixed. Carefully pour over crust. Bake in 400°F (205°C) oven for 10 minutes. Reduce heat to 325°F (160°C). Bake for about 40 minutes until center is almost set. Turn heat off. Let stand in oven for 10 minutes. Remove to wire rack. Run knife around sides to allow cheesecake to settle evenly. Cool. Chill for several hours or overnight. Spoon remaining cranberry topping onto individual servings. Cuts into 12 pieces.

1 piece: 401 Calories; 19.2 g Total Fat; 486 mg Sodium; 13 g Protein; 44 g Carbohydrate; 1 g Dietary Fiber

Pictured on page 181.

Left: Almond Zucchini Cake, below   Top Right: Carrot Coffee Cake, page 180   Bottom Right: Cranberry Cheesecake, page 180

Almond Zucchini Cake

Shhh…Still have some zucchini in the freezer?
No one has to know there's zucchini in this moist cake.

Large eggs	3	3
Brown sugar, packed	1 1/2 cups	375 mL
Cooking oil	1/2 cup	125 mL
Almond flavoring	1 tsp.	5 mL
All-purpose flour	2 1/4 cups	550 mL
Baking powder	2 tsp.	10 mL
Baking soda	1/2 tsp.	2 mL
Salt	1/2 tsp.	2 mL
Peeled and grated zucchini	2 1/2 cups	625 mL
Ground almonds	3/4 cup	175 mL
GLAZE		
Icing (confectioner's) sugar	1 cup	250 mL
Water	1 tbsp.	15 mL
Almond flavoring	1/2 tsp.	2 mL
Sliced almonds, toasted (see Tip, page 28)	1/4 cup	60 mL

Beat eggs in large bowl until frothy. Add brown sugar, 1/4 cup (60 mL) at a time, while constantly beating until thick and brown sugar is dissolved.

Beat in cooking oil and almond flavoring.

Combine flour, baking powder, baking soda and salt in separate large bowl.

Add flour mixture to batter in 3 parts, alternately with zucchini in 2 parts, beginning and ending with flour mixture. Beat well.

Stir in almonds. Pour into well greased and floured 12 cup (2.7 L) bundt pan. Bake in 350°F (175°C) oven for 45 minutes until wooden pick inserted in center comes out clean. Cool in pan for 15 minutes. Turn out onto wire rack to cool until warm to touch.

Glaze: Mix icing sugar, water and almond flavoring in liquid measure, adding more water if necessary to make thick but pourable glaze. Makes about 1/2 cup (125 mL) glaze. Pour in thick layer around top of warm cake, allowing some to run down sides.

Sprinkle with almonds while glaze is still soft. Cuts into 16 pieces.

1 piece: 310 Calories; 12.7 g Total Fat; 183 mg Sodium; 5 g Protein; 46 g Carbohydrate; 2 g Dietary Fiber

Pictured above.

Valentine Cake

If you don't have a heart-shaped pan,
here is a simple way you can make a heart cake.

CAKE

Yellow cake mix (2 layer size)	1	1
Instant vanilla pudding powder (4 serving size)	1	1
Large eggs	4	4
Cooking oil	1/2 cup	125 mL
Water	1 cup	250 mL

ICING

Icing (confectioner's) sugar	3 1/2 cups	875 mL
Hard margarine (or butter), softened	1/4 cup	60 mL
Drops of red food coloring	2	2
Vanilla	1 tsp.	5 mL
Water	1/4 cup	60 mL

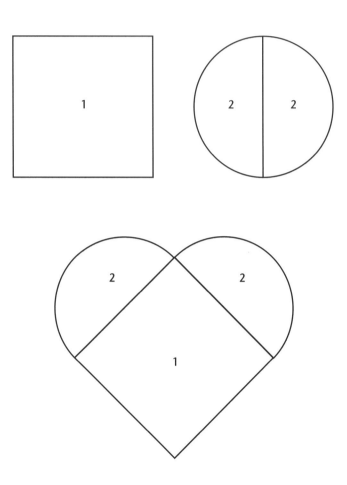

Cake: Empty cake mix into large bowl. Add next 4 ingredients. Beat on low until just moistened. Beat on medium for about 2 minutes until smooth. Measure 2 1/2 cups (625 mL) batter into greased 8 × 8 inch (20 × 20 cm) pan. Pour remaining batter into greased 8 inch (20 cm) round pan. Make sure batter is equal depth in each pan. Bake in 350°F (175°C) oven for about 30 minutes until wooden pick inserted in center comes out clean. Let stand in pans for 15 minutes. Turn out onto wire racks to cool. Cut round cake in half. Place square cake on foil-lined cake board or heavy cardboard to form diamond shape. Place cut sides of round cake on adjacent sides of square cake to form heart shape (see Diagram, this page). Trim top of cake to make flat if necessary.

Icing: Combine all 5 ingredients in medium bowl. Beat, adding more icing sugar or water until spreading consistency. Makes 1 3/4 cups (425 mL) icing. Ice cake. Decorate. Serves 10 to 12.

1 serving: 613 Calories; 24.6 g Total Fat; 574 mg Sodium; 5 g Protein; 95 g Carbohydrate; 0 g Dietary Fiber

Pictured on this page.

Valentine Cake, this page

Measurement Tables

Throughout this book measurements are given in Conventional and Metric measure. To compensate for differences between the two measurements due to rounding, a full metric measure is not always used. The cup used is the standard 8 fluid ounce. Temperature is given in degrees Fahrenheit and Celsius. Baking pan measurements are in inches and centimetres as well as quarts and litres. An exact metric conversion is given on this page as well as the working equivalent (Metric Standard Measure).

Oven Temperatures

Fahrenheit (°F)	Celsius (°C)	Fahrenheit (°F)	Celsius (°C)
175°	80°	350°	175°
200°	95°	375°	190°
225°	110°	400°	205°
250°	120°	425°	220°
275°	140°	450°	230°
300°	150°	475°	240°
325°	160°	500°	260°

Spoons

Conventional Measure	Metric Exact Conversion Millilitre (mL)	Metric Standard Measure Millilitre (mL)
1/8 teaspoon (tsp.)	0.6 mL	0.5 mL
1/4 teaspoon (tsp.)	1.2 mL	1 mL
1/2 teaspoon (tsp.)	2.4 mL	2 mL
1 teaspoon (tsp.)	4.7 mL	5 mL
2 teaspoons (tsp.)	9.4 mL	10 mL
1 tablespoon (tbsp.)	14.2 mL	15 mL

Cups

1/4 cup (4 tbsp.)	56.8 mL	60 mL
1/3 cup (5 1/3 tbsp.)	75.6 mL	75 mL
1/2 cup (8 tbsp.)	113.7 mL	125 mL
2/3 cup (10 2/3 tbsp.)	151.2 mL	150 mL
3/4 cup (12 tbsp.)	170.5 mL	175 mL
1 cup (16 tbsp.)	227.3 mL	250 mL
4 1/2 cups	1022.9 mL	1000 mL (1 L)

Pans

Conventional - Inches	Metric - Centimeters
8x8 inch	20x20 cm
9x9 inch	22x22 cm
9x13 inch	22x33 cm
10x15 inch	25x38 cm
11x17 inch	28x43 cm
8x2 inch round	20x5 cm
9x2 inch round	22x5 cm
10x4 1/2 inch tube	25x11 cm
8x4x3 inch loaf	20x10x7.5 cm
9x5x3 inch loaf	22x12.5x7.5 cm

Dry Measurements

Conventional Measure Ounces (oz.)	Metric Exact Conversion Grams (g)	Metric Standard Measure Grams (g)
1 oz.	28.3 g	28 g
2 oz.	56.7 g	57 g
3 oz.	85.0 g	85 g
4 oz.	113.4 g	125 g
5 oz.	141.7 g	140 g
6 oz.	170.1 g	170 g
7 oz.	198.4 g	200 g
8 oz.	226.8 g	250 g
16 oz.	453.6 g	500 g
32 oz.	907.2 g	1000 g (1 kg)

Casseroles

Canada & Britain

Standard Size Casserole	Exact Metric Measure
1 qt. (5 cups)	1.13 L
1 1/2 qts. (7 1/2 cups)	1.69 L
2 qts. (10 cups)	2.25 L
2 1/2 qts. (12 1/2 cups)	2.81 L
3 qts. (15 cups)	3.38 L
4 qts. (20 cups)	4.5 L
5 qts. (25 cups)	5.63 L

United States

Standard Size Casserole	Exact Metric Measure
1 qt. (4 cups)	900 mL
1 1/2 qts. (6 cups)	1.35 L
2 qts. (8 cups)	1.8 L
2 1/2 qts. (10 cups)	2.25 L
3 qts. (12 cups)	2.7 L
4 qts. (16 cups)	3.6 L
5 qts. (20 cups)	4.5 L

Recipe Index

Tip Index